CREED & CULTURE

CREED & CULTURE

A Touchstone *Reader*

EDITED BY

JAMES M. KUSHINER

ISI BOOKS
WILMINGTON, DELAWARE
2003

Cataloging-in-Publication Data:

Creed & culture : a Touchstone reader / edited by James M. Kushiner. —
    Wilmington, Del. : ISI Books, c2003.

        p.   ; cm.
Essays originally published in the newsletter Touchstone.

    ISBN 1932236058
        1. Christianity. 2. Christian life. 3. Christian literature. 4. Essays.
    I. Kushiner, James M. II. Creed and culture. III. Title: Touchstone

BR53 .C74 2003   2002115033
808.8 / 03823 — dc21   CIP

Published in the United States by:

    ISI Books
    Intercollegiate Studies Institute
    Post Office Box 4431
    Wilmington, DE 19807-0431

Manufactured in the U.S.

IN MEMORIAM

Russell Amos Kirk († 1994)

Fr. Paul M. Quay, S.J. († 1994)

CONTENTS

Introduction   xi

James Hitchcock
CHRIST & CULTURE: A DILEMMA RECONSIDERED
A New Look at Culture, Christians & the State   I

Huston Smith
SCIENTISM: THE WORLD'S LITTLEST RELIGION
How Theology Must Confront the New Global Religion   14

Patrick Henry Reardon
CLASSROOM CHAOS
Atheism & the Public Schools   23

Leon J. Podles
NO PLACE LIKE HOME
A Personal Look at the Education of Children:
Public, Private & Domestic   32

Steven Faulkner
THE CENTURY OF THE CYCLOPS
On the Loss of Poetry as Necessary Knowledge   44

Steven Faulkner
THE WORKSHOP OF WORSHIP
On Recovering Poetry for Our Children   51

Russell Kirk
T. S. ELIOT ON LITERARY MORALS
T. S. Eliot's After Strange Gods   58

Thomas Howard
BRIDESHEAD REVISITED REVISITED
Moral Imagination & the Catholic Faith
in Evelyn Waugh's Modern Novel   63

James L. Sauer
LESSONS FROM THE NURSERY
The Catholic Imagination Encounters Bambi   75

Philip G. Davis
THE SWISS MAHARISHI
The Religion of Carl Jung & His Legacy Today   81

Vigen Guroian
FAMILY & CHRISTIAN VIRTUE
IN A POST-CHRISTIAN WORLD
Reflections on the Ecclesial Vision of John Chrysostom   93

James L. Sauer
AN EVERLASTING LIFE
Remembering Mary Denise Sauer: July 12, 1995 – August 26, 1995   108

Thomas Howard
RECOGNIZING THE CHURCH
A Personal Pilgrimage & the Discovery of Five Marks of the Church 115

Leon J. Podles
ALL THAT SEPARATES MUST CONVERGE
The Fragmentation of Christianity & the Unity of Faith   129

David Mills
THE BIBLE TELLS ME SO
Everything You Need to Know About Morality & the Bible   139

Patrick Henry Reardon
CHRISTOLOGY & THE PSALTER
The Church's Christian Prayer Book   153

S. M. Hutchens
THE PROFESSOR & THE UNICORN
Reality, Revelation & the Seductions of Abstract Thought   162

David Mills
MEET THE LATCONS
The Trouble with Latitudinarian Conservatives   179

David Mills
EVADING THE CREED
The Various Attacks on the Faith of the Church & Why They Fail   188

Paul V. Mankowski
A FIG LEAF FOR THE CREED
"Inclusive Language" Comes to Mass   200

James R. Edwards
NEW QUEST, OLD ERRORS
The Fallacies of the New Quest for the Historical Jesus   208

Contributors   225

Index   229

INTRODUCTION

THE LATE RUSSELL KIRK was noted for planting trees for those who would come after him. *Touchstone* in part owes its existence to such foresight. The journal was a sapling when brought to his attention, to which he directed water and nourishment at a critical stage.

In 1986 a group of earnest young Christians, mostly from a Protestant Evangelical background, started a newsletter called *Touchstone*, seeking to address topics of concern to us and a small circle of friends. We were reading history and tradition for answers to questions about the divisions between Christians, as well as about the challenges of living and raising families in a secular, post-Christian culture.

Touchstone grew from a 12-page newsletter into a quarterly journal. In the early 1990s Dr. Kirk kindly arranged for some modest financial support for our fledgling publication (which helped us continue until 1997, when we attracted even more substantial funding).

To encourage us on the way, Kirk also wrote this endorsement in 1990: "In a bent time, *Touchstone* speaks up courageously for sound doctrine. It does not evade the great questions at issue. Through its pages a conscience speaks to a conscience." It has been our constant endeavor to do just that.

We realized then that many Christians, despite belonging to different churches, share an adherence to a common Great Tradition, arguably what C. S. Lewis called "mere Christianity." Such Christians, whether Protestant, Catholic, or Orthodox, have much more in common with each other than they do with the members of their own churches who accept liberalism's refashioned Christian gospel and no longer espouse the historic Christian creeds with integrity. We realized also that the culture in which we live has likewise fallen prey to the secularists' gospel of mere pluralism and moral relativism. Hence, both creed and culture have been of central concern in the pages of *Touchstone* from the beginning.

Of course, there were others who were writing about these concerns. Early on, we attracted writers—some of stature, such as Dr. Kirk, and some new and lesser known—who wrote in defense of both the "permanent things" and the Christian faith. Our writers came from various traditions, giving the magazine an ecumenical breadth then rare (and still uncommon) among conservative Christians.

Many of the essays we published in our first ten years are no longer available but are no less valuable today than when they were originally published. In this book we offer a selection of the finest essays published during *Touchstone*'s first decade—essays that speak conscientiously for the gospel in a still bent time in which creed and culture seem to be at grave risk.

The Essays

We begin with James Hitchcock's reconsideration of the perennial question of "Christ and Culture," given that "modernity has now exhausted itself."

Next, both Huston Smith in "Scientism: The World's Littlest Religion" and Patrick Henry Reardon in "Classroom Chaos: Atheism & the Public Schools" deal with the dominant materialist philosophies of our day. Smith notes that "theology should recognize scientism as its principal enemy." Reardon considers scientism and atheism in the context of public school education.

Having moved on to the matter of education, we next offer Leon Podles's "No Place Like Home," which recounts the advantages of home-schooling his six children and discusses the issues of faith and character formation in the education of children.

In two essays, "The Century of the Cyclops" and "The Workshop of Wonder," Steven Faulkner points out the limitations of technological, scientific, and secular knowledge and the human need for "poetic knowledge" in "ordering the soul"—and its importance in the education of children (and adults).

We then feature Russell Kirk's first (and only) original *Touchstone* essay, "T. S. Eliot & Literary Morals," a provocative discussion of Eliot's "forbidden" book, *After Strange Gods*.

Thomas Howard follows, opening "*Brideshead Revisited* Revisited" with a discussion of "moral imagination" and literature, then describing the religious accomplishment of Evelyn Waugh's most famous novel.

James Sauer engages our Christian imagination in "Lessons from the Nursery," which contrasts the Christian faith with certain appealing notions of romanticism in Felix Salten's *Bambi*. Such notions still persist in various forms.

In "The Swiss Maharishi," Philip G. Davis outlines the religious legacy of Carl Jung and shows how its appeal, especially in the face of a failed modernism, can only be effectively answered by an authentic Christian faith.

With the next two essays, both having a vantage point from within the Christian family, we move closer to exclusively "in-house" Christian concerns. In "Family & Christian Virtue in a Post-Christian World," Vigen Guroian describes the role of the Christian family as a sacred institution in the world, as articulated by John Chrysostom in the fourth century. James Sauer's "An Everlasting Life" is a deeply moving tribute to his daughter's brief life and death within a Christian family, seen in the light of the Apostles' Creed and the greater Christian Church.

The remaining essays treat specifically Christian concerns and challenges *within* the Church. We begin with Thomas Howard's "Recognizing the Church," a personal account of his discovery of the "five marks of the Church." Leon Podles's "All That Separates Must Converge" considers the problems of Christian disunity and the unity of the faith, particularly as they apply to Eastern and Western Christianity.

David Mills, in "The Bible Tells Me So," describes modern challenges to biblical morality and how best to confront them through a faithful reading of the Scriptures. In "Christology & the Psalter," Patrick Henry Reardon articulates the vital role of the Psalms in Christian prayer and shows how the traditional christological reading of them is being lost because of a "present impiety."

In "The Professor & the Unicorn," S. M. Hutchens provocatively discusses the problem posed to Christian thinkers in "telling where revelation leaves off and speculation . . . begins." In "Meet the Latcons," David Mills describes so-called conservatives whose "moderation" endangers the faith they think they are defending. In "Evading the Creed," Mills describes the liberals' methods for getting around the dogmas of the Church and explains the ultimate failure of such methods.

In "A Fig Leaf for the Creed," Paul Mankowski clearly shows the mistaken notions behind "inclusive-language" translations for the Church. Finally, James R. Edwards, in "New Quest, Old Errors," describes and analyzes the errors of modern "scientific" treatment of the Gospels. Thus, our *Touchstone* Reader, which began with "Christ and Culture," ends with a defense of the Christ of the Gospels, the Fount of all Christian culture.

These essays are, then, offered as "first fruits," so to speak, of a small journal planted in the late 1980s and later watered by Dr. Kirk and others, not least those writers who so generously contributed these fine articles to *Touchstone*. It is our hope that this collection of essays will be read profitably by many new readers in the years to come.

Acknowledgments

Thanks to the generous support of many, *Touchstone* now flourishes. It became a bimonthly in 1998 and a monthly in 2000, now reaching more than seven thousand readers.

I am indebted to all of the senior editors—James Hitchcock, Steven M. Hutchens, David Mills, Leon J. Podles, and Patrick Henry Reardon—for their vital assistance and crucial support in developing *Touchstone* into a substantive monthly journal. I am especially grateful for their friendship; working with them has proven to be an encouraging example of Catholics, Protestants, and Orthodox working together without compromising their beliefs.

Also invaluable in nurturing *Touchstone* early on have been associate editor Thomas Buchanan and his wife, Gaye, as well as Lynnette Hoppe and John Thompson. In addition, there have been many volunteers, and not least were the many writers who contributed their labors during that critical period—all too numerous to mention.

In addition, I thank those providing invaluable aid in the production of this book, particularly our managing editor, Anita Kuhn, and intern Mary Kushiner. The design and layout are by Sam Torode, our design editor since 1999.

I am grateful to the publisher for its willingness to publish a collection of essays (often a risky proposition), and also to Kenneth Tanner for suggesting ISI Books and to Geoffrey Battersby for his encouragement.

Finally, and most especially, I wish to thank Patricia, my wife of thirty years, for her many editorial and office hours over the years, absolutely critical to *Touchstone*'s success.

This book is dedicated to two extraordinary men, Russell Kirk and Fr. Paul Quay. Dr. Kirk's writings are well known (*The Conservative Mind* and *T. S. Eliot & His Age,* to name just two), and I have already said something about his early support for *Touchstone*.

Fr. Paul Quay was a Jesuit professor at Loyola University in Chicago. He was thoroughly orthodox and ecumenical, a mere Christian and robust Catholic. Fr. Quay had agreed to join the board of *Touchstone* in 1994 but soon discovered he was suffering from an incurable cancer, to which he succumbed shortly thereafter. His literary legacy is small but rich, including *The Christian Meaning of Human Sexuality* and his magisterial *The Mystery Hidden for Ages in God.* His love for Christ and the Church was apparent, his concerns for both creed and culture genuine.

Like Dr. Kirk, Fr. Quay was humble and wise and faithful in a time of unbelief. We were blessed to have known them both. It is our hope, then, that this collection dedicated to their memory will encourage readers in the Christian faith, which is the only true hope for mankind.

—James M. Kushiner
Executive Editor, Touchstone
Chicago, Illinois
September 2002

JAMES HITCHCOCK

CHRIST & CULTURE: A DILEMMA RECONSIDERED

A New Look at Culture, Christians & the State

ULTURE, SOCIETY, AND STATE are commonly distinguished by social scientists, with the first the most difficult to define. The state—the apparatus of political organization—is obvious. Society is somewhat less so, but it involves visible, even measurable, realities—the family, economic institutions, social classes. Culture in a sense merely comprises everything else, although in a way it also includes the first two. It is the totality of a people's communal life in all its manifestations.

The great historian Christopher Dawson devoted his entire career to studying the relationship of religion to culture, in works such as *Progress and Religion* (1929), *Enquiries into Religion and Culture* (1933), *Religion and the Modern State* (1936), *Religion and the Rise of Western Culture* (1950), and *The Historic Reality of Christian Culture* (1960).

Because of his acute sense of the importance of religion as the foundation of human culture, Dawson was perhaps the first modern critic to point out the ways in which the state is often antagonistic to culture. Among other things, religion teaches that there is a divine purpose to history, that man owes God collective as well as individual worship, and that the human race must be obedient to a law

I

higher than that of the state, all of which make the relationship between religion and the state problematical and, to the degree that religion inspires the culture and is part of it, makes culture also a danger to the authority of the state. The Roman Empire persecuted Christianity not because Christians held different beliefs from the Romans but because the state could not control the Church.

Culture & the Modern State

Although seldom cast in these terms, in a sense one of the important "conservative" tasks in the modern West is the struggle to maintain not only the distinction between culture and politics but also the priority of culture over politics, the merging of the two being one of the principal characteristics of modern totalitarianism.

This merger is most easily seen in such things as the official art fostered by Communist and Fascist dictatorships, or by the official science that for a long time was the only kind tolerated in the Soviet Union. However, the claim of totalitarianism to extend its vigilance literally to every obscure corner of people's lives necessarily destroys culture by sucking it into the constantly expanding political vacuum machine.

But the apparent defeat of totalitarianism in Europe does not mean the end of danger because, as Dawson once again pointed out, there has existed in the West for some time a kind of "soft" totalitarianism that ultimately has the same effect, although it is achieved more circuitously and slowly, and less painfully.

Again art offers the most obvious window. Beyond the controversy over the specific kinds of art supported by the National Endowment for the Arts is the larger question of whether a government agency should decide which kind of art is deserving of encouragement, a power that establishes certain styles, themes, and techniques as privileged, seeks to shape public taste by determining what is to be made available, and penalizes artists who do not conform to those expectations.

The politics and economics of art are hardly new. But, as with fascism and communism, the real totalitarianism lies in the assumption that government officials possess a wisdom lacking to ordinary citizens, and that they should use their power to force changes on people that the people would not otherwise accept—what is sometimes called social engineering.

The modern state aspires to fill the role historically filled in culture by the Church, that of offering to its people not only support and protection but also spiritual guidance through continually expanding public agencies armed with coercive power.

The word *culture* as used by biologists implies a more or less spontaneous growth under controlled circumstances, and anthropologists and others who use the term mean something similar. Culture is the totality of the life of a people, shaped and guided by their institutions but also to some extent a spontaneous development from the people themselves—their moral and religious beliefs, their social customs, their attitudes towards each other and towards the universe, their sports and games, their community mores, and many other things.

Except when immediately usable, culture in this sense is intolerable to the totalitarian mind because of the danger that it will produce ideas and movements inimical to the regime. In soft totalitarianism there is a similar, if less virulent, suspicion, since the social engineer assumes that, left to themselves, people will continue to resist the progressive movement of society.

Cultural Elitism & the New Class

One of the classic arguments against democracy is that the common people are fickle and unstable, easily swayed by demagogues, and that only an elite can preserve the values upon which a society rests. But as numerous observers have pointed out, in modern America the reverse is true—an attachment to traditional values is mainly found among the masses; it is certain elites that seek to transform traditional ways of thinking and acting.

The specific cases of this need no rehearsal. It is especially characteristic of people in the "New Class," whose professions have to do with words and ideas— educators, journalists, those recognized as intellectuals, many social workers, many lawyers, many clergy. Numerous opinion polls have demonstrated how far such people are at odds with common opinion on a range of questions, and it is a central irony that most of those who extol "diversity" as a moral imperative (on university campuses, for example) hold almost identical opinions, one with another.

In part, this situation is the natural result of such people's defined social roles. Their claim to authority is the ultimate realization of the Enlightenment dream of meritocracy—power accorded to those who deserve it by their talent, such talent having now been defined largely in terms of education and intelligence. This being the case, such people must by definition always be "ahead" of the masses; otherwise, they would have no claim to authority. The basis of their self-esteem is the belief that they understand the needs of the world more authentically and more deeply than most other people and that they deserve to be listened to.

The temptation to resort to the power of government to implement one's vision of the good society is therefore almost overwhelming—people can be forced by laws, by regulations issued by government agencies that circumvent the electoral process, and, above all, by courts to alter their behavior and even their beliefs, an effort that has been going on for at least six decades. Since the time of Constantine, Christians usually have not had to take seriously the biblical warning that the mighty of the earth are the enemies of the faith, but in this neo-pagan era that warning is once again becoming relevant.

It is the unstated and perhaps sometimes unconscious assumption of the New Class that culture as independent of, and prior to, politics cannot be permitted, since it fosters ideas and actions detrimental to the best future of society. (Christopher Dawson offered the homey example of the Boy Scouts as an instance of culture independent of the state, and it is good to recall that efforts have been made in the courts, so far unsuccessfully, to force the Boy Scouts to abandon their explicitly theistic creed.)

The mass media play a crucial and paradoxical role here. They are fiercely resistant to any kind of outside control, especially any that might come from the government. But at the same time the media seek to mold a uniform mass consciousness. Rather than dictatorship, it is this uniform consciousness, Dawson pointed out, that is the real essence of modern totalitarianism. For most of those who speak through the media, the modernist agenda is merely self-evident and those who resist it are strange or perverse.

Beyond the fact that such an outlook is inherent in the role of the modern social engineer is the reality of modernism itself, modernism being distinguishable from modernity by the fact that the latter is merely the reality of modern life as it is, while the former is a powerful ideology that has unfolded over three centuries or more. It is no longer necessary to trace particular radical ideas to particular historical sources, to ask why a certain venerable institution, or a certain accepted belief, has suddenly been subject to attack. The essence of modernism is, in the words of the Freudian sociologist Philip Rieff, the "systematic hunting down of all settled convictions." Only the person who joins in such assaults can think of himself as truly enlightened, and traditions are attacked for the same reason that mountains are climbed—because they are there. Occasionally the iconoclasts go too far and provoke a reaction even among progressive-minded people, as presently in the matter of pederasty. But even as the practice is widely condemned, its devotees continue to propagandize for it, confident that, the next time around, they will prevail.

For the enlightened class, therefore, the only culture worth the name is not at all spontaneous, much less traditional, but consciously constructed by governing elites according to a rational and comprehensive plan. For example, it is the obvious goal of the educational bureaucracy, already realized to a great extent, to ensure that public education everywhere in the United States is absolutely homogenized and nowhere reflects local peculiarities. Thus, the schools are being rapidly turned into agencies for disseminating the "good news" of the sexual revolution to younger and younger children, while the introduction of various kinds of therapeutic services into education gives practitioners of those techniques unlimited opportunity to become involved in the personal lives of students.

If this understanding of modernism is correct, there will simply be no rest, nor can there be a viable compromise that finally brings cultural iconoclasm to an end and lays the foundation for a new stability. Modernism in its fullness celebrates precisely the extreme and marginal figures of the culture, the wholly alienated men, not only as a way of undermining the culture's traditional certainties but also as a prelude to a new enforced conformity in which there will be no toleration of alienation.

The sociologist Peter Berger has summed up the most important dimension of this in his well-known quip that, if India is the most religious nation in the world and Sweden the most secular, America is a nation of Indians ruled by Swedes.

The Christian Right

No one who pays attention to the media can fail to be struck by the hysterical abuse heaped on the Christian Right, an abuse far out of proportion to whatever faults that movement may have, and certainly out of proportion to its demonstrated political importance. In most newspapers, for example, hardly a week passes without letters by citizens, and essays by professional journalists, condemning the Christian Right as intolerant, fascist, deranged, sinister, and many other things. Something about the phenomenon arouses a fury and fear that exceed any rational cause.

The root of this reaction is the fact that the Christian Right contradicts the official "enlightened" history of the modern world whereby, as human discoveries advance, religion necessarily recedes, becoming less and less credible, more and more marginal, until it is merely the refuge of a few elderly people who will soon pass from the scene. It is the fact that the Christian Right is correctly perceived as a resurgence, that it attracts many young people to its ranks, and that it has growing strength, that arouses such antagonism.

The Christian Right is a genuine emanation of American culture in that it enjoys no support from those who strive to shape the future of American society, fits no familiar theory of modernity, replenishes itself from reservoirs filled centuries ago yet still flowing, and at the same time shows a sometimes baffling capacity for innovation and surprise. It is the ultimate uncontrolled cultural emanation that above all threatens the hegemony of the New Class and the social engineers. (For years the Supreme Court has routinely spoken of religion as a dangerous substance, rooted in mere emotion, likely to break forth at any time in murderous strife.)

While shaped by centuries of institutional history, much of American religion at present is also a genuinely spontaneous emanation from culture, precisely because it goes so much against the worldview taken for granted among the dominant classes of society. Evangelical Protestantism is like petroleum deep in the cultural soil, often declared to be used up, then erupting in unexpected places and with surprising strength. The nondenominational character of so much of contemporary religious life also reflects this—spontaneous religious upsurges often only thinly connected to any tradition or established institution.

For the same reason the most common kind of conversion story over the past 30 years has been in the evangelical mode, in contrast to the sacramental-doctrinal mode, because the latter has had the social and cultural supports yanked out from under it, while the evangelical mode flourishes in an atmosphere of individualism, of preoccupation with one's subjective spiritual state, of being at odds with the larger culture.

In terms of H. Richard Niebuhr's famous typology of *Christ and Culture* (1951), in one sense the Christian Right must be said to believe in the union of

Christ and culture. Thus it speaks about a "Christian America" and justifies its program as representing authentic America against those who would undermine it. There are of course varying degrees of sophistication on this point, and an accurate historical assessment must be complex—in certain ways the Christian Right legitimately claims that it is merely defending things that have been traditional in American life, while it also misses important indications to the contrary; this ambiguity is embodied in the thought of the Founding Fathers themselves.

The Right's Embrace of Technology

Besides its general acceptance of democracy and capitalism, the Christian Right, as has often been noted, has embraced technology, if anything, even more enthusiastically than have liberal Christians. The Right's effective use of the electronic media is the most dramatic example, and there is an impression that people in technologically advanced fields, such as engineers and computer experts, are disproportionately represented in its ranks. Almost the last category of people one would expect to find are those in traditional humanistic disciplines often regarded as in rivalry with the technological worldview, such as poets and artists.

This uncritical embrace of technology is in some ways mysterious, but its roots may go back several centuries. On one level, the Puritan critique of Catholicism and Anglicanism was that these faiths did not go far enough in the process of the "disenchantment of the world," still believing that there was spiritual meaning in material things. Catholics even had what seemed like a quasi-magical view of the world, while Puritanism held that divine reality was only accessible in purely spiritual modes, without tangible symbol or support. Thus, if the material world is devoid of sacramental meaning, it may be the object of technological control without scruple.

Thus, once again, the attitudes of both the Christian Right and the Christian Left towards culture are ambivalent. Not all of the Christian Left inclines towards radical ecologism, but much of it does. Meanwhile, the Christian Right, while condemning many features of contemporary culture, especially its morals, has no serious quarrel with the force that has to so great an extent shaped that culture.

Surprisingly, the spiritual effects of technology have not been systematically explored in religious circles, perhaps because in their very act of discussing them,

Christians can hardly avoid making use of airplanes, computers, fax machines, and many other things, and because of the illogicality of drawing the line of technological limit at some arbitrary historical point, as the Amish seem to do.

But the Christian Right's failure to identify technology as the source of many of the features of modernity that it condemns may not be illogical, once it is recognized that modernity has been shaped by many factors, and overtly intellectual and spiritual causes should not be slighted. The conscious philosophical and moral outlook of modernism has been shaped by intellectuals, many of whom have themselves been indifferent to technology, some even quite hostile. Although it may be a mistaken assumption by the Christian Right, it is at least a defensible one that technology is not responsible for the decay of culture so much as the intellectual movement of cultural modernism is.

Varieties of Political Engagement

Self-proclaimed secularists are relatively rare in America, and the most potent opposition to the Christian Right comes from the Christian Left, really a continuation, on the stage of the larger society, of internal religious quarrels dating back a century. Both kinds of Christians (here divided more along theological than political lines, in terms of the weight given to the idea of a fully authoritative divine relation) see the other as inauthentic, which, given each side's theological assumptions, is a logical conclusion.

The antagonism between these two branches of Christianity, which, as many people have pointed out, crosses most denominational lines, is itself one of the most revealing illustrations of the reality of the "culture wars." The Christian Right defends what it regards as the authentic America rapidly slipping away, while the Christian Left casts its lot with an ideal future America already partly realized through political action. The conflicts are not illusory.

Much of the hysteria provoked by the Christian Right comes from the fact that it not only is based on a theology that was supposed to be dying, but it also has managed to use the political process for its own purposes, the process that modernist reformers long assumed rightly belonged to themselves. Thus, words like *insurgent* are often used to describe successful movements of the Christian Right. The modernist agenda seemingly triumphed permanently with the election of John F. Kennedy in 1960, and for many modernists the political history of the nation since 1968 seems like a nightmarish and almost inexplicable detour in the march of history.

The entry into politics by the Christian Right is open to criticism on a number of scores, including theological ones, and such criticisms are familiar enough not to require summation here. In terms of Niebuhr's categories, this entry into politics by fundamentalists and Evangelicals in part reveals the belief that Christ and American culture are united, or at least used to be, but also shades into the mode of Christ against culture, since the Right's agenda rests on perceptions of a corrupt culture in need of redemption.

The Christian Right is often accused of advocating theocracy, and probably in its broad folds there are some who do hope for such a thing. (However, what is a theocracy? Historians have never agreed, for example, whether the term should be applied to Calvin's Geneva or Puritan New England, to say nothing of less obvious candidates.) To the degree that Christians do harbor such dreams it is fair to say that they have fated themselves to suffer bitter disappointment, perhaps most of all should they ever attain their goals.

The Christian Right is quite obviously a product of culture by the fact that it is, as it claims to be, a genuine manifestation of the modern democratic principle according to which, if a particular social group feels itself aggrieved, the solution is to organize itself politically and take its case to the public. This has been the whole point of the Moral Majority and the Christian Coalition, although it would have been incomprehensible to religious leaders prior to the modern era. Far from being a threat to democracy, the Christian Right with touching faith reaffirms its belief that democratic action is the best way to correct social wrongs.

Political Withdrawal?

Religious critics of the Religious Right are correct in warning that political action can be, and often has been, corrupting of religious purity, and it would be a naïve enthusiast indeed to suppose that somehow such activity can substitute for formal worship, private prayer, personal acts of charity, and everything else that comprises a truly Christian way of life.

But the call for conservative Christians to withdraw from politics must be recognized for the radical demand that it is—perhaps the ultimate case of Christ versus culture as Niebuhr defined it. For such a withdrawal would mean a withdrawal from the democratic process itself, essentially from modern society itself, the rejection of one of the important dimensions of modernity that even most orthodox Christians have found acceptable. The Christian Coalition is playing according to the rules of a democratic society and, were they to dissolve themselves, would be negating those rules.

The only possible alternative is some kind of monasticism, including the kind of monasticism lived by groups like the Amish. In every age, some are called to live the monastic life, which the Catholic Church has always taught is the Christian life in its fullness and purity. But the corollary is that in every age most Christians are not called to live such a life and, even if they were, would not do so. But in modern democratic societies there are no viable alternatives between monasticism and democratic participation. (It should be noted that in the Catholic Church even monks usually vote in civil elections.)

If a new Dark Age is indeed coming over Western society, then of necessity the monastic path will probably be the only one open to Christians, and they will once again find themselves, willy-nilly, the saviors of culture as well as of faith, just like the monks of a thousand years ago. However, this is a path that will be imposed by Divine Providence acting through historical events, and it would be presumptuous and irresponsible merely to assume it at present.

If there is a new Dark Age, it will differ in one important respect from the previous one, in that the Dark Ages of the period circa A.D. 500–1000 came about largely because of the collapse of the Roman Empire, which plunged most of Europe into chaos. There is no sign today that powerful governments are going to wither away, as Karl Marx foretold, or be destroyed by force. Thus, a cultural and spiritual Dark Age would occur within the confines of an all-powerful state quite capable of maintaining its laws by force.

Politics as Defense of Life & Family

The abortion issue illustrates the dilemma of democratic participation by Christians. Many people accuse pro-lifers of wanting to "impose" their own moral views on the rest of the society, even of wanting to establish a theocracy. Pro-lifers respond that they only wish to regain for the unborn the protection that the law offers all human beings and that they fight for a principle that was not even questioned in American life until barely 30 years ago. In Catholic terms, the struggle is not to impose religious dogma but to force society to recognize moral principles accessible to reason itself. (There is an occasional atheist who sees the evil of abortion.)

The best argument for Christian participation in politics is the simple one that Jerry Falwell offered when he founded the Moral Majority—although fundamentalists wanted to stay out of politics, they found that politics would not let them alone. Political action has become a defensive activity.

Thus, not only is abortion legal, but it is also argued that taxpayers must fund it and that its "benefits" must be made available to girls without their parents' knowledge or consent. The public schools at all levels are centers of bureaucratic experiments in social engineering, especially in changing children's moral perceptions, even as government regulation and the taxing power can be used to drive private schools out of existence.

The definition of child abuse can be expanded to include parents accused of "imposing rigid values" on their children. The work of evangelization is systematically thwarted by the fact that the media often do not treat Christianity with even minimal fairness and can choke the message of the gospel before it can even be proclaimed. (Fundamentalists have, once again, successfully gotten around this barrier through their creation of an alternative media, another example of generating new things spontaneously from the culture without regard for the dominant institutions of the society.)

The Christian Right has above all claimed for itself the title "pro-family," a claim that enrages critics who insist that they are no less so. But one of the major fronts in the culture war is, of course, precisely the drive to redefine the family as virtually any community of persons with more than ephemeral ties to one another.

The redefinition of the family is essential to modernism both because such a redefinition is the essence of social engineering and because the family as traditionally understood is the final and most deep-seated institution of a culture independent of the state. If "it takes a village" to raise children properly, then the authority of the parents will be steadily diminished by that of the village elders, in this case primarily government bureaucrats.

There is a long history of modernism's assault on the family, because it recognized almost from the beginning that the family is indeed the center of the most stubborn resistance to social engineering. Thus, even those Christians who are tempted to eschew politics in favor of turning inward, into their families and their religious communities, will eventually hear the knock on the door. (The Supreme Court once considered the question whether Amish parents have a right not to send their children to school after a certain age. A divided court ruled that they do, but it is not at all certain that the issue will not arise again, and be decided in a different way.)

The Christian Right is often accused of being reactionary, which, in a literal sense, it is. But one of its strengths, and one of the guarantees of its authenticity, is the fact that it does not attempt to forge its own proactive agenda for American society but contents itself with reacting against perceived assaults by others, a democratic way of acting and one that undercuts any temptation to theocracy. In effect, the Christian Right promises to be a force in politics only so long as it senses the need to defend its members in their way of life. That is likely to be a long time.

Christ & the Salvation of Culture

Plastic statues on the dashboards of pious Catholic drivers, or homey religious slogans on the wall plaques of Protestant kitchens, may elicit superior smiles or shudders of distaste from the sophisticated, including sophisticated believers. But in assessing the relationship between Christ and culture it is important to recognize a simple but startling fact—although Christ is everywhere, his presence is explicitly acknowledged mainly in the lives of ordinary people, in ways it is never acknowledged in gatherings of the sophisticated. It may seem gauche, and more than a little theologically perplexing, for a high-school football team to huddle in prayer before taking the field, but it is an important fact about the culture that no one would even dream of suggesting such a thing in, for example, the boardrooms of Microsoft or the editorial offices of the *New York Times*.

Salvation will not come through politics, and in a sense the renewal of the society must come from the renewal of culture, a task in which few Christians seem to be consciously engaged and for which perhaps few are suited. However, before Christians can even think about transforming culture, they must first act to protect culture from the voracious appetite of the modernist state, must tenaciously affirm the autonomy of culture, which at the deepest level means affirming and securing the autonomy of religion.

Modernity has now exhausted itself and has no more powers of revitalization. The modernist trail, whatever good it has led to over the past almost five centuries, has at last petered out in compulsory skepticism and the substitution of raw power for free human action.

The salvation of culture does not lie in a return to the past, which is always impossible, nor can it be achieved even by a renewed attention to the wellsprings of the culture, such as Greek philosophy. Bold and radical actions alone will serve, inspired by that mysterious power that always holds out the promise of throwing off the old man, of making all things new.

Reprinted from Touchstone: A Journal of Mere Christianity, *Winter 1997, Volume 10, Number 1. Originally given as a lecture at* Touchstone's *conference, "In the World: The Gospel of the Resurrection in a Culture of Death," Chicago, Illinois, 1996.*

SCIENTISM: THE WORLD'S LITTLEST RELIGION

*How Theology Must Confront
the New Global Religion*

TRADITIONALLY, when people wanted to know the big picture or ultimate nature of things, they turned to their sacred texts or, if they were primal peoples, to the great orienting myths that their ancestors bequeathed to them. Since modern science arose, however, Westerners have looked increasingly to it to tell them what things are like. An intellectual historian has estimated that already a hundred years ago more Westerners believed in the periodic table of chemical elements than believed in any of the distinctive things the Bible speaks of. The reason for the shift is obvious. Modern science can prove its theses through controlled experiments. A moment's reflection on how much those theses have changed our world will convince anyone that they have a firm grip on the way nature works.

This about-face from Scripture to science has worked heavily against theology's overview. In his *Understanding the Present: Science and the Soul of Modern Man*,[1] Brian Appleyard asks us to imagine a missionary to an African tribe. Conversion is slow work until a child comes down with an infectious disease. The local medicine men are summoned and do their best, but to no avail. The child's condition steadily worsens until the missionary administers the penicillin she thought to bring with her, whereupon the child recovers.

With that single move, Appleyard concludes, it is all over for the tribe's traditional culture. Elijah has challenged the priests of Baal, and has won. "Elijah" is science here, and its victories continue both at home and abroad. Stephen Carter reports a discernable increase in America's culture of disbelief in the last twenty years alone. "There is less respect for religion, less of an appreciation of it as an important force that can genuinely be the motive force in people's lives without being somehow a symptom of something neurotic."[2]

How should theology conduct itself in a global village in which religion is increasingly on the defensive? I will propositionalize my proposals. They are heavily opinionated and eschew nuances. I shall state them categorically to make the issues stand out as starkly as possible.

1. *Theology should recognize scientism as its principal enemy.*
Science deserves no reproach, but scientism goes beyond the findings of science to assume that the scientific method is the only reliable (or at least most reliable) road to truth, and that the things science deals with are the most fundamental things that exist. In slipping into these assumptions, it turns into a religion that challenges traditional, orthodox ones to the core. Rarely is its position stated. It proceeds surreptitiously, by innuendo and surmise, and this makes it difficult to combat. If it came out into the open, the arbitrariness of its premises would become apparent and it would cease to be the problem that it is. It would be wrong to blame scientists for scientism; the proportion of them who are taken in by it is no greater than that of the population at large.[3] No individuals or groups are responsible. It is the marvels of science and its technology that have made scientism the working assumption of our era.

2. *In addition to the foregoing marks of scientism, theologians should be aware of its inherent imperialism.*
The imperialism is not calculated, so again blame is out of place; but the imperialism proceeds anyway, and Spinoza helps us to see why. Everything, the blessed Spinoza taught, possesses an inbuilt *conatus,* a propensity not just to maintain itself but to enlarge its domain until it runs into something that stops it. This holds for institutions as well as organisms, and, as there is nothing currently strong enough to stop science, it crests into scientism.

I have already pointed out that many scientists as individuals recognize scientism for what it is, but two things keep going on. From the inside, loyalty to their profession pressures scientists to exaggerate their abilities in the public eye, for this brings both prestige and funding. Concomitantly, from the outside, the public at large virtually requires scientists to behave that way, for the world is always in need of salvation, gods are salvation's agents, and science is the current god. So scientists are not allowed to point out that their competence covers only the physical world. They must pronounce on the whole of things, for a restricted god is no God at all. "The Cosmos [understood as what cosmologists deal with] is all that ever was or ever will be," Carl Sagan declaims,[4] and at the conclusion of *A Brief History of Time*,[5] Stephen Hawking speculates on science's end: a set of equations which, because they could implicitly account for everything that ever happened or ever could happen, would be a Theory of Everything. In *Darwin's Dangerous Idea*, cognitive scientist Daniel Dennett asserts flatly that Darwinism—"as secure an idea as any science," he claims—shows conclusively that mind derives from "mindless, purposeless forces," rather than, as theologians had supposed, the other way around.[6]

It would be a mistake to dismiss spokesmen like these as extremists, for—superstars that they are—they do more to shape the public image of science than their reasonable counterparts do. Brian Appleyard, whom I have already cited, summarizes this second of my points as follows: "Spiritually corrosive, burning away ancient authorities and traditions, science has shown itself unable to coexist with anything."[7]

3. *Theology should expose its enemy for the paper tiger that it actually is.*

Stripped of science's prestige, which it battens on but has no right to, scientism does not have a leg to stand on. The astounding power of science to probe the workings of nature gives it zero credentials for pronouncing on the whole of things, unless one assumes that nature is the whole, which begs the question.

Nothing would do more to restore society's respect for theology than a clear recognition of this point, so I shall address it head-on with an expanded syllogism.

    a. Science is our sacral mode of knowing.

    b. The crux of science is the controlled experiment.

    c. We can control only what is inferior to us.

    d. Conclusion: Science discloses only our inferiors, from which God is excluded by definition.

No science course or textbook ever informs us of beings that are superior to us in the traits we most prize, including intelligence, wisdom, and compassion, for as far as science can make out, the human species is the noblest thing in existence. And it is clear why science must so conclude, for it cannot see beyond us when it comes to values. To mount a controlled experiment of the sort that gives science authority to speak, one must know what the relevant variables are, and if grander beings than us exist—angels? God?—their variables elude us in the way those relating to human consciousness elude the sniff tests of dogs. Our superiors, if they exist, dance circles around us, not we them.

Obviously, that science cannot speak to God's existence does not prove that he does exist. It does, though, leave the question wide open, for as the saying goes, absence of evidence is not evidence of absence.

4. *Recognizing that universities are scientistic and hence secular to the core, seminaries should stop tailoring their theologies to academic styles of thought.*
At his inauguration, a recent president of Johns Hopkins University, Steven Muller, made a pithy statement that speaks tomes. "The trouble with today's university," he said, "is that it is rooted in the scientific method, and the trouble with the scientific method is that it cannot deal with values." Strictly speaking, Muller should have said that it cannot deal with intrinsic and normative values, for it can deal with descriptive and instrumental ones. With that qualification, however, he could have gone on to list five other things it cannot deal with: existential meanings, teleology, qualities as distinct from quantities, invisibles that are not strictly entailed by the behaviors of visible objects in the way electromagnetic fields are entailed, and (as my previous point noted) our superiors.

That is a huge omission: virtually our entire lived world. Yet the social, self-styled human sciences ape the methods of the natural sciences in the hope of approximating their successes. In doing so, they leave the larger part of our humanity unaccounted for. Robert Bellah tells the story:

> The assumptions underlying mainstream social science are positivism (the assumption that the methods of natural science are the only approach to valid knowledge); reductionism (the tendency to explain the complex in terms of the simple and to find behind complex cultural forms biological, psychological or sociological drives, needs and interests); relativism (the assumption that matters

of morality and religion cannot be judged true or false, but simply vary with persons, cultures and societies); and determinism (the tendency to think that human actions are explained in terms of "variables" that will account for them). The upshot is that what social scientists teach and write undermines all traditional thought and belief.[8]

Even the humanities feel the methodological suction of science's Black Hole. To speak only of religious studies, Marcus Borg reports that "to a large extent, the defining characteristic of biblical scholarship in the modern period is the attempt to understand Scripture without reference to another world because in this period the visible world of space and time is the world we think of as 'real.'"[9]

Arthur Green describes the consequences for Jewish studies as follows:

> The emergence of *Wissenschaft* brought forth the bifurcation between the study of Torah as a religious obligation and the forging of scholarly research into a surrogate religion of its own. We are forced to "bracket" for the purposes of teaching and research our faith in God. The methods by which religion is studied in the university are those of history and philology (in the humanities) and anthropology, psychology, and sociology (in the social sciences). Their impact has been to discount Torah as a divine creation. A scholar who has submitted an article to the *Journal of the American Academy of Religion* or the *Journal of Biblical Literature* assuming that Scripture was quite literally the Word of God would be a laughingstock.[10]

In *The Soul of the American University*, the historian George Marsden sums up the situation by saying that in five short generations, American universities have gone from "Protestant establishment to established non-belief."[11] Given this switch, it is ironic to find seminaries routinely importing university styles of thought, but psychologically the move is understandable. Mainline seminaries ring the universities, whose greater prestige causes seminary professors to look up to their closest university counterparts and hope that they will consider theology too to be a respectable intellectual endeavour.

Our century has witnessed Heidegger shaping Bultmann and New Testament studies, Whitehead spawning process theology, Darwin inspiring Teilhard and the theology of hope, Marx prompting liberation theology, and multiculturalism and political correctness powering feminist theology.

Influences of these sorts have been so strong that they have turned seminaries into subcultures for breeding new religions, William Abraham of Southern Methodist University argues. As these religions are mostly fathered by the secular university, it is not surprising that they are theologically anemic. Changing the subject (without notice) from cosmology to metaphysics, Bultmann argued (spuriously) that the collapse of the pre-Copernican three-story universe retires ontological hierarchies as well; but is Heidegger's Being (that this left him with) a match for the God of the Bible or the *ens perfectissimum* of medieval theology?

If, as existentialists would have us believe, to objectivize is to be inauthentic, what does this do to our thought about God as he exists in his own right? Both Whitehead and the theology of hope historicize God and turn him into something that in ways is "not yet." In this account God did not create time; he is caught in its net. John Cobb says we should "accept without hesitation or embarrassment the distinction between ultimate reality and God,"[12] and Teilhard's notion of Christ as "the term of evolution" upsets God's alpha-omega balance and makes meaning turn on the fate of nature. If science's actual findings required such diminishings, we should have to put up with them, but they do not. The influences rise from universities like vapors, beclouding theological vision.

I do not include feminist and liberation theologies in the losses I just listed because they have religious as well as academic roots and do good as well as harm. Their objectives are admirable, but their strategies raise serious questions. Thomas Oden of Drew University thinks that a version of political correctness he calls "ultrafeminist" has vitiated the theological institutions,[13] but I will withhold judgment on that and confine myself to what feminism is doing to language. Turning *hierarchy* and *patriarchy* into dirty words seriously affects the religious future.

Hierarchy was originally one of the noblest words in language, holding out (as it does etymologically) for power that is suffused with holiness. The eclectic Left redefines the word to mean the exact opposite: oppressive, abusive power. To do so, it resolutely closes its eyes to the fact that hierarchies can empower as well as oppress. A loving family with small children is an empowering hierarchy, as is a well-run classroom. The paradigm of a benevolent, empowering hierarchy is God's relation to the world: "God became man that man might become God." Without worthy hierarchies we have no one to look up to. We are stripped of empowering role models.

As for *patriarchy*, whether there have even been any other than patriarchal societies is unclear; definitions enter, and pre-history remains pretty much pre-history. Even if there have been, however, the enduring historical religions were for the most part patently fashioned by men—God's workings don't figure much in feminist accounts. So if patriarchy is bad, so are its products, the religions it fashioned. Intended or not, this is the message of feminist and liberation theology that falls on public ears, which are poorly tuned to nuances and qualifications. Whether the mainline churches can survive this broadside remains to be seen, for beginning with the family, tradition turns on respecting one's elders who have given us life, and historians are reporting that no generation has regarded its heritage as re-proachfully as ours does.[14] Some words that Walter Lippmann penned a half-century ago echo ominously here.

> Socialization has to be transmitted from the old to the young, and habits and ideas must be maintained as a seamless web of memory among the bearers of the tradition, generation after generation. If this does not happen, community will break down into factional wars and the new generation will be faced with the task of rediscovering, reinventing, and relearning by trial and error most of what it needs. No one generation can do this.[15]

That injustice exists, and probably always has, is beyond question, but the lines of causation are tangled and obscure. We are back with Karl Popper's counsel: It is safer to work for specific immediate objectives than to pour energies into ideologies that presume to understand the complicated forces that went into the making of earlier societies and the way the world works. Such ideologies convince less by their logic than by their violent voicing of partially legitimate causes.

Up to this point I have focused on problems. It is time for the good news: theology's opportunity.

5. *Amid the bewilderment that almost everyone feels today, theology has the answer people are waiting to hear.*
I say this because theology is the custodian of the wisdom traditions of mankind. Not everything in them is wise. Modern science has retired its cosmologies, and its social blueprints, for example, master/slave and gender relationships, need to be

reviewed in the light of changed circumstances and our continuing search for justice. But on the nature of ultimate reality and the way human life can best be comported in its context, there is nothing outside the abiding religions that rival their truth.

Currently, we are in the best position we have been in for four centuries to recognize this fact, for though scientism is still with us, frontier thinkers now recognize that science cannot provide a worldview and "leaves the problems of life completely untouched," as Wittgenstein pointed out. This is what, philosophically, has moved us from the modern into the postmodern era. But postmodernism is in no better position to compete with the wisdom traditions, because it rejects worldviews in principle. More concerned with justice than with metaphysics— "society is the magic world of our times," George Will reports—postmodernism dismisses metanarratives on grounds that they "totalize," and thereby marginalize minorities.[16] This leaves theology without serious metaphysical rivals. *Carpe diem!* Seize the day! Some think that differences among the world's religions make it inappropriate to speak of theology in the singular in the global village, but I find a common conceptual spine underlying them all: the Great Chain of Being.[17]

My *Forgotten Truth*[18] is devoted to a cross-cultural discussion of that spine, but here I can only mention its pivotal point. There is an alternate reality to the one we normally experience and expand through science. It is momentously better, more powerful, and more real than our quotidian world, and the chief reason the mainline churches are losing ground is that scientism and the academy have loosened their grips on it, leaving them with no clear alternative to the liberal intellectual ethos of our day. They continue to use the word *God,* but what is the cash value of that word when it is injected into a world that is basically vectored by Darwin, Marx, Nietzsche, Freud, and the Big Bang?

That world is too small for the human spirit. To the degree that the mainline churches accept it, their parishioners will go elsewhere. In North America today, this means going to conservative churches (fundamentalist, Evangelical, or Pentecostal), to Asian religions, or to New Age enthusiasms, all of which do challenge the naturalistic outlook of mainstream intellectuals.

Reprinted from Touchstone: A Journal of Mere Christianity, *Summer 1997, Volume 10, Number 3. Adapted from the author's 1995 lecture, "Doing Theology in the Global Village," at the University of Saskatchewan, and published in* Religious Studies and Theology.

ENDNOTES

1. New York: Doubleday, 1993.

2. Interview with Stephen Carter in the *Harvard Divinity School Forum,* vol. 2, no. 1 (1993).

3. John Polkinghorne's assessment of the matter is as clear-eyed as one could wish to find: "Science's great success is purchased through the modesty of its ambition, restricting the phenomena it is prepared to discuss to those of an impersonal, and largely repeatable, character." (*The Faith of a Scientist* [Princeton: Princeton University Press, 1994], p. 5).

4. Carl Sagan, *Cosmos* (New York: Random House, 1980), p. 4.

5. David Hickman [producer] (U.S.: Triton Pictures, 1992).

6. New York: Simon & Schuster, 1995.

7. Brian Appleyard, op. cit., p. 9.

8. Robert Bellah, National Institute of Campus Ministries *Journal,* Summer 1981, pp. 10–11.

9. Marcus Borg, "Root Images and the Way We See," *Fragments of Infinity* (Dorset, U.K. and Lindfield, Australia, 1991), p. 38.

10. Arthur Green, in *Tikkun,* I.1, 1968.

11. George Marsden, *The Soul of the American University* (New York: Oxford University Press, 1994). Page Smith covers much the same ground in his *Killing the Spirit* (New York: Viking Press, 1990). Supporting evidence for this arrives as I write this paragraph. In the October 19, 1995 issue of the *New York Review of Books,* the university presses in America join forces to run an eight-page advertisement for their books. The 24 categories into which the titles are divided include dance, ethnology, general interest, and even photography. Religion is not among them.

12. John Cobb, "Can a Christian Be a Buddhist, Too?" *Japanese Religions* (December 1978), p. 11.

13. Thomas C. Oden, *Requiem: A Lament in Three Movements* (Nashville, Tennessee: Abingdon Press, 1995).

14. For documentation, see Richard M. Weaver, *Visions of Order: The Cultural Crisis of our Time* (Bryn Mawr, Pennsylvania: Intercollegiate Studies Institute, 1995): "I do not find any other period in which men have felt to an equal degree that the past either is uninteresting or is a reproach to them."

15. Walter Lippmann, *The Public Philosophy* (Boston: Little, Brown, and Company, 1955).

16. For an elaboration of this point, see my essay, "The Religious Significance of Postmodernism," *Faith and Philosophy,* vol. 12, no. 3 (July 1995), pp. 409–422.

17. Those who want my thoughts on religious pluralism will find them touched on in "Bubble Blown and Lived In: A Theological Autobiography," *Dialog,* vol. 33, no. 4, pp. 274–279; and presented in greater detail in my "Introduction to Fritjof Schuon," *The Transcendent Unity of Religions* (New York: Pantheon, 1953).

18. New York: Harper & Row, 1976.

PATRICK HENRY REARDON

CLASSROOM CHAOS

Atheism & the Public Schools

O VER THE PAST COUPLE OF DECADES many Christians in this country, feeling a great deal of frustration with our public education, have attempted to deal with the problem in various ways. Some have assumed the enormous task of educating their children at home (cf. Leon J. Podles, "No Place Like Home," pp. 32–43 in this volume), while others, as though shaking the very dust from their feet, have taken the more public stand of establishing independent Christian schools, following a long tradition of Roman Catholics and certain Lutherans.

The frustration that Christians feel about our public schools is certainly understandable. Not only does the steady annual decline in SAT scores show that these schools are largely failing in their task of education, but a large body of sociological data indicates that they have become spawning beds of violent and other undesirable behavior. The full significance of these phenomena hits us when we ponder that 90 percent of American students are enrolled in these schools. Indeed, it appears to some of us that, were there afoot an actual conspiracy involving the American Federation of Teachers, the National Education Association, the American Civil Liberties Union (ACLU), the Surgeon General, and the Supreme

Court to sabotage the education, moral well-being, and physical safety of American children, the results would be close to what we have now.

Even without a conspiracy theory (to which I do not subscribe), it is difficult to avoid the impression that our public schools have been turning large numbers of kids into barbarians and atheists. Leaving aside barbarism, which experience suggests that children can generally manage on their own, something really does need to be said about the privileged place of atheism in the public school systems of this country. Unlike barbarism, atheism does not come naturally. It must be taught, and right now it is certainly being taught.

Three established policies in particular combine to give substance to my contention that atheism is now the dominant ideology in our public schools: the emphasis on evolution in science classes, the departure from the ethical perspectives of the Bible, and the prohibition of public prayer. I propose to comment briefly on each of these policies and on some of the corresponding reforms suggested by Christians in response to them.

Cosmic Chaos

First, there is evolution. Teaching philosophy in a local college over the past several years, I've discovered that many of my students are, from an early age, spoon-fed a theory according to which the universe and everything in it resulted from a series of accidents occurring over "millions of years." (They employ this last expression, by the way, as though it actually corresponded to some real concept of which their heads were in firm and serene possession. Like too many of their teachers, you see, college kids nowadays succumb on occasion to a sort of nominalism, in the sense that they do not always distinguish sharply between the exercise of the mind and the running of the mouth.) They have sometimes been brainwashed with this theory, accepting it with a mindless faith beyond any that a religious institution would dare require of its members.

These young people have been brought to imagine that, while the evidence of intricate design in eyeglasses and hearing aids, for example, is a sound premise for concluding that these things were fashioned with intelligence and on purpose, no similar argument can be reasonably advanced about the formation of eyes and ears. Such a fancy is so radically at variance with "the instinct for probabilities that we call common sense" (Chesterton) that the participle "brainwashed" is almost too weak to describe its victims. Discussing evolution with me, one of my students confidently affirmed that a group of monkeys, were they left with a typewriter long enough, would eventually reconstruct the entire Bible by pure chance. When I simply replied, "No, they wouldn't," I rejoiced to detect in his eyes the sudden dawning of a new day.

Often, however, when I draw attention to the a priori implausibility of claiming that the myriad complex systems of the universe are the result of accident (appealing to St. Thomas's fifth proof), my students sometimes react in disbelief at my daring, as though I had trespassed, still shod, the vicinity of some burning bush. No one seems ever to have suggested to them that the considerable evidence for evolution, both cosmic and biological, is quite compatible with the presumption of teleology, and therefore with the existence of the wise Creator.

There is, moreover, an obvious epistemological difficulty in holding to random evolution. Even the ancient atomist Democritus realized that if the whole universe is haphazard, so are all processes of human thought taking place within it, a conclusion that inevitably introduces solipsism and the impossibility of communication. That line of non-thought was long ago laid to rest by Socrates when he gently dismembered poor Gorgias.

In response to the reckless indoctrination of our children with this science fiction version of evolution, many conservative Christians urge that "Creation Science" be taught in school as an alternative explanation of the universe, and they resent the 1987 Supreme Court decision striking down a Louisiana law making such teaching a requirement. Personally, however, I resist the idea of teaching Creation Science, not because of scientific reservations (such as those of Austin L. Hughes, "Creation, Science, and the New Gnosticism," *Touchstone,* Fall 1993), but for theological and philosophical considerations.

Relative to theology: We Christians affirm creation as a mystery of the Faith, a doctrine of the church's creed. Flesh and blood have not revealed it to us. We know it in the same way that we know the identity of Christ—through the grace and "obedience of faith," by the testimony of the Holy Spirit in the church's proclamation of the gospel. It is a mystery pertaining to the glory of God shining on the face of Jesus Christ. We believe in creation because we know the Creator: "The God who said 'let light shine' in darkness, hath shown in our hearts. . . ." Creation is a theological reference in the strict sense, a component of the biblical truth perceived in Christ.

Consequently, the doctrine of creation should not be identified or confused with any theory derived from a scientific analysis of the physical world (nor even with the classical "cosmological arguments" for God's existence, as valid and cogent as I think some of them to be). The very name "Creation Science" encourages such a confusion. Following the example of those conservative Christians who study extra-biblical sources of ancient history to prove that "the Bible got it right," some Christians imagine that they can do the same thing with a scientific study of the "origins of the universe." With all due respect to the sincerity of that apologetic intention, there are more serious limits to the latter enterprise.

Relative to philosophy: Since the fatherly framers of the creed understood the act of creation to be "from nothing," there is a mammoth problem with attempting its empirical examination. Just how does one inductively track the "transition" from nothing to something, or even ask the question without seeming foolish? Even with the best of optic advantages, it is hard to gain a sharp gaze at "nothing." Indeed, the effort is manifestly utopian in the literal sense that there is "no place" (*ou topos*) to look. Whatever Creation Science thinks it is studying, it is not studying creation. If, as Christians believe, all things are created ex nihilo, it is obvious that no empirical science can examine the "motion" (Aristotle's *kinesis*) by which they exist, the divine act by which they are separated from nothingness.

The manifest impropriety and analogy marking my language here should suggest that we are talking of a divine mystery when we use the word *creation*. It has no more business in a science course than do *Incarnation* and *Redemption*. Whatever their frustration with the atheism currently favored by the arrogant treatment of evolution in our public schools, I submit that Christians should be very careful lest they come to confuse just another scientific theory with divinely revealed truth.

Moral & Cultural Chaos

Second, there is the departure from biblical norms on moral questions in our public schools. The enormity of this problem is evident in the statistics relative to premarital sex, condoms, abortion, theft, cheating, and violence. Correctly judging that these evils are partly caused by the enforced absence of Holy Scripture from our public schools, many Christians have sought to bring it back somehow.

For example, several years ago the legislature of my native Kentucky passed a bill requiring that the Decalogue be posted in every public school classroom. The legislators hoped, of course, that this procedure might lead to a lessening of social scourges like murder, adultery, stealing, bearing false witness, and the failure to honor fathers and mothers. Almost immediately, however, a hardly surprising conjunction of the ACLU and the federal courts removed the Decalogue from those classroom walls. Thus, kids in Kentucky got the message that murder, adultery, stealing, bearing false witness, and the failure to honor their parents are somehow integral to their civil rights.

While the courts challenged that legislation on constitutional grounds, it seems that it could also be challenged for theological reasons. The individual requirements of the Decalogue, after all, are not ethical standards in a vacuum. Based on that initial self-proclamation of the saving God and its concomitant interdiction of idolatry, the Ten Commandments are components of a divine covenant. Thus, the action of the Kentucky legislature could have accomplished only one of two things: It could have removed the Decalogue from its defining covenantal context and thus distort it, or it could have suggested that the commonwealth of Kentucky enjoys some special covenant relationship with God. Certain thorny questions would appear to escort either option.

The real task, I believe, is to make our public schools deal realistically with what Russell Kirk called "the moral conversation of mankind." Can that be done with no reference to the Bible, the major and defining moral text of Western civilization? I don't see how.

To remove the Bible from the established education of 90 percent of American school children is to deprive them of familiarity with the chief literary font of their own inherited culture. We simply cannot do such a thing and simultaneously describe it as "education." By analogy, I would insist that my own Christian children, were I raising them in an ambient Hindu or Moslem culture, should learn the Upanishads or the Qur'an respectively, in order to be literate and culturally functional.

We should not underestimate, however, the difficulties attendant on putting the Bible back in public schools. Even if we were able to persuade the public that ignorance of the Bible is incompatible with being a literate and even modestly educated person (which seems obvious to me), just how would we teach the Scriptures in public school?

The usual answer is that we should simply expose children to the Bible as inherited literature, without interpretation or evaluation. Maybe, but permit me a doubt. Can this kind of biblical reading be effected in the public schools when it really hasn't been done in denominational seminaries, even in those that think they are doing it? Ingenious are the ways already devised to bypass the Bible in courses ostensibly devoted to its study. Given the climate of contemporary education, how long would it be before our kids were learning about J, E, P, D, and Q, Proto-Luke, Pseudo-Zechariah and the rest of it? (All with a proper *Sitz im Kindergarten,* doubtless, so that the little ones could make their existential decision on the authentic *Urgrund,* if you catch my drift.)

Then again, what translation would be used? A thoroughgoing Protestant kind, like the New International Version? One of the "supermarket English" variety, such as the New American Bible? A feminist rendition that avoids those dreadful, oppressive, degrading pronouncements like "The Lord is King" and "Behold the handmaid of the Lord" and "Abba, Father"?

Finally, if a return to the Bible in our public schools is truly to be part of "the moral conversation of mankind," which sections would be presented? For example, would that high moral colloquy be significantly enriched by a non-evaluative reading of Amnon's incestuous rape of Tamar, Jacob's deception of Isaac, Phineas's quick action with his trusty spear, or that little incident involving Judah with his daughter-in-law? In short, while we may agree that American kids are being deprived of their cultural and moral birthright by not being taught the Bible as a regular part of their education, it is not yet clear how to implement a remedy for the current misfortune as it pertains to the public schools.

Prayer in Chaos

Third, there is the recently renewed question of authorized prayer in public school, outlawed by the Supreme Court since 1962. (Going even further in 1985, the Court struck down an Alabama law authorizing one daily minute of silence "for meditation or voluntary prayer.") A national poll reported in the *Pittsburgh Post-Gazette* (Nov. 27, 1994) shows that a whopping 80 percent of Americans favor a return to prayer in public schools, while political support for this proposal is wide enough to include figures as diverse as Newt Gingrich and Marion Barry. The general idea seems to be that prayer in school would encourage students to presume the existence of God, a presumption already made by the Pledge of Allegiance, the Declaration of Independence, the inscriptions on American currency, the normal procedures in both legislatures and courts, and other common expressions of theism in American life. All this would seem reasonable enough.

The negative response of civil libertarians, however, sometimes borders on hysteria. For instance, when President Clinton modestly suggested that the matter was open to dialogue ("I'll be glad to discuss it with them. I want to see what the details are"), Arthur Kropp of People for the American Way promptly denounced his "gestures to the right wing." Evidently this "American way" does not include a rational exchange of views.

Leaving aside the "moment of silence" option, I have my own reasons for opposing the recent efforts to return authorized prayer to our public schools. Once again, the reasons are religious rather than political. I appeal to a theological principle, *lex orandi est lex credendi,* which I would paraphrase as "our prayer says what we believe."

I am very strict on this point. My wife and I taught our children to invoke no divinity but the God and Father of our Lord Jesus Christ. Relying on the teaching of Holy Scripture, we believe that our prayer must be based on the two defining affirmations given by the Holy Spirit: "Abba, Father" and "Jesus is Lord." In short, Christian prayer must be Trinitarian. A general, all-purpose godhead will not do. The substance of my opposition to the return of school prayers is that the God that I believe in may not be the one invoked in those prayers.

This is the reason I try to avoid "ecumenical" worship services where I cannot be sure which divinity will be invoked. Thus, I do not participate in annual interfaith Thanksgiving Day services, high-school baccalaureate celebrations, the dedication of local municipal buildings, and so forth. Whatever godhead is being invoked on those occasions, in my experience, the wording of the prayers does not even faintly hint that it might be the God whose glory shines from the face of Jesus Christ, the only name under heaven by which we must be saved, and the one Mediator between God and man.

Let me candidly illustrate my point, even at the risk of giving further offense. Until recently I experienced no scruples at worshipping with my Methodist friends when they invited me to their church for some special occasion. I regret to say that my conscience can no longer make that safe presumption. Since the publication of the new Methodist service book about three years ago, I might now find myself invoking God as "Grandfather, Great Spirit," "God, our grove," "Jesus our Mother," "our father and mother God," and (everybody's all-time favorite) "Bakerwoman."

Even worse, perhaps, are the "trial liturgies" inflicted on some long-suffering Episcopalians in the past few years, where the divinity is described in terms scarcely rising above animism.

Now my question is this: If such idolatry and syncretism have found their way even into those sanctuaries dedicated to the God professed in the Apostles' Creed, how can I feel any confidence in prayers written by some secular agency? Consequently, in the present circumstances I would be very reluctant to see public prayer returned to public schools.

Striving for Real Education

It is obvious that I perceive no way to correct the three major policies contributing to the atheism of our public schools. If Christians decide to stick with those schools, they are simply going to have to remedy the influence of those policies within the contexts of their homes and the catechetical programs of their congregations. As traditional parochial schools and more recent efforts among Evangelical Protestants have shown, moreover, those catechetical programs can be expanded into full-scale educational enterprises.

The fundamental presupposition of both religious schools and home-based education deserves more attention. Each of these endeavors is based on the persuasion that religious instruction should not be simply tacked onto an otherwise secular education. Ever since Socrates taught that the cultivation of one's soul is the purpose of life, education has meant, rather, the formation of *charakter* (internal shape, the moral integration of personality) by the encouragement of *arete* (virtue, excellence). Real education is qualitative: not how much (*quantum*) a person knows, but of what sort (*qualis*) a person becomes. Following the useful distinction of Irving Babbitt, a truly educated person's ethical "selection" must give form to his intellectual "sympathy." The full and proper structuring of conscience is the goal of education. Though we may compensate for their deficiencies, I do not see any way that our public schools can become the instruments for that sort of education in a way satisfactory to Christians.

So, is there no way out? Perhaps there is. We may with profit look at how other Western democracies handle the problems arising from the state's legitimate interest in mandatory education. In Great Britain, Canada, Australia, France, Germany, Holland, and Denmark, the state itself estimates that its own goals of educating the public are well served by providing government assistance, in various ways, for those parents who decide to send their children to religious schools of their own choosing. Why can't Christians in this country strive politically for this type of arrangement? The slight impulses we have recently seen in this direction in our own country would be greatly strengthened if serious Christians would look more closely at our public schools, ask some uncomfortable questions, and then summon imaginative resources that are committed to the gospel.

Reprinted from Touchstone: A Journal of Ecumenical Orthodoxy, *Winter 1995, Volume 8, Number 1.*

LEON J. PODLES

NO PLACE LIKE HOME

A Personal Look at the Education of Children:
Public, Private & Domestic

WHILE FEW OF US greatly enjoyed the school classroom, most of us accept it as something that our children will have to experience and no doubt be the better for it. Most people are content with the public schools. This complacency led to the defeat of tuition vouchers in a recent California referendum.

Most Americans live in homogeneous suburbs in which the education of their children is paid for by taxes, without the extra expense of private-school tuition. The others who can afford private school and choose it for their children are at least satisfied enough with their children's schools to pay both the tax for public education and the tuition for private education. The poor, often single mothers, are grateful for whatever help they can get in raising their children, and are not in a position to demand academic excellence, even if the schools could achieve it.

But a growing number of students (estimates range from 300,000 to 2,000,000) are taught at home. Their parents mostly are Evangelical Protestants. But there is a generous sprinkling of atheists, Buddhists, New Agers, and other fringe types. What has led the parents to abandon communal schooling, even under private auspices?

Are they doing what is best for their children? How hard is it to do? Is it worth doing, from the points of view of the children and of the parents?

Public & Private Schooling

Suburban parents generally are satisfied with the academic standards of their local public school. The schools do not do a very good job by world standards, but they educate the masses of the middle class to a degree that allows them to function in our economy. The parents' own education was never up to the best European standards, but the European standards were always meant for a small elite, which was rigorously winnowed out by examinations at each level. Those who did well went to the lycées and gymnasiums and thence to university and professional life. Those who did poorly were put into vocational training.

The American system always has been more forgiving, and gives late bloomers second, third, and fourth chances. Nor should the idea of socialization be totally despised. The common public-school culture may not have produced academic excellence, but it did help insulate America from the sectarian and class conflicts that have poisoned modern European life. When the 1941 graduates of a Washington, D.C. public high school returned for a fiftieth reunion, they had only vague memories of their classes; real school life revolved around dances and sports. But such a school life, while lacking in academic rigor, produced a sense of social unity among the various (white) ethnic groups of the neighborhood, a sense of community that helped America weather the challenges of the Depression and war. The school they returned to was now over 99 percent black; socialization by public-school education largely has been defeated by the black-white separation in American society.

The private schools also do what they are expected to do: give their students the advantage of social contacts. They rarely perpetuate the old elite, which doesn't reproduce itself very well. The parents' money is mostly new money, that of doctors and lawyers and members of the "chattering classes" (as the British call those who make their living by the sweat of their jaw: professors and television commentators and such).

The private schools share the general American guilt about elitism, and often make a sincere effort to recruit scholarship students from the scheduled castes of American society. At a private school my wife went to in Pittsburgh, there was much fuss about racial integration, but not a single Slavic name was to be found among the students—in Pittsburgh about half of the population comes from Eastern Europe. The minority scholarship students generally are well motivated and on their best behavior, so the atmosphere at private schools is somewhat more conducive than that of the public schools to learning, and very much conducive to carving out comfortable niches in the power structure of American society.

The schools of America in general do not do that bad a job academically or socially in preparing students for middle-class life, except for the inner-city schools, which have largely given up any function beyond providing salaries for teachers and administrators. The responsible parents of children at these urban schools are the ones clamoring for vouchers to help their children escape, but they are powerless against teachers' unions and satisfied suburbanites. It is clear why such parents, if they had the ability and the confidence, would want to teach their children at home, so that the children would both be literate and reach graduation alive. But why would anyone who has access, because of the location of his home or the size of his pocketbook, to decent schools bother to teach children at home? Is there some problem intrinsic to school as such?

The Old Schools & the New

Schools originally were set up for specific purposes, to teach rhetoric or doctrine. They were like our driving schools. A pupil went to one to learn a specific skill or body of knowledge. The schools of the Middle Ages taught pupils what they needed to know to become clerics in major or minor orders: reading, Latin, music. Later, secular subjects such as science were added to the curriculum.

The one-room schoolhouse in America offered children instruction in many subjects. Because of the small size of the school and the irregularity of attendance, pupils were largely taught individually or in small groups in which not age but mastery of material was determinative. Despite the poverty of material resources, the schools did a much better job than modern schools because they practiced what is now called "child-centered education." Laura Ingalls Wilder, after attending such schools intermittently, was examined by a state official and found "competent to give instruction in Reading, Orthography, Writing, Arithmetic, Geography, English Grammar, and History"—at the age of fifteen (*Little Town on the Prairie*)! However, the future of the nation was not to be agrarian.

As America developed its industries, it needed masses of immigrants to staff them. Urban schools tried to Americanize the children of the immigrants. The schools were set up on the new model of the factory. Children entered as raw material, were processed on an assembly line of classes, and graduated as a finished product.

Along with industrialization came bureaucratization, an ugly word for an ugly thing. Ivan Illich in *Deschooling Society* claimed that the schools set themselves up as the controllers, dispensers, and certifiers of knowledge. He wanted to deschool society and to allow everyone to control his own education. He proposed free schools that offered instruction in whatever one wanted to learn, at whatever age one wanted to learn it. The community colleges are the closest system we have to his ideal, and for the amount of money spent they probably do a better job than Harvard does at helping their students learn interesting and useful things.

The fallacy of the industrial, bureaucratic, mass school is assuming that children are raw material to be processed, and that they all learn in basically the same way. Every child learns at a different rate, and there seem to be different types of intelligence and an infinity of strategies for learning. Factory seconds can be destroyed. What can we do with children who can't be successfully processed by the educational factory?

The Dynamics of School Learning

In home schooling my children, and in my prior teaching at a private school, I have noticed that learning does not progress at an even rate. A child will plod along for a while, regress a bit, then have a sudden insight and zoom ahead. Each child follows a different pattern in different subjects, depending on his interest, aptitude, health, worries, and an infinity of influences that help make him a unique person.

There are even different types of intelligence. The most obvious is that boys tend to learn by physical activity, and find sitting in a classroom to be torture. When we still had one child in school, our eight-year-old son, who had never been to school, decided he wanted to see what it was like. He went for one day, and came home complaining that he had muscular cramps. His legs bothered him for several days, and he correctly diagnosed the source as having to sit still for six hours. He said he wouldn't mind an occasional visit to school (once every two or three years) but that he definitely did not plan to make a career of it.

In a group of children of mixed abilities (and there is no other type), what can a teacher do? If he teaches to the fastest learners, everyone else will be lost. If he teaches to the slowest learners, everyone else will be bored. If he teaches to the middle, some will be bored and the others lost. If he keeps the boys busy and out of trouble, the girls will feel neglected. In any case, classroom lecturing may not be the best way for some or many of the children to learn.

Many times I have heard parents complain that their children used to be active and bright but have now lost all interest in school. I suspect that teachers are busily trying to pound square pegs into round holes, but I try to refrain from immediately offering the advice, "Try home schooling, and find out what your child wants to learn and how he can learn it." Social and sexual development also proceeds at different paces in different children. For those out of step, school can be a very unhappy experience.

Most children will be out of step in one way or another, academically or physically or socially. They therefore dislike what they learn in school, even if what they are being taught is basically sound. Americans insist on the necessity of universal schooling, but the object of school is not intellectual attainment. Americans are anti-intellectual; their popular culture is crude, vulgar, sex-obsessed, and consumerist. In part, Americans always have disliked the European high culture they left behind, with its monarchical and aristocratic assumptions. But in part, the rebellion against high culture may be caused by an exposure to it (or some facsimile thereof) in the context of the classroom, which most dislike.

Once I attended a matinee showing of Mel Gibson's *Hamlet*. A high-school class filed in and started to fool around. I consoled myself that groundlings added a touch of Elizabethan authenticity to the experience. But when the film started, everyone was transfixed. Both those who knew every word of dialogue by heart and those who had only a vague idea that the play was about a guy who thought his dad had been knocked off sat in stunned silence before the power of the play. In the 1970s Pachelbel's Canon was a pop hit, and Gregorian chant CDs now are bestsellers. Queues form in front of museums with blockbuster exhibits. Americans can respond to the deep and high moments in Western culture, if only they encounter it away from the dead hand of school.

My previous use of the generic *he* to refer to teachers is misleading, because most teachers are women, and school is a feminine environment. Boys do not fit in very well. They have a higher dropout rate than girls, and currently 55 percent of college students are women. Among blacks, more men are in prison than in college. School is an excellent way of alienating young men from normal, civilized existence and of cultivating a criminal underclass, which has damaged American blacks and is beginning to spread among poor whites.

Teaching Children at Home

It is difficult to teach children at school. Is it possible to do it at home? Yes, provided the needs of the children, rather than educational theories, determine what the parents do. Some children need a highly structured environment, almost like a classroom. However, most need a greater amount of freedom to study what they are interested in, when they are interested in it, in the manner they find most fruitful. Some structure and some parental supervision are usually necessary, especially if a child has learned bad habits in school. We find that the less time our children have spent in school, the more independently they can work. Mathematics is necessary for modern life, and almost all children need some prodding and assistance in mastering its elements. Languages also are hard to study independently, and need parental or other adult involvement.

Even in a good school, a child may get at most 10 or 15 minutes a day of personal attention, the attention he needs so that the teacher can ascertain what the child does or doesn't understand. If a parent daily spends a half-hour to an hour per child in formal instruction, that is enough for most children. If there are several children, the older ones usually end up teaching the younger ones, and teach more effectively than a parent could. To a small child, a parent belongs to a different order of being, and adult attainments may seem hopeless. However, the younger child usually feels that he can do the same thing that a slightly older child is doing.

We were astonished when our five-year-old suddenly announced that he could read, and read things like *The Chronicles of Narnia* and *National Geographic*. We had not taught him to read. As far as we can determine, his sister read stories to him at night after they went to bed, and he played with a pre-computer that had a spelling program. His ability to understand words did not always match his judgment. When he was five and we were visiting relatives, he announced that a flying saucer had landed in a city in the Soviet Onion. We asked him where he had learned this interesting fact, and he announced it must be true, because he had read it in the newspaper; when pressed for the name of the newspaper, he said it was something called the *Weekly World News* (my brother-in-law, a graduate of Harvard and Harvard Law, is a connoisseur of tabloids). Children will need some guidance from parents in making judgments about the things they encounter, but the thrill of discovery is always great.

In teaching children at home, I spend a little less than an hour in formal instruction with the oldest boy, now 14, and my wife less than three hours with the remaining five younger ones. She is usually finished by lunch. The children have some independent assignments, and lots of time for sports, including skiing, ice skating, recreation league baseball, and soccer; for reading (our children take out about 700 books a year from the local library); for Scouts, piano lessons, visits to neighbors, projects (making brownies and selling lemonade to passersby), computers (we have two that are fully occupied all day), serving as altar boys, and anything else they are interested in.

Some education goes on inside the house, but only part of this is formal. Chores, for example, can teach: The oldest boy pays the bills and runs our house finances from the computer. A lot of education goes on outside the house and introduces them to the wider community, giving them a wider experience than children have who are in school six hours and then have homework.

Our children are doing well by grade-level norms, but even if they were behind, I wouldn't worry. Some children, boys especially, are not ready to read until they are 10 or 11, when in their brains occurs the mysterious process of neural development that makes reading possible. They would be miserable in school, but enjoy playing and learning crafts until the brain is ready, and then they read at or above grade level within a few months. This is even more true of children with real learning disabilities or mental limitations. The practice of mainstreaming them into regular school often leads to acute misery.

For the lower grades, we use structured material from the Calvert School, which has been in the business of home schooling for almost a century. The middle children can use the materials on their own. As they get older, we use Saxon Mathematics, which has books from advanced arithmetic through calculus. In studying pre-algebra with one son, I finally understood addition in base 2, an operation that had escaped me 30 years ago. Cambridge University has a Latin series for middle school, which we have used successfully with nine-year-olds.

Parental ignorance of a subject is not an obstacle. The parent should demonstrate to the child that adults, too, have a willingness, indeed, an eagerness to master new and difficult material. Such an attitude is one of the most important lessons a child can learn. Some parents of our acquaintance are successfully teaching themselves Latin as they teach their children. This is the system used by St. John's College in Annapolis, Maryland, known for its Great Books program. I interviewed for a position there, and the dean explained to me that all teachers were expected to teach all material, including Greek and French. I said that, alas, my languages were Latin and German. She assured me that all I had to do was keep a page or two ahead of the students. I was doubtful, but St. Johnnies are among the few American undergraduates who seem to be genuinely educated.

Obstacles & Benefits

Some parents, although their children are having problems at school, and home schooling looks attractive, are put off by practical difficulties or fears. Is it possible to maintain a house and teach children at the same time? We have a part-time housekeeper, but this is a luxury, and we could have the children do more of the cleaning. Other families we know successfully do without outside help. It seems that in any large family, parents must develop a certain tolerance of mess (this tolerance comes naturally to children).

The fear of denying their children socialization also scares some parents away from home schooling. Socialization usually means learning to succumb to peer pressure, and to the material and sexual competitiveness of adolescence. After leaving school, how many people spend all their time with their peers, that is, those of the same age? Children taught at home are also taught by other members of the community in formal and informal ways, and have a pattern of development saner than that of children who associate almost exclusively with their peers.

One common concern is, can we afford it? One parent, usually the mother, has to be home in order to supervise the children, and many families feel they cannot do without two incomes. Although all family circumstances differ, the financial savings derived from home schooling—such as not having private-school expenses, or being able to live in an area, which although pleasant, does not have a good public school and is therefore less expensive, or being able to get along without a second car—sometimes can help the family do without a second income.

After the expenses added on by working—childcare, clothing, lunches, transportation, higher taxes—are deducted, wives often are surprised to discover that they are working for less than minimum wage. There may be some things a family has to go without, but they gain something that is precious and irreplaceable: time together when the children are young.

The children also are less demanding of material possessions if they are not exposed to school. In my family's case, the difference may not be entirely caused by home schooling. We differ in two additional ways from other American families. We are numerous by American standards (six children, and occasional long-term guests, including my retarded sister who lived with us for several years), and we have never had a television. In addition to exposing children to questionable programs, television cultivates their avarice. Why else do advertisers spend billions each year to reach children?

Although we are moderately affluent, our family income is below the per-capita average of the metropolitan area. We do not have six private-school tuitions to pay, and can therefore afford to live in a neighborhood in which Jaguars dot the street. I was concerned that the children would pick up tastes from neighborhood children that we could not afford to indulge, but my children have never been materialistic. In fact, it is hard to extract requests for birthday presents. My wife's friend, who was in the diplomatic corps in Africa, visited us once and remarked that our children were more like African children than American children. The older ones took care of the younger and played with them, and they had endless fun with a few sticks and a cardboard box.

Our life is hardly monastic; apparently, children have to be trained in the American fixation with material objects—and television and school are two of the main agents of propaganda. Since home schoolers from smaller families and from families that allow the occasional use of television often exhibit this lack of interest in possessions, school seems to be the main culprit. By home schooling one can save money and help save the child's soul at the same time (a combination that should appeal to the Scottish Presbyterians among us).

I have noticed several distinctive personality traits in our children and in other home-schooled children, both those I have known and those about whom I have read. Our children have remained more childlike: They don't exhibit precocious maturity. They like playing with their bunnies, and even the four-teen-year-old seems to enjoy playing cars with the five-year-old. But they also are more independent and more self-confident in dealing with adults than most children are.

Our daughter was terribly shy at school. After a year at home, she began making expeditions around the neighborhood with a home-schooled friend and independently arranged to participate in a fashion show at a fabric store where she shopped. When my then thirteen-year-old discovered a virus in a laptop computer his uncle had brought home from work, he fixed it and told his uncle to have the mainframe checked. There was indeed a virus, and the computer expert called my son to see what had happened. My son told the expert what he had done and suggested alterations to a command path that the expert did not know were possible. We learned later that not only was he impressed by my son's expertise, but he was also even more impressed by the self-confidence with which he talked to an adult about technical matters.

Wellesley, my wife's alma mater, has a student who had never attended school before going to college. Her parents were sixties types who had moved to the mountains. When their children were old enough for school, they were appalled by the condition of the local schools and decided to teach their three children at home. She had a rigorous and structured education at home with her brother and sister. When she came to Wellesley, there were several surprises. She had never heard of eating disorders, but they were common among Wellesley students. She found incomprehensible the complaints that teachers in school had neglected girls; she was relieved by the relative anonymity and lack of attention in the college classroom compared to the scrutiny she had received at home. She did not feel at all socially awkward because she lacked the experience of school. Most of all, she discovered that she was more capable of independent thought than her classmates.

Faith & Love at Home

I have not touched on religion. Our children were in Roman Catholic schools, but we had already started taking them out one by one because they were so academically out-of-step, although the school is good by American standards.

The final straw was a letter that the eighth graders (mostly girls) wrote, under the direction of their teacher, to the local Catholic newspaper, saying that middle-school students were going to have sex anyway and that the schools should give them condoms. This letter (with some assistance from my fax machine) caused a furor among our school's parents. The official explanation from the damage-control people at school headquarters was that many of the students were Protestant and had picked up these ideas at home. Somehow I couldn't imagine the black Baptist parents who were paying for a Catholic school telling their daughters this; surveys have shown that Evangelical Protestants are more conservative than Catholics in sexual matters. I decided that I did not want my daughter to pick up these attitudes, whatever their source.

Unfortunately, because of the massive confusion about doctrine and morality in all denominations, no religious school can be fully trusted to transmit its heritage faithfully. Perhaps the fundamentalist schools do, but their rigidity creates its own problems.

We use orthodox religion textbooks (the Ignatius Press *Faith and Life* series) and read Scripture at several points during the day, but the main religious education comes from our use of folk traditions that the liturgical churches in Europe, especially the Catholic and Lutheran, have preserved. We celebrate St. Nicholas with shoes and presents and St. Lucy with the Lucia crown and saffron rolls. Evelyn Vitz's cookbook, *A Continual Feast,* is full of useful suggestions. She has tested them in her family of six children whom she is raising in Manhattan. The customs of Christmas have done much to keep a vestige of Christianity alive in American culture; the customs that used to fill the year can implant a deep memory of Christian life in children, whatever they encounter later in life.

But the chief religious role of home schooling is not in imparting instruction. The family is the social structure that cultivates pietas, and that binds, *religare,* generation to generation. We desire to spend time with those we love, so that we can get to know them and help them in an intelligent fashion. Teaching, as David Guterson says, "is an act of love before it is anything else." His book, *Family Matters: Why Homeschooling Makes Sense,* is the best introduction to the legalities, advisability, and desirability of teaching at home, and is suffused with a charm that stems from his delight in his children.

Guterson emphasizes that being independently wealthy is not a requirement to teach your children at home; he makes $30,000 a year, and his wife does not work outside the house. He insists that it is not a sacrifice to spend your time with your children, with those to whom you have given existence and whom you love more than anyone in the world. He also teaches at a good public high school, so he knows both types of teaching, and calls for the reform envisioned by Ivan

Illich, in which the schools provide opportunities to learn for all. A few enlightened public-school districts have begun a sincere cooperation with home-schooling families, providing them with opportunities to participate in such activities as they desire.

Much may be made of a child if, like Johnson's Scot, he is caught early enough. But what will catch him? A parent's love, which created him and called him into being from nothingness, and that surrounds him every hour of the day, that studies his needs and desires, and tries to help him grow into a being that expresses a unique idea, an idea that Christians know exists in the mind of God? Or will it be what used to be called the world, a society that lives by frivolity and the competitive multiplication of possessions, that forgets to delight in God's creation and in the summit and crown of that creation, the human person?

Both socialism and capitalism tend to view human beings as ciphers who can be manipulated in the service of economic efficiency. Capitalism is better at creating wealth, but at what cost? First, fathers were taken away from their children more than primitive societies had ever done. Now, mothers are being taken away from their children, and the children turned over to strangers.

A child must learn that he is loved if he is to have a chance to know, by analogy, what God's love is, attentive and ever present, yet giving us freedom to grow, and being confident in us, easily pleased, yet never really satisfied until we grow up to the full stature of his sons. Often a home is the best environment in which to raise and instruct a child in the household of the faith.

Reprinted from Touchstone: A Journal of Ecumenical Orthodoxy, *Fall 1994, Volume 7, Number 4.*

STEVEN FAULKNER

THE CENTURY OF
THE CYCLOPS

On the Loss of Poetry as Necessary Knowledge

S OMEONE RECENTLY WON a $75,000 poetry prize. I don't recall the poet's name. The sponsors of the prize thought that big bucks would help revive interest in poetry. The winner of the Ruth Lilly Poetry Prize for $25,000, Charles Wright, admitted that this country's interest in poetry is in something of a free fall, but he hoped these large prizes would arrest that fall. I doubt it will help.

Who reads modern poetry? A reporter for National Public Radio interviewed another poet who said that people may no longer know why "The woods—are lovely, dark and deep," but they do understand the money message. If someone forks out 75 big ones for poems, poems must be valuable property.

These are cries of desperation. One comes to love poetry as a man comes to love a woman, by first catching her eye in passing, by stumbling through a few embarrassing conversations with her, by listening to her, attending to her, getting caught up in the mysteries of love. If someone offered us money to take an interest in a woman, we would know that something was drastically wrong.

Like modern art, modern poetry began to lose its audience almost a century ago. Indecipherable and egocentric, impressionistic poetry does not catch the eye, much less bear listening to. The old standards of Beauty, such as clarity and coherence, have fallen to the shifting winds of subjectivism, relativism, and

44

skepticism. What beauty remains has been stripped from reason, severed from its old Platonic mates, the Good and the True. Our modern poetry is in pieces.

This makes a defense of poetry difficult. But defend it we must, for poetic knowledge is an essential kind of knowledge. Without it, our understanding of the world suffers a severe distortion. It is as if we have grown up in an age of one-eyed men who have heard rumors that people could once judge distances, depths, and colors by the use of two eyes, but are now reduced by this flat, prosaic information age that relies on scientific analysis as virtually our only source of knowledge. We are a century of Cyclops.

Poetry as a way of knowing is essential to the human being. Modern thinkers, the heirs of Immanuel Kant, have come to depend almost entirely on discursive reasoning, packing journals and academic books with complex analysis, deduction, demonstration, abstraction, and argumentation. This is necessary in its place, but it is not the only necessary knowledge.

Sir Philip Sidney, in his *Defense of Poetry*, written when Shakespeare was young, said the poet "yieldeth to the powers of the mind an image of that whereof the philosopher bestoweth but a wordish description, which doth neither strike, pierce, nor possess the sight of the soul so much" as poetry does.

Linear, rational discourse is the domain of philosophy and rhetoric. "The philosopher teacheth," said Sidney, "but he teacheth obscurely, so as the learned only can understand him; that is he teacheth them that are already taught. But the poet is the food for the tenderest stomachs; the poet is indeed the right popular philosopher." The reason for this is that poetry appeals to the whole person, not merely to reason. Even the young and the uneducated can appreciate it. Jacques Maritain wrote: "Poetry is the fruit neither of the intellect alone, nor of imagination alone. Nay more, it proceeds from the totality of man, sense, imagination, love, desire, instinct, blood and spirit together." Poetry can of course be highly intellectual, demanding much from the mind, but it is always more than intellectual; it is intuitive. It is a way of seeing and admiring the whole without taking it apart by analysis. It is a taking into the self that which cannot be fully explained, a way of observing with silent attention rather than active inquiry, what Wordsworth called a "wise passivity," or "passionate regard."

This distinction between discursive knowledge and intuitive or poetic knowledge is a very old idea. German philosopher Josef Pieper explains this at some length in his book, *Leisure, the Basis of Culture:*[1]

The Middle Ages drew a distinction between the understanding as *ratio* and the understanding as *intellectus*. *Ratio* is the power of discursive, logical thought, of searching and of examinations, of abstraction, of definition and drawing conclusions. *Intellectus*, on the other hand, is the name for the understanding in so far as it is the capacity of *simplex intuitus*, of that simple vision to which truth offers itself like a landscape to the eye. The faculty of mind, man's knowledge, is both things in one, according to antiquity and the Middle Ages, simultaneously *ratio* and *intellectus*; and the process of knowing is the action of the two together.

It is difficult to stress this point enough in this hardworking, scientific age that seeks to dissect and define all mysteries, leaving no room, not even a category, for the effortless awareness, the contemplative vision of the ancient Hebrews, Greeks, and medieval Christians. The Hebrew poets who wrote great sections of the Bible understood the necessity of contemplative knowledge. Thomas De Quincey, in *The Poetry of Pope*, wrote of them:

> The Scriptures themselves never condescended to deal by suggestion or cooperation with the mere discursive understanding; when speaking of man in his intellectual capacity, the Scriptures speak not of the understanding, but of "the understanding heart"—making the heart, i.e., the great intuitive (or non-discursive) organ to be the interchangeable formula for man in his highest state of capacity for the infinite.

Thus the Psalms and prophets express more of a contemplative vision of God than a view merely doctrinal or dogmatic. Certainly there is doctrine there, but the truths of the Psalms and prophets are not expressed as systematic theology, but as poetry. Job, overwhelmed with loss and suffering, asks God for a rational explanation. He demands to know the reason for his afflictions. But God's answer is given in rich, ironic poetry:

> Then the Lord answered Job out of the whirlwind:
> "Who is this that darkens counsel by words without knowledge? Gird up your loins like a man, I will question you, and you shall declare to me.
> "Where were you when I laid the foundation of the earth? Tell me, if you have understanding. Who determined its measurements—surely you know!

Or who stretched the line upon it? On what were its bases sunk, or who laid its cornerstone, when the morning stars sang together, and all the sons of God shouted for joy?" (Job 38:1–7)

And so, for chapter after chapter, God speaks forth a landscape of great majesty and beauty until Job says quite simply, "I lay my hand on my mouth. . . . I had heard of thee by the hearing of the ear, but now my eye sees thee; therefore I despise myself, and repent in dust and ashes." This is the knowledge that simply sees, that contemplates even the transcendence of God in the minutiae of creation and somehow comprehends the incomprehensible.

This word *comprehend* is a good one. It means "to take in." This is knowledge by union, rather than knowledge by analysis. Analysis always breaks the object of its inquiry in pieces in order to examine the constituent parts. Examine the idea, the economic plan, the political policy, the piece of vegetation, the animal, the machine, all in the same way. It is Descartes' methodology. Take it apart and put it back together again. But there is a knowledge by union which, as Karl Stern says, is contrary to knowledge by disassembly:

> Simple self-observation shows that there exist two modes of knowing. One might be called "externalization," in which the knowable is experienced as an object, a *Gegenstand*, something which stands opposed to me; the other might be called "internalization," a form of knowledge by sympathy, a "feeling with"—a union with the knowable.

Thomas Aquinas, often accused of being merely rationalistic, called this intuitive kind of knowledge connatural knowledge: "The spiritual man knows divine things through inclination and connaturality; not only because he has learned them, but because he experiences them." This is knowledge by participation. We have an inherent relationship with all things in nature; we are co-natured and thus our knowledge of such things is a kind of natural sympathy. Stern goes on to quote Henri Bergson:

> By intuition is meant the kind of *intellectual sympathy* by which one places oneself within an object in order to coincide with what is unique in it and consequently inexpressible. Analysis, on the contrary, is the operation that reduces the

object to elements already known, that is, to elements common both to it and
other objects.

Dissecting analysis produces the categorizing of commonalities; poetic intuition
simply sees or takes in what we can never fully define.

A horse, for example, is more than the sum of its parts. In Charles Dickens's
novel *Hard Times*, a model student named Bitzer describes a horse in this way:
"Horse: Quadruped. Graminivorous. Forty teeth, namely twenty-four grinders,
four eye-teeth, and twelve incisive. Sheds coat in the spring in marshy countries,
sheds hoofs, too. Hoofs hard, but requiring to be shod with iron. Age known by
marks in mouth." But this is not a horse; it is nothing but a list of a horse's parts.
Better the warhorse in Job that "paws in the valley, and exults in his strength. . . .
With fierceness and rage he swallows the ground."

Poetic knowledge, as Sidney said, gives sight to the soul in a region of mysteries. We cannot reduce everything we experience to precise definition. C. S. Lewis
noted this in an essay on language. He gave three examples of language:

(1) It was very cold.
(2) There were 13 degrees of frost.
(3) "Ah, bitter chill it was!
   The owl, for all his feathers was a-cold;
   The hare limped trembling through the frozen grass,
   And silent was the flock in wooly fold:
   Numb'd were the Beadsman's fingers."

The first example is what Lewis calls ordinary language. The second, the scientific description, gives a precise measure to the cold. The third is knowledge by
connaturality, by sympathy.

Where science seeks to master the knowledge of things with weights, measure-
ments, mathematics, statistics, poetic knowledge humbly understands the world as
"vast, immeasurable, impenetrable, inscrutable, mysterious," to quote John Henry
Newman. Thus, says Newman, science results in system; poetry leads to admiration, enthusiasm, devotion, and love. Science can be very useful; poetry is essential.

Wonder, humility, admiration, praise, gratitude, love—these are the proper
responses to poetic knowledge. The scientist seeks to understand and control na-

ture. But in doing so, as C. S. Lewis powerfully argued in *The Abolition of Man*, humanity may lose its better self, for man's conquest of nature ultimately results in his conquest of himself. Lewis quotes Bunyan: "It came burning hot into my mind, whatever he said and however he flattered, when he got me to his house, he would sell me for a slave." Science has tried to reduce humanity to a complex, genetic machine. If anyone doubts this, he should read Nobel Prize winner Francis Crick's assessment of the human soul as "no more than a vast assembly of nerve cells." Crick thinks he has identified the part of the mind where free will exists. But, of course, if we are no more than a complex soup of nerves and chemicals, free will is no longer free. Of such analysis is slavery made.

Mark Twain recognized that scientific knowledge, as useful as it is, can actually deprive us of a greater vision. As a young, novice riverboat captain on the great river, he describes a sunset: "There were graceful curves, reflected images, woody heights, soft distances: and over the whole scene, far and near, the dissolving lights drifted steadily." His response reveals he has seen poetically: "I stood like one bewitched. I drank it in, in a speechless rapture. The world was new to me, and I had never seen anything like this at home." But years later, as an experienced captain, he had learned the practical meaning of every ripple, every floating log, every variation in color:

> Now when I had mastered the language of the water, and had come to know every trifling feature that bordered the great river as familiarly as I knew the letters of the alphabet, I had made a valuable acquisition. But I had lost something too. I had lost something which could never be restored to me while I lived. All the grace, the beauty, the poetry, had gone out of the majestic river!

Charles Darwin, near the end of his life, felt the same way. He complained that he no longer took pleasure in poetry or music, and little delight in scenery. "My mind," he said, "seems to have become a kind of machine for grinding general laws out of a large collection of facts."

Our schools teach almost only the scientific mode of knowing. We no longer teach our children poetry, but we cram them full of numbers and definitions. Our academic journals and journals of opinion are largely analytic. A hundred years ago, journals commonly printed poetry, but now the public doesn't know what to do with a poem when one is printed. The culture has lost in a trice the wisdom of millennia.

Poetic knowledge, connatural knowledge, intuitive knowledge, call it what you will, plays an immense role in our lives: the child who laughs at his first sight of a bee, the woman who weeps at her lover's approach, the soldier numbed by his friend's sudden death cannot explain what they see. They may later attempt some explanation of one facet or another of their experience. They may attempt analysis, but the immediate experience in its totality is beyond such dissection. The immediate awareness of a complex and mysterious reality impresses not only the mind but also the emotions, the desires, and the memory.

Only poetry can sing of such things in any way commensurate with the immediate experience, for poetry appeals to the whole man. And because the poetic experience is not limited to linear thought, it hears countless echoes that correspond to other experiences and other existent realities so that the mind and soul naturally reach beyond the thing observed, listening intently toward the whole, inquiring after the Source and Meaning of things. Again Maritain: "Poetic intuition makes things which it grasps diaphanous and alive, and populated with infinite horizons. As grasped by poetic knowledge, things abound in significance and swarm with meanings."

But the culture and its intellectuals have thrown all of this into near oblivion; we have lost sight of it, and, in doing so, we have lost an important way of seeing. Blinded in one eye, we have lost the ability to admire, which means to look upon with praising wonder. While we increase our mastery of the world through science, we lose the vocation of the soul, which is to see and contemplate that which is around us as it leads to that which is beyond us. We must reclaim its place in modern thought. We must recognize that poetic knowledge is not mere sentimentality, but a real and necessary knowledge.

Reprinted from Touchstone: A Journal of Ecumenical Orthodoxy, *Winter 1996, Volume 9, Number 1.*

ENDNOTES

1. Trans. Alexander Dru (London: Faber and Faber, 1952)

STEVEN FAULKNER

THE WORKSHOP OF WORSHIP

On Recovering Poetry for Our Children

I DRIVE MY CHILDREN several miles every school day to a brick, one-room schoolhouse. On the way, I turn off the radio and ask them to teach me the poems they have been memorizing. At first they thought this was splendid fun, teaching slow-witted Father the poems they pick up so quickly.

But children tire easily, and now they often don't feel like going to the trouble of repeating, "Blow, blow, thou winter wind;/ Thou art not so unkind as man's ingratitude." But I usually press on and begin repeating the lines myself. Soon they chime in, and we are off and running together again, shouting, "Hey ho, the holly! This life is most jolly!"

Children love poetry. They love the sound of it, even when they have no idea what is being said. The rhythms of the meter and the sounds of well-chosen words naturally appeal to them. Plato said that this was a gift from the gods intended to charm us toward the Good.

Plato thought that children should be taught to sing poems in chorus and dance to music so as to bring order to their wild little souls. He said that since virtually all children find it impossible to keep their bodies still and their tongues quiet, they need rhythm and harmony to order their movements and voices. For Plato, education was more than filling little minds with information; it was a training in the virtues, an ordering of the appetites, for which poetry was necessary.

Of course, not all rhythm and music is good for the soul. In Book Two of *The Laws*, Plato investigates the kinds of music and dance that move the soul toward the Good and those that debase the soul. It is an obvious indictment of our times that young people are given over to every kind of perverse lyric, sensual music, and chaotic dance that disorders the appetites, while adults shrug this off as impossible to change.

We seem to think this a new problem, that other ages did not have to contend with children's proclivity to sensual music and barbaric dance. Five hundred years ago, in the age of Shakespeare, Sir Philip Sidney was complaining that "measure, order, proportion be in our own time grown odious." It is a persistent problem that many through the ages have recognized as typical of youth.

Plato thought that a society concerned about the virtues must seek to order the passions of their children by teaching them good music and good dancing. If the definitions of "good" dance and music "give us the slip and get away," Plato said, "it will be pointless utterly to prolong our discussion of correct education, Greek or foreign." If Plato is right, educational reform in this country is in a lot of trouble.

One way of charming children toward a good and ordered life is to teach them to memorize poetry. Most parents and teachers today would probably respond that their children are not charmed by poetry, that poetry is difficult and boring. And their children would agree. There are many obvious reasons for this attitude, including television and parents who themselves do not love poetry. Another reason is that the schools teach children to analyze poems before teaching them to memorize them.

Once when I was tutoring Kansas University football players, a massive linebacker, who had never met a poem he didn't want to smash, handed me a sheet of some 70 terms a poetry teacher wanted him to memorize, terms like *trochee*, *anapest*, *dactyl*, *spondee*, *onomatopoeia*. I handed him a poem by Langston Hughes that takes the reader on a walk girl-watching in Harlem. It is not an erotic poem, but one that revels in all the shades of color we reduce to "black." After a time, the linebacker's face lit up like a child's; he laughed and wanted to read the poem to me; he wanted to share his delight in a kind of beauty he had not recognized before. Perhaps a professional teacher might have some use for those verbosaurs, *dactyl, spondee,* and *anapest,* but most of us just need to read and speak the poems. Better yet, memorize them; get them by heart.

I have had the good fortune of taking classes at the University of Kansas from two professors who made us memorize poems. Over the years, college students who rarely have been required to memorize anything but facts, dates, and theorems have been learning poems by Shakespeare, Milton, Tennyson, Frost, and many others.

The effect has been startling. Many former students say this was the best thing they learned in college. Students steeped in computer science, business, biology, and social sciences are unexpectedly caught up into regions mysterious. One of these students is now my children's teacher, passing on to them (and to me) poetic words that, as Christopher Lasch put it, "order experience and evoke its depths."

But it is unfortunate that so many have had to wait until college to learn what Plato said should be taught when the mind is supple and the imagination is alive to the wonders of the world. Too many college students already have grown cynical and are much too proud to appreciate poetry.

Parents should read aloud to their children. It is as delightful for the parent as it is for the child, for the parent not only learns the poems, but also gets to participate in the sparkle and laughter the children bring to the poems. "That's my favorite part!" my six-year-old daughter always would say with a giggle and a bashful smile as we finished reciting Robert Louis Stevenson's poem about the cow that "walks among the meadow grass,/ And eats the meadow flowers."

The rhythms and music of good poetry are essential to the enjoyment of the poem. For this reason, poems should be spoken aloud. In a 1977 interview, Robert Penn Warren was asked how important the sound of poetry is. He responded, "No sound, no poetry." English poet Walter de la Mare said the same: "Needless to say, we may value poetry more for its ideas, its philosophy, its message, its edification than for the delight which the mere music of its language may bestow. But that music absent, poetry, in the generally accepted meaning of the word, is absent."

Of course, like Plato, we must make the necessary distinctions between good poets and bad. Too many modern poets have abandoned meter and rhyme. Free verse is something like music without a beat and without a distinguishable melody. It is difficult to read, almost impossible to memorize, and may in fact contribute to a child's confusion.

Following Descartes, modern poets have split thought from objective reality so that their poetry becomes nothing but the expression of their own feelings, merely sentiments, not re-presentations of, or judgments about, existences beyond the poet's mind. Like Walt Whitman, they focus on the self and elevate the self to a godlike status. The poet becomes a creative deity who endows things with significance rather than a student, a lover, or a child who discovers the significance already there. The poet's creative Self begins to loom larger than the universe.

But this creative Self is an idiot giant who cannot be counted on to make truthful statements about the existent world or moral judgments about right and wrong, because he records the wanderings of a mind awash in relativism. The old poets knew better. C. S. Lewis notes in his essay, "The Poison of Subjectivism": "Until modern times no thinker of the first rank ever doubted that our judgements of value were rational judgements or that what they discovered was objective." Aristotle's famous dictum was that art imitates or re-presents nature. In such a context, poems open the eyes to the mysteries of the world, rather than trapping the reader in the mind of the poet.

Of course, one does not need to entirely do away with subjectivity. In reading a poem, we are seeing through another's eyes so that what we see is a reflection of both objective existences and a poet's inspiration about those existences. Jacques Maritain put it this way: A painting or a poem "is a sign—both a *direct sign* of the secrets perceived in things, of some irrecusable truth of nature or adventure caught in the great universe, and a *reversed sign* of the subjective universe of the poet, of his substantial Self obscurely revealed." Subjectivity, the reader's and the poet's, are the lenses we use to view the cosmos. But a grand and mysterious cosmos it is where there are incredible secrets to be found, undeniable truths to be investigated, and adventures that take the breath away.

From Wonder to Worship & Love

We must leave those modern poets who have botched up the musical sound of poetry with free verse and have gutted it of real meaning with subjectivism; we must leave them to wander in the labyrinth of their own exclusionary minds so that we, and our children, may wander through the earth and, looking up at the stars, fall to musing with King David the poet:

When I look at thy heavens, the work of thy fingers,
The moon and the stars which thou hast ordained;

What is man that thou art mindful of him,

And the son of man that thou visitest him?

The classical poets introduce the young to reality through delight. It is, as one
of my professors has written,

> a total education including the heart—the memory and passions and imagina-
> tion—as well as the body and intelligence. The nursery rhyme and fairy tale first
> present the phenomena of nature to the child. "Twinkle, twinkle, little star" is a
> Musical . . . introduction to astronomy that includes some primary observations
> of the heavenly phenomena and stirs the appropriate human emotion—wonder.
> Now it is precisely this emotion that provides the motivating energy of educa-
> tion. . . . Mistake me not: wonder is no sugary sentimentality but, rather, a mighty
> passion, a species of fear, an awe-full confrontation of the mystery of things.
> [Through it] the fearful abyss of reality first calls out to that other abyss that is the
> human heart; and the wonder of its response is, as the philosophers have said, the
> beginning of philosophy—not merely the first step; but the arche, the principle,
> as one is the principle of arithmetic and the fear of God the beginning of Wis-
> dom. Thus wonder both starts education and sustains it.

Poetry, even children's nursery rhymes, introduces a child to nature in a way
that often evokes that proper response of wonder. A child who learns that a star is
a gaseous ball of a certain mass and density and distance from the earth may have
his curiosity satisfied by the information, but he will not respond like Robert Louis
Stevenson's child, who, walking outside his house at bedtime, sees:

> . . . High overhead and all moving about,
> There were thousands of millions of stars.
> There ne'er were such thousands of leaves on a tree,
> Nor of people in church or the Park,
> As the crowds of the stars that looked down upon me,
> And that glittered and winked in the dark.

> The Dog, and the Plough, and the Hunter, and all,
> And the star of the sailor, and Mars,

These shone in the sky, and the pail by the wall
Would be half full of water and stars.
They saw me at last, and they chased me with cries,
And they soon had me packed into bed;
But the glory kept shining and bright in my eyes,
And the stars going round in my head.

This knowledge does not dismiss the stars with a few statistics, but generates awe that one day might lead to the musings of the psalmist. Not only this, but the child also learns to see the miracles of the cosmos in all the little complexities of everyday life: that pail by the wall that is "half full of water and stars."

Wonder is the workshop of worship. The child who wonders is moving toward worship. John Henry Newman spoke of the difference between scientific knowledge and a poetic knowledge that generates an attitude appropriate to worship:

> The aim of science is to get a hold of things, to grasp them, to master them, or to be superior to them. Its success lies in being able to draw a line round them, and to tell where each of them is to be found within that circumference, and how each lies relatively to all the rest. Its mission is to destroy ignorance, doubt, surmise, suspense, illusions, fears, deceits. But as to the poetical, very different is the frame of mind which is necessary for its perception. It demands as its primary condition, that we should not put ourselves above the objects in which it resides, but at their feet; that we should feel them to be above and beyond us, that we should look up at them, and that, instead of fancying that we can comprehend them, we should take for granted that we are surrounded and comprehended by them ourselves. It implies that we understand them to be vast, immeasurable, impenetrable, inscrutable, mysterious; so that at best we are only forming conjectures about them, not conclusions, for the phenomena which they present admit of many explanations, and we cannot know the true one.

The child who learns the numerical dimensions of a thing may be tempted to think that his knowledge gives him a kind of control over it. But what real control does the knowledge that the sun's light takes eight minutes to reach the earth give us?

We may be tempted to think that once we know this, we can keep the sun in its place, which is out of our thoughts, but why should such knowledge reduce wonder? The flight of light through millions of miles is still a marvel.

And wonder leads to love. Mary Midgley seems to echo Newman in saying:

> It is an essential element in wonder that we recognize what we see as something we did not make, cannot fully understand, and acknowledge as containing something greater than ourselves. This is not only true if our subject-matter is the stars; it is notoriously just as true if it is rocks or nematode worms. Those whose pearl is the kingdom of heaven, or indeed the kingdom of nature, follow it because they want to drink in its glory. Knowledge here is not just power; it is a loving union, and what is loved cannot just be the information gained; it has to be the real thing which that information tells us about. . . . The student will learn the laws and practice the customs belonging to the kingdom of heaven or of nature, trying to be more fit to serve it.

Which brings me back to my original point. In a chaotic world where our children are pushed to give vent to their desires and indulge their appetites, reading and memorizing poetry can be one way of ordering the soul, of disciplining feeling with form. More than this, poetry evokes wonder, and wonder leads to love, so that child and parent might find their place at the feet of God. As Josef Pieper put it: "Now, as always, the workaday world can be transcended in poetry and the other arts. In the shattering emotion of love, beyond the delusions of sensuality, men continue to find entrance to the still point of the turning world."

Reprinted from Touchstone: A Journal of Ecumenical Orthodoxy, *Spring 1996, Volume 4, Number 3.*

T. S. ELIOT ON
LITERARY MORALS

T. S. Eliot's After Strange Gods

T S. ELIOT'S SLIM BOOK about moral and immoral fiction may surprise anyone who first comes upon a copy. *After Strange Gods: A Primer of Modern Heresy* consists of three lectures delivered at the University of Virginia in 1933. These present an uncompromising denunciation of liberalism—both the liberalism of the nineteenth century and that of the twentieth (the two differing little, in Eliot's judgment); both liberalism in the Church and liberalism in the secular commonwealth.

Fifteen hundred copies of the first edition were printed in New York; no later edition has been published in this country. Why have these lively lectures been virtually suppressed? Chiefly because of an aside on page 20. There Eliot is discussing the conditions necessary for a tradition to develop and survive, with particular reference to Christian tradition and to Virginia. For tradition to endure, he remarks,

> The population should be homogeneous; where two or more cultures exist in the
> same place they are likely either to be fiercely self-conscious or both to become

adulterate. What is still more important is unity of religious background, and reasons of race and religion combine to make any large number of free-thinking Jews undesirable.

Howls of rage, in New York especially, arose at this passage when Eliot's little volume was published in 1934; the same fulminations against Eliot were uttered in 1989, when the first volume of his letters was published. The *New York Times*, never forgiving Eliot for his Charlottesville lectures, thereafter dealt him a knock whenever opportunity occurred. Actually this alleged "anti-Semitism" was merely an illustration of the principle that a culture—which arises from a cult—cannot well abide two radically different religions. It would be equally true that a community of orthodox Jews would be distressed and resentful, were they to find themselves beset by a Comus's rout of free-thinkers nominally Christian. The religion, or anti-religion, of the "free-thinking Jews" that Eliot had in mind was not Judaism, but rather *secular humanism* (a term employed by Eliot's friend Christopher Dawson). It was the predominance of this secular humanism (or *humanitarianism*, the term preferred by Irving Babbitt) that caused Eliot to remark, later, that the worst form of expatriation for an American writer is residence in New York City.

The Evil Spirit & Decadence

There being nothing more in the pages of *After Strange Gods* about Jews, whether free-thinking or orthodox, it is absurd to cry anathema and to keep from others' eyes this outspoken little book. Does literature have an ethical end? Should books be judged by the moral suppositions they implicitly affirm or deny? Do Good and Evil matter? And may the operations of the Evil Spirit (capital letters Eliot's) be discerned among us in the twentieth century? May they be descried, indeed, among men of letters whose talents are high and whose private characters are commendable? These questions are raised perceptively in *After Strange Gods*.

As orthodoxy had been Samuel Johnson's doxy, so was she Eliot's, in 1933 and so long as he lived. Heresies among men of letters in his time infected even his mentor Irving Babbitt, his helpful friend Ezra Pound, and such eminent contributors to Eliot's *Criterion* as William Butler Yeats and D. H. Lawrence: Eliot is very blunt about this.

It is characteristic of the more interesting heretics, in the context in which I use the term, that they have an exceptionally acute perception, or profound insight, of some part of the truth; an insight more important often than the inferences of those who are aware of more but less acutely aware of anything.

So Eliot said in his first Page-Barbour Lecture. "So far as we are able to redress the balance, effect the compensation, we may find such authors of the greatest value."

So Eliot finds George Eliot, William Butler Yeats, Thomas Hardy, and D. H. Lawrence, none of whom wrote within true tradition.

The general effect in literature of the lack of any strong tradition is twofold: extreme individualism in views, and no accepted rules or opinions as to the limitations of the literary job.

Thus Eliot puts it in his second lecture. A little later,

It is true that the existence of a right tradition, simply by its influence upon the environment in which the poet develops, will tend to restrict eccentricity to manageable limits; but it is not even by the lack of this restraining influence that the absence of tradition is most deplorable. What is disastrous is that the writer should deliberately give rein to his "individuality," that he should even cultivate his differences from others, and that his readers should cherish the author of genius, not in spite of his deviations from the inherited wisdom of the race, but because of them.

James Joyce, Eliot instructs us, is the most ethically orthodox of the writers of his day; but Thomas Hardy and D. H. Lawrence represent "the intrusion of the *diabolic* into modern literature." In his third lecture, he reproaches Hardy for cruelty and moral nihilism.

The work of the late Thomas Hardy represents an interesting example of a powerful personality uncurbed by any institutional attachment or by submission to any objective beliefs; unhampered by any ideas, or even by what sometimes acts as a partial restraint upon inferior writers, the desire to please a large public.

As for Lawrence—on behalf of whom Eliot was a witness at the trial for alleged obscenity in *Lady Chatterly's Lover*—"It would seem that for Lawrence any spiritual force was good, and that evil resided only in the absence of spirituality. . . . The man's vision is spiritual, but spiritually sick."

The Ruin of Imagination

What disease of mind and heart brings on this literary decadence? Why, deliquescent Protestantism.

> The chief clue to the understanding of most contemporary Anglo-Saxon literature is to be found in the decay of Protestantism. I am not concerned with Protestantism itself. . . . I mean that amongst writers the rejection of Christianity— Protestant Christianity—is the rule rather than the exception; and that individual writers can be understood and classified according to the type of Protestantism which surrounded their infancy, and the precise state of decay which it had reached.

After Strange Gods would be no more approved by the National Council of Churches than by the Anti-Defamation League or the American Humanist Association. It is a very Catholic piece of criticism. And what with the depravity in prose and verse that has flourished during the past several decades—especially since Eliot's death—this forbidden little book deserves careful reading nowadays.

Literary decadence commonly is bound up with a general intellectual and moral disorder in a society resulting, presently, in violent social disorder. The decay of literature appears often to result from a rejection of the ancient human endeavor to apprehend a transcendent order in the universe and to live in harmony with that order; for when the myths and the dogmata are discarded, the religious imagination withers. So it had come to pass with twentieth-century Protestantism, Eliot believed.

Religious assumptions about the human condition having been abandoned by men of letters, the moral imagination starves. And presently the moral imagination gives way, among many people, to the idyllic imagination; and after they have become disillusioned with Arcadia, they turn to the diabolic imagination, which afflicts both the best-educated and the worst-schooled classes in Western society today. Upon this corrupted imagination the clever charlatan and the nihilistic writer prey. Unscrupulous originality thus terminates in a universal boring nihilism—or, yet more catastrophic than the listlessness of nihilism, the common collapse of all standards, of all authority visible or invisible, the ruin of culture, the ruin of life.

Eliot foresaw this in 1933. It is unpopular teaching still, but painfully true.

Reprinted from Touchstone: A Journal of Ecumenical Orthodoxy, *Summer 1991, Volume 4, Number 3.*

THOMAS HOWARD

BRIDESHEAD REVISITED REVISITED

*Moral Imagination & the Catholic Faith
in Evelyn Waugh's Modern Novel*

THE LATE RUSSELL KIRK spoke often of "the moral imagination." By it he referred to that whole backdrop, or set of underpinnings, that corroborates for us mortals the fixities of the moral law. We are not angels; hence, we do not encounter Reality directly. We are protected ("from heaven and damnation," says T. S. Eliot) by the merciful arch, or filter, we might say, of the temporal and spatial, which bring with them the forms and colors that address our imaginations.

When we use this phrase, "moral imagination," we do not mean that the moral world exists only in the realm of fancy. Rather we refer to the vision of good and evil that we find in works of fiction. It is a vision that not only suffuses these works, but also presides over the terms of these fictions, nay, that determines the very stuff and texture of them.

Take, for example, the fourteenth-century *Vision of William Concerning Piers the Plowman*: Here we have, in an allegory to be sure, not merely the picture of a personality, or of a whole world, but, beyond these, the vision of what constitutes goodness and badness. Or take *Gawain*: The trouble in that poem is that Gawain

63

has sinned (not that he is "out of touch with his feelings," or that he has been "victimized"). There is a moral litmus test brought to bear on his behavior. In *The Faerie Queene*, all the thick woods and grottoes and hags and perils are to be understood in moral, and not merely psychological, or linguistic, terms. In *Measure for Measure*, the thing that has them all apoplectic in Vienna is the matter of sin and its punishment. We playgoers may enjoy the leisure and luxury of beholding fascinating personalities at work—Isabella and Angelo and Lucio and Claudio—but the nub of the drama is a moral matter.

It is not without significance that we often reach for Renaissance and pre-Renaissance fiction when we speak of the moral imagination. By the time we get to Henry Fielding, and then Jane Austen, Anthony Trollope, Henry James, and Virginia Woolf, we are not sure that *moral* is altogether the apt word. To be sure, all of these authors undergird their stories, in some sense, with a world of moral suppositions. Trollope, for example, shows how all the dramatic currents and countercurrents flow over a bed, so to speak, of moral assumptions. The sanctity of marriage is there, for example, and truthfulness, and generosity, and fidelity to one's duties, and benevolence: It is all there. But the main thing that engages our attention in Barset, or among the Pallisers, is not a rock-bottom question about goodness and evil; Trollope has not set out primarily to extol morality or religious truth.

Walker Percy makes this distinction, speaking of fiction:

> Let me define the sort of novelist I have in mind. . . . He is . . . a writer who has an explicit and ultimate concern with the nature of man and the nature of reality. . . . One might apply to the novelist such adjectives as "philosophical," "metaphysical," "prophetic," "eschatological," and even "religious." . . . Such a class might include writers as diverse as Dostoevsky, Tolstoy, Camus, Sartre, Faulkner, Flannery O'Connor. Sartre, one might object, is an atheist. He is, but his atheism is "religious" in the sense intended here: that the novelist betrays a passionate conviction about man's nature, the world, and man's obligation in the world. By the same token, I would exclude much of the English novel— without prejudice: I am quite willing to believe that Jane Austen and Samuel Richardson are better novelists than Sartre and O'Connor. The 19th-century Russian novelists were haunted by God; many of the French existentialists are haunted by his absence. The English novelist is not much interested one way or

another. The English novel traditionally takes place in a society as every one sees it and takes it for granted. If there are vicars and churches prominent in the society, there will be vicars and churches in the novel. If not, not. So much for vicars and churches.[1]

Waugh's Unthinkable Strategy

It is not to be urged that Evelyn Waugh should be thought the equal of Tolstoy, or even of Jane Austen. Nevertheless, his fiction raises piquant questions, if we are speaking of the moral imagination and twentieth-century English-language fiction—particularly *Brideshead Revisited*. But his *Sword of Honor* trilogy also would certainly raise similar questions, most notably in the figure of the protagonist's father, old Gervase Crouchback. We would need to undertake a wide canvass in order to discover another character in recent fiction who exhibits in such stark colors the quality that we can only call holiness. We, jades that we moderns are, find ourselves hailed, against all plausibility, with holiness—that is the only word for it—in the figure of Gervase Crouchback. And it is done, *mirabile dictu*, without the faintest whiff of sentimentality.

But in *Brideshead Revisited*, Waugh has done the almost unthinkable. He has given us (jades, if the accusation is not too fierce) a full-blown acclamation of Catholic piety, vision, morals, and dogma, but in terms that steal a march past merely modern sensibilities, and in fact virtually swamp those sensibilities.

It might be put this way: We are a skeptical epoch. Waugh's book is full of skepticism; indeed, the narrator is a card-carrying skeptic. Charles Ryder, the protagonist, is a thoroughly modern man. We might congratulate ourselves on being a somewhat cynical epoch—and the book is redolent of cynicism. Again, we are an unbelieving era, and the whole drama in *Brideshead* is seen through the lens of unbelief. Yet again, we are most certainly a highly self-conscious era—and the narrator in *Brideshead* is agonizingly self-conscious, almost paralytically so. (In the BBC television series, Jeremy Irons, in depicting Charles Ryder, displayed incredible dramatic prowess by making the reticent, self-conscious, laconic Charles a figure who seizes and holds our attention, and affection even.)

Oddly, *Brideshead* would seem able to take its place entirely comfortably on the shelf of modern fiction (as opposed to other fiction which has religious overtones, like that of Tolkien or Williams or Chesterton, for whom categories like

CREED & CULTURE

"fantasy" and "metaphysical thriller" have to be invoked). And yet *Brideshead* takes us all the way in to the world of Christian belief, piety, and dogma.

How does Waugh do it? My hunch is that he does it by *bravado*. It is bravado that is Waugh's trump card. Knowing that he is writing in a highly blasé, weary, and urbane world (and 50 weary years have passed since then), he first of all trumps that world, so to speak. He upstages us all by making his novel 10 times more blasé, weary, and urbane than we are.

For example, the tale is set in the 1920s, in Oxford, London, and Venice, and at a great country house. Any reader ignorant enough to congratulate himself on his own cleverness is very quickly left in the dust by the sheer agility, the prowess, the vivace tempo of the badinage flying about his ears. You thought you were urbane? Meet Sebastian: You will feel yourself an oaf. You thought you were witty? Meet Anthony Blanche: You will retire in confusion from the lists. You thought you had fine sensibilities? Next to Charles you are a churl. You thought you were civilized? In the family circle at Marchmain House you find that you are the merest rustic, left mute by your own solecisms.

But Waugh's strategy goes much further than this. After upstaging our sup-posititious urbanity, he goes on to disarm our routine and self-congratulatory un-belief, again by sheer bravado. That is, we find ourselves in thick Catholic piety and faith, but deprived, somehow, of our usual ability to patronize that piety and faith. We have lost our vantage point, and it is no longer these pious people who are under our avuncular surveillance, but we who are under theirs. For example, in one conversation with Lord Brideshead, Charles announces that he is an agnostic. Bridey is only mildly diverted by this, the way he would be if Charles had an-nounced himself a vegetarian or a necrophiliac. "Really?" says Bridey. "Is there much of that at your college? There was a certain amount at Magdalen. . . . It's everywhere."

Now that is bravado. But it is not bravado from the characters themselves. Indeed, there is nothing ostentatious, or swashbuckling, about any of them. The bravado is at work in the challenge that the narrative mounts against the reader. We find that we have been angled into the uncomfortable position of being the ones under scrutiny. We no longer have the luxury of patting faith on the head. Faith is looking at us, quizzically, ironically, and slightly incredulously. "An unbe-liever?" it seems to say. "Fancy." Somehow "unbeliever" and "bumpkin" seem to have become synonymous here.

The Catholic Gauntlet

But a much greater subtlety is at work in Waugh's narrative than any brief exchange like that might suggest. The subtle strategy comes in the form of a challenge: The reader finds himself drawn into the story, and losing thereby his agnostic footing. (This, of course, is to assume, for the argument, that your archetypal "modern" reader is agnostic.) We enter a brilliant world in the story, but it is a peculiar world, namely, the world of the Catholic aristocracy in England. By locating his story here, Waugh throws down a gauntlet.

Catholicism in England always has been in the minority: For some centuries it was a beleaguered minority. So to be Catholic in England was to be entirely free from the burden under which the Church of England always seems to stagger, namely, the burden of being agreeable. Anglican bishops seem anxious to assure everyone that what they are retailing is, after all, nothing but good, modern, sensible English fare. Don't for a moment suppose that I am purveying zeal, or miracles, or revival. To be Anglican is to be *au courant*.

This is an unfair caricature, of course, but one which, for good or ill, finds itself echoed in English fiction (and also in television: the late Malcolm Muggeridge was wickedly merciless in tweaking the noses of just this sort of churchman).

By locating his story among the English Catholic aristocracy, Waugh has, with one leap, made it immune from having to be acceptable. Catholicism through the centuries has not ordinarily been found pawing the arm of contemporaneity, as it were, and pleading, "But you can be Catholic without crowding your Englishness, or your respectability." To be Catholic is to be different—but not different, Waugh would have urged, in the way cults, sects, or conventicles are. It is easy to dismiss the religion in those quarters by pointing out that it is tacky, or marginal, or haywire, or arriviste, whereas to be Catholic is to belong to the most ancient and august organism in the world. It is older than the oldest dynasties and universities. To be Catholic is to be free from ever having to temporize. (If this sounds triumphalist, we may remind ourselves that Waugh might not have demurred at the charge.) To be Catholic is to be identified as someone who espouses a whole fabric of ideas—Virgin Birth, miracles, transubstantiation, and so forth—but who cannot be dismissed with exactly the same insouciance with which one might dismiss you if you belonged to a sect.

This matter never comes up in the story in so many words: but the way in which the Flyte family hold their faith is a vastly different business from the way in which, say, a devout Evangelical middle-class family might hold theirs. The Flytes are immemorially at home in their serene and lofty faith, and entirely untroubled by the disjuncture between that faith and the rest of England. They have, as it were, nothing to prove.

Thus Waugh outflanks his readers. He does not have to try to weasel religion into the narrative: It is of the very texture—a highly civilized texture—of the narrative. But there is more. Waugh manages a sort of narrative alchemy, so to speak, whereby the troubles of the Flyte family take on the aspect of *sin*.

This is unheard-of in modern fiction. Which of the characters of Henry James or D. H. Lawrence or E. M. Forster must make his agonizing choices in life under the scrutiny of the church's teaching on sin (unless it be by shucking off that teaching)? Stephen Dedalus must leave the world of Jesuit sermons. But in *Brideshead*, we find that everyone, sooner or later, must come to terms with God, not in an attenuated or leeched-out version that might be acceptable to William Ellery Channing's Boston or our own New Age sibyls. No. What is asked of the characters is that they squeeze through the needle's eye of sacramental confession and absolution, and thus find dignity and freedom and authenticity. It offends our fastidiousness.

This tactic, or alchemy, if you will, whereby Waugh obliges us to take seriously the demand laid on his characters that they face their choices in the light of Catholic teaching, is paralleled by another tactic, namely, that even though the faith is, in some sense, the heroine of the story, nevertheless, every single exemplar of that faith is a very poor icon.

The Poorest of Icons

We may survey the characters to see if this is so. First, of course, there is Sebastian. What a dazzling, coruscating figure he is. Young, beautiful, witty, acerb, cavalier, infinitely cultivated: which of us is not left plodding in the dust as his barouche-landau whirls by? He seems to know, and be long since at home in, everything that marks the precincts where life is lived with grace and civility: cigars, wine, clothes, art, repartee, persiflage, eccentricity—Sebastian is the very avatar of all of this. He would seem to stand at a polar extreme from the dowdy world of religious belief. But when Charles ventures to raise the matter of Sebastian's faith, ever so gingerly, we have this:

"Oh dear, it's very difficult being a Catholic!"

"Does it make much difference to you?"

"Of course. All the time."

"Well, I can't say I've noticed it. Are you struggling against temptation? You don't seem much more virtuous than me."

"I'm very, very much wickeder," said Sebastian indignantly.

". . . I suppose they try to make you believe an awful lot of nonsense?"

"Is it nonsense? I wish it were. It sometimes sounds terribly sensible to me."

"But my dear Sebastian, you can't seriously believe it all."

"Can't I?"

"I mean about Christmas and the star and the three kings and the ox and the ass."

"Oh yes. I believe that. It's a lovely idea."

"But you can't believe things because they're a lovely idea."

"But I do. That's how I believe."

This is the note struck in *Brideshead Revisited*. Whereas religion ordinarily has to creep apologetically, or lurch awkwardly, onto the stage, here it dances out in front of our eyes, daring us to cavil or carp. We haven't often encountered religion in these bravura terms. We are not sure how we might gainsay it.

And there is Sebastian's older brother, Lord Brideshead (Bridey). The satanically witty Anthony Blanche, in his thumbnail sketch of the whole family, says Brideshead is "something archaic, out of a cave that's been sealed for centuries. He has the face as though an Aztec sculptor had attempted a portrait of Sebastian; he's a learned bigot, a ceremonious barbarian, a snowbound lama." And indeed, we find ourselves writhing at times over Brideshead's lack of apparent tact.

But there is something vastly civilized about Bridey at the same time. He has no vanity at all, and he is transparent and utterly without malice. But he can be heavy-footed. We find this when Bridey explains why his fiancée, Beryl Muspratt, must not visit the Flyte household, where Julia is now present with her husband and Charles, her lover: "You must understand that Beryl is a woman of strict Catholic principle, fortified by the prejudices of the middle class. I couldn't possibly bring her here. It is a matter of indifference whether you choose to live in sin with Rex or Charles or both—I have always avoided inquiry into the details of your menage—but in no case would Beryl consent to be your guest."

So far, Catholicism is not being very compellingly, or attractively, represented by the Catholics among whom our agnostic narrator Charles finds himself. Sebastian's Catholicism seems to exist in a category with Mother Goose, and Brideshead sounds like an inquisitor. But there is their wonderful little sister Cordelia. She promises to pray for Charles, and tells him she can't spare a whole rosary for him, only one decade. She also thinks it would be a good idea if Charles chipped in five shillings so she can buy yet another African goddaughter. "You send five bob to some nuns in Africa and they christen a baby and name her after you. I've got six black Cordelias already. Isn't it lovely?" It seems that we are being invited to write Catholicism off with our worst prejudices confirmed about how mercenary and idolatrous it is.

But Cordelia turns out to be a girl, and presently a young woman of vast integrity, generosity of spirit, joy, and self-effacement. Much later in the story, speaking to Charles of the disordered lives of her older brother and sister, Sebastian and Julia, she says, "There's Sebastian gone and Julia gone. But God won't let them go for long, you know." Then she quotes Chesterton's Father Brown: "'I caught him with an unseen hook and an invisible line which is long enough to let him wander to the ends of the world and still to bring him back with a twitch upon the thread.'" With charity and faith like this at work in Cordelia, we readers scarcely feel inclined to snipe at her five-shilling goddaughters in Africa.

In this same conversation with Charles, she speaks of Lady Marchmain, their mother. Lady Marchmain has died by this late point in the story. Cordelia says to Charles, "You didn't like her. I sometimes think when people wanted to hate God they hated Mummy. . . . You see, she was saintly, but she wasn't a saint. No one could really hate a saint, could they? They can't really hate God either. When they want to hate Him and His saints they have to find something like themselves and pretend it's God and hate that. I suppose you think that's all bosh."

The reader, it seems, has been angled into Charles's position: Do I wish to sit in judgment on such sentiments as these, when the thing that so patently glimmers through it all is goodness?

Enigmas & Death

But what are we to make of Lady Marchmain? Early in the story, Charles, the narrator, says this: "Religion predominated in the house; not only in its practices—

the daily Mass and rosary, morning and evening in the chapel—but in all its intercourse. 'We must make a Catholic of Charles,' Lady Marchmain said." In one conversation with Charles, speaking of the tremendous wealth that their family enjoys, she says this: "Now I realize that it is possible for the rich to sin by coveting the privileges of the poor," and goes on to point out that paradox is of the essence of the gospel: "It's not to be expected that an ox and an ass should worship at the crib."

This is all innocent enough; but we discover in the story that Lady Marchmain is something of a dragon. It may be because of her sheer power over her children, exercised ever so softly and elegantly, that they all have such problems. And so once again, we find a reason why Catholicism need not win us over. Look at what a termagant Catholic piety has made of Lady Marchmain.

But then we come to this, uttered after Lady Marchmain's death by Julia, through bitter tears of remorse over her own sinful and adulterous life:

> "Mummy carrying my sin with her to church, bowed under it and the black lace veil, in the chapel; slipping out with it in London before the fires were lit; taking it with her through the empty streets where the milkman's ponies stood with their forefeet on the pavement; Mummy dying with my sin eating at her, more cruelly than her own deadly illness. Mummy dying with it; Christ dying with it, nailed hand and foot; hanging over the bed in the night-nursery; hanging year after year in the dark little study at Farm Street . . . hanging in the dark church where only the old charwoman raises the dust and one candle burns; hanging at noon, high among the crowds and the soldiers; no comfort except a sponge of vinegar and the kind words of a thief. . . ."

Which brings us to Julia, long since deeply embroiled in a life of sexual havoc. At the end of the story, she renounces Charles, for whom she has divorced her husband:

> "I can't marry you, Charles. . . . I saw today that there was one thing unforgivable . . . the bad thing I was on the point of doing, that I'm not quite bad enough to do; to set up a rival good to God's. Why should I be allowed to understand that, and not you, Charles? It may be because of Mummy, Nanny, Cordelia, Sebastian—perhaps Bridey and Mrs. Muspratt—keeping my name in their

prayers; or it may be a private bargain between me and God, that if I give up this one thing I want so much, however bad I am, He won't quite despair of me in the end."

Just a day or two earlier, when the family insists that their father, the renegade Lord Marchmain, be given the last rites on his deathbed and Charles fiercely objects—"Can't they even let him die in peace?"—Julia replies, "They mean something so different by 'peace.'" And when Charles objects that extreme unction is "a lot of witchcraft and hypocrisy," Julia asks, "Is it? Anyway, it's been going on for nearly two thousand years."

The scene at Lord Marchmain's deathbed is one of the most delicate in all of fiction. Waugh's tact as a narrator is put to the fiery test here. How do you present a drawn-out, highly charged deathbed scene without sloshing into the worst sort of bathos and treacle? Victorian novels and Hollywood movies have made us all quite justifiably skittish about deathbed scenes.

But Waugh seems to bring this one off. It is doubly threatened with sentimentalism, since not only do we have the dying man surrounded by his family, but we also have our agnostic Charles, having reached the crisis in his own recalcitrant itinerary. He has been scandalized, through all the action, with this dogged faith of the family; but now, at Lord Marchmain's bedside, with the family kneeling and the priest making the sign of the cross over the dying man, we have this:

> Then I knelt, too, and prayed: "O God, if there is a God, forgive him his sins, if there is such a thing as sin. . . ." I suddenly felt the longing for a sign, if only of courtesy, if only for the sake of the woman I loved, who knelt in front of me, praying, I knew, for a sign. . . . All over the world, people were on their knees before innumerable crosses, and here the drama was being played again . . . the universal drama in which there is only one actor. . . . Suddenly Lord Marchmain moved his hand to his forehead . . . the hand moved slowly down his breast, then to his shoulder, and Lord Marchmain made the sign of the cross. Then I knew that the sign I had asked for was not a little thing, not a passing nod of recognition, and a phrase came back to me from my childhood of the veil of the temple being rent from top to bottom.

The Unseen Hand

How do you do a conversion scene? The perils are legion. But Waugh's tact is in control: We never see Charles converting. Only in the epilogue, when we are back in the bleak present with Charles, 19 years later, do we find him, in 1943, with his army unit having been ordered to bivouac, unbeknownst to him, on the immense Brideshead estate. He steps into the little chapel in the house.

> There was one part of the house I had not yet visited, and I went there now. The chapel showed no ill-effects of its long neglect; the art-nouveau paint was as fresh and bright as ever; the art-nouveau lamp burned once more before the altar. I said a prayer, an ancient, newly-learned form of words, and left, turning towards the camp. . . . Something quite remote from anything the builders intended had come out of their work, and out of the fierce little human tragedy in which I played; something none of us thought about at the time: a small red flame—a beaten-copper lamp of deplorable design, relit before the beaten-copper doors of a tabernacle; the flame which the old knights saw from their tombs . . . that flame burns again for other soldiers, far from home. . . . It could not have been lit but for the builders and the tragedians and there I found it this morning, burning anew among the old stones.

That is language that sails very near the wind. One false word, and we would capsize into sentimentalism. But I think Waugh brings it off. Reticence is what saves it all. We are not given the conversion scene: That would have been unmanageable (we may recall similar reticence on Shakespeare's part, in refraining from giving us the marriage scene of Romeo and Juliet, and in having Falstaff's death scene only reported by the maladroit Mistress Quickly). But we do see Captain Charles Ryder, in the chapel, offer an ancient prayer, newly learned. Somebody has been teaching him the prayers of the Church. Obviously he has been received into that ancient Church.

Brideshead Revisited is the story of a religious conversion, whatever else it may be. Conversion is one of the topics that is most intractable, and most inhospitable to any attempt to come at it narratively. There is one sense in which the Catholic faith itself may be said to be the heroine of the story. Certainly Charles is the protagonist. But the victor is the faith that, in spite of—or, paradoxically, and far more profoundly because of—its shabby look when clothed with the flesh of Catholics themselves, triumphs, both in Charles, and also in each of the characters before they make their exits.

Waugh would have urged that this is the way it is. God shows up in the most inauspicious precincts: Israel—not one of the more impressive tribes of antiquity; Bethlehem—not one of the watering spots of the world; Calvary—scarcely an appropriate purlieu for the King of Heaven; the Church—not exactly a select group; and a flat, white, tasteless wafer—not a hopeful entry in the baked-goods sweepstakes. But the thing about all of these items is that God is to be found there.

Waugh has caught this in his novel and consequently offers the modern reader a work of moral imagination rare in modern fiction. The squalor, the bad taste, the *stürm und drang*, the ineptness, show up, not just in remote contrast to some austere vision of the faith. They are the very modality in which that faith is, as often as not, mediated to us.

Reprinted from Touchstone: A Journal of Ecumenical Orthodoxy, *Summer 1996, Volume 9, Number 3.*

ENDNOTES

1. *The Message in the Bottle* (New York: Farrar & Giroux, 1982), p. 103.

JAMES L. SAUER

LESSONS FROM
THE NURSERY

The Catholic Imagination Encounters Bambi

I N MY FAMILY, it is our habit to read to the children before we put them to bed. Usually, it's a few picture books without much substance, which move along fairly quickly—though the *Pokey Little Puppy* never seems to move quite fast enough for me. I must say, however, that I do enjoy the earlier Dr. Seuss material—especially the moralistic stuff—*Horton Hatches the Egg* ("I meant what I said and I said what I meant, an elephant's faithful 100 percent") and *Horton Hears a Who* ("A person's a person. No matter how small"—a small didactic point for our generation).

We also have been reading our children some more substantial works—short novels like George MacDonald's *The Light Princess*, a most happy allegory; and a children's version of *Pilgrim's Progress*. But a truly wonderful and unexpected pleasure, one could almost say an aesthetic experience, came to me recently through my parental reading of Felix Salten's *Bambi*.

Now like most of you, the title *Bambi* immediately conjures up visual associations of the full-length Disney cartoon by that name. There is a certain romance to that version of the tale—but it is a Disney romance. We are subject to the childish delight in the wide-eyed Bambi, the frolicsome rabbit Thumper, and the shy little skunk, appropriately named Flower. These two last characters don't even appear in the Salten text. In fact, there is so much alteration in tone and content that one ought to view the novel and the cartoon as two separate works, rather like two different versions of a myth.

Salten writes in the tradition of Aesop, but it is Aesop with a Wagnerian soundtrack. His word pictures of animals distill the spiritual substance of life. The reviewer in the *Catholic World* of 1928 said that Salten's "approach to his subject is marked by poetry and sympathy and there are charming reminders of German folklore and fairy tale in his nature world."[1] E. H. Walton in the *Bookman* held that "the story is told with an enchanting clarity and simplicity. It creates its own atmosphere and its own terms."[2] Salten has given us a prose poem.

Hidden in our humanity, like some vestige of Adamic headship, is our unity with the animal world; there we find the imaginative ability to see through beastie eyes. It is not only pleasing, it also is almost necessary. Seeing with the animals reminds us of our creaturehood. Salten understands this preternatural link. This same perceptual power is seen in the modern fiction of Richard Adams's *Watership Down* and Walter Wangerin, Jr.'s *Book of the Dun Cow*.

The lyrical power of *Bambi* in English came through the translating pen of Whittaker Chambers. A Communist at the point of translation, Chambers "thought the story rather sentimental, but it brought back to me my boyhood days in the woods, when I was watching the flight and pursuit of creatures under the ponds or among the grass stems. I made the translation. *Bambi* was an instant success. . . ."[3] Even a dialectical materialist recognizes the romance.

Visions of Eros & Freedom

As I read *Bambi,* a number of emotion-charged visions made me pause. I literally stopped reading and set the book down more than once, overcome with a kind of aesthetic shock that takes the wind out of you.

The first experience occurred in the chapter on leaves. Hardly what one would consider the most promising topic for high art. Nevertheless, the chapter on leaves forms a picturesque parable of the problem of our existence. Two leaves discuss mutability and the afterlife:

> They were silent a while. Then the first leaf said quietly to herself, "Why must we fall? . . ."

The second leaf asked, "What happens to us when we have fallen?"

"We sink down."

"What is under us?"

The first leaf answered, "I don't know, some say one thing, some another, but nobody knows."

The second leaf asked, "Do we feel anything, do we know anything about ourselves when we're down there?"

The first leaf answered, "Who knows? Not one of all those down there has ever come back to tell us about it."[4]

Not one? Well, Salten is defining the human predicament, not presenting the gospel. And as a definition of the human situation, it is marvelous. The parable goes on and achieves that brave agnosticism that is found in parts of the Old Testament Wisdom literature. There is a sad, solitary pain as the leaves fall one by one. And so we will wither; all flesh is grass. Vanity of vanities, saith the Preacher.

The second vision revolves around, of all things, the power of Eros. Faline is Bambi's mate. Bambi awakes from sleep and finds that his Faline is not to be found. Frantic, he hears Faline's voice in the distance and begins to rush toward it, only to have his path blocked by the Great Stag. He must get to her. He must. The Stag tells him that it is not Faline. Bambi argues with the Stag. Can it be true? But Faline calls him. She calls. Finally, the Great Stag shows him that it is not Faline, but a man making her voice—a deceptive imitation from Bambi's natural enemy. The Stag's wisdom has preserved Bambi from death. Later he finds his lovely Faline safe and sound:

He was breathless, tired and happy and deeply stirred.

"Please, beloved," he said, "please don't ever call me again. We'll search until we find each other, but please don't ever call me . . . for I can't resist your voice."[5]

I don't think there can be a more evocative expression of Eros. This is not lust, but pure holy desire: "please don't ever call me . . . for I can't resist your voice." I am undone. My children yawn. They turn over and go to sleep as I read. I lay down the book, while my imagination flies to her form with whom I share my bed and life. I hear her move to the stairs. She is a poem. Her voice calls me from a distance. "Are the children asleep?" She calls. O Lord, I cannot resist her voice.

The third vision occurs with the return of Gobo and reflects the problem of freedom and slavery in a bare, unadorned way. With one little word picture, Salten devastates our self-delusion of freedom in a world that offers no guarantee from risk.

Gobo, a fawn who had been presumed dead, returns after having been captured by men and tamed. The Old Stag is again the voice of Wisdom in this age of moronic youth:

> "What kind of band is that you have on your neck?"
>
> Everybody looked at it and noticed for the first time the dark strip of braided horsehair around Gobo's neck.
>
> Gobo answered uneasily, "That? Why that's part of the halter I wore. It's His halter and it's the greatest honor to wear His halter, it's . . ." He grew confused and stammered.
>
> Everyone was silent. The old stag looked at Gobo for a long time, piercingly and sadly.
>
> "You poor thing!" he said softly at last, and turned and was gone.[6]

The Old Stag is not angry; he does not lecture; he merely gazes, understands, and pronounces judgment. Gobo is a deluded fool: a once free deer whose heritage was to range the forest, now an apologist for tyranny. He rejoices in his slavery. He wears his chain as a mark of honor. He has achieved Orwellian doublethink: "Freedom is Slavery." Gobo is the embodiment of all modern men who have given up the wild liberty of their forefathers for the security of a little food, a little credit, a little health insurance, a little pension. Gobo is Esau selling his birthright.

The fourth aesthetic experience occurs in the fox hunt scene—the problem of treachery forms the basis for a heroic last stand. Chased by the barking dogs, the cornered fox pleads for his life:

> ". . . [L]et me go." He spoke softly and beseechingly. He was quite weak and despondent.
>
> "No! No! No!" the dog howled.
>
> The fox pleaded still the more insistently. "We're relations," he pleaded, "we're brothers almost. Let me go home. Let me die with my family at least. We're brothers almost, you and I."
>
> "No! No! No!" the dog raged.

Then the fox rose so that he was sitting perfectly erect. He dropped his handsome pointed muzzle on his bleeding breast, raised his eyes and looked the dog straight in the face. In a completely altered voice, restrained and embittered, he growled, "Aren't you ashamed, you traitor!"

"No! No! No!" yelped the dog.

But the fox went on, "You turncoat, you renegade." His maimed body was taut with contempt and hatred. "You spy," he hissed, "you blackguard, you track us where He could never find us. You betray us, your own relations, me who am almost your brother. And you stand there and aren't ashamed!"[7]

In the face of tyranny there are only two responses: acquiescence or sacrificial fortitude. Life is a choice between a Vichy existence or a Warsaw ghetto uprising. Salten teaches us that it is better to die with the honor of self-respect and truth than to live as a treacherous dog.

Mortality & Life

And finally, there is the scene in which Bambi confronts a Dead Man—and all of his notions of mankind's divinity are toppled. In one great iconoclastic blast, Salten has the Great Stag say of man:

"Listen, Bambi. He isn't all powerful as they say. Everything that lives and grows doesn't come from Him. He isn't above us. He's just the same as we are. He has the same fears, same needs, and suffers the same way. He can be killed like us, and then He lies helpless on the ground like all the rest of us. . . ."[8]

The toppling of man from the Temple of Animal-land parallels for the Romantic mind all rebellion against divinity. But it is important to notice that it is false divinity that Salten has removed from the center of worship. In spite of this orthodox truth, we must recognize that Salten has given us a sub-Christian, and indeed a sub-Hebraic view of man: placing man and animal on a common plane below their Creator. Man certainly is an animal, but he is the divine animal—the Imago Dei. Salten asserts an egalitarianism of all species that is at odds with the Judeo-Christian hierarchical model recounted in Lovejoy's *Great Chain of Being* and established in the biblical literature.

Salten's haunting treatment of the woodland ought not to blind us to the errors of his theology. Not everything that Mr. Salten has said is true. Indeed, he is the perfect example of the dictum that "the poet tells lies." But they are pleasing lies, the fictions that bear fragments of truth.

The smell of Judeo-Christian sentiment mingles with the green-gray Northland forests. Yet it is ironic that Felix Salten, pseudonym for the Jewish journalist Siegmund Salzmann, and a refugee from Nazi Austria, should write a text that celebrates, however so slightly, the notion of the *Overman*—the individual, the Steppenwolf. This German Romanticism runs through Salten's work. Nature is celebrated; wildness is placed above domesticity. The lone silent Stag is given the place of heroic center.

Salten has made me think and feel life's struggle; he has moved my heart through forest parable. I have learned to see through a children's book the problem of life and the hereafter; the power of Eros; the dignity of liberty and the sadness of servility; the nobility of death nobly faced and the curse of existence treacherously lived. And I have learned to see Man, that god of animals, stretched and bleeding on the ground—impotent, mortal, most unworthy of worship. Like Bambi, I am forced to confess when I survey the frailty that is Man that "there is Another who is over us all, over us and over Him."[9]

These are good lessons to learn, especially in the nursery of life.

Reprinted from Touchstone: A Journal of Ecumenical Orthodoxy, *Summer 1991, Volume 4, Number 3.*

ENDNOTES

1. M. C. M., *Catholic World,* vol. 128 (December 1928), p. 376.
2. Walton, E. H., *Bookman.* vol. 68 (September 1928), p. 99.
3. Whittaker Chambers, *Witness* (New York: Random House, 1952), p. 239.
4. Felix Salten, *Bambi* (New York: Simon & Schuster, 1929), pp. 106–109.
5. Ibid., p. 192.
6. Ibid., p. 210.
7. Ibid., p. 274.
8. Ibid., p. 286.
9. Ibid., p. 286.

PHILIP G. DAVIS

THE SWISS MAHARISHI

Discovering the Real Carl Jung
& His Legacy Today

C ARL GUSTAV JUNG (1875–1961) has become one of those cultural giants whose influence extends far beyond the field of his own professional activity. He is best known as one of the key figures in the development of modern psychology and psychiatry, but the traces of his distinctive ideas can be found in fields as varied as archaeology, personnel management, criminal investigation, and liberal theology. Now, decades after his death, newly accessible information indicates that Jung's life and work were guided by religious, even occult, considerations and need to be reassessed in that light.

Jung had a consuming interest in the functions of the mind, and trained originally in medicine. Between 1905 and 1912, he was so close a disciple of Sigmund Freud that the master anointed him as "son" and "crown prince," the Gentile successor who would carry Freudianism beyond its original circle of Viennese Jews. The pair fell out quite dramatically, however, and spent the rest of their lives as antagonists. The generally accepted explanation is that Jung came to doubt Freud's conviction that sexuality is the key to most mental problems, and developed instead a broader, more "spiritual" perspective.

Naturally, they remained in agreement on some matters. Both Freud, the secularized Jew, and Jung, the discontented son of a Swiss Protestant pastor, developed a deep antipathy towards the Judeo-Christian tradition, especially its standards of sexual morality. As E. Michael Jones showed in his book *Degenerate Moderns*, their theories on human sexuality reflected the most pressing sexual concerns in their own private lives.[1]

Part of Freud's fame rose from his idea that incestuous desires are universal in children; by the time he published this theory, he already had been passionately involved with his own sister-in-law, Minna Bernays. Jung, by the same token, undertook a sustained investigation of human inclinations towards polygamy, and launched a long series of extramarital affairs with patients and colleagues; he went so far as to claim that "the prerequisite for a good marriage . . . is the license to be unfaithful."[2] In both cases, as Jones showed, the personal temptation preceded the formulation of a general, exonerating theory.

Of the two, Freud has since predominated in "orthodox" psychology; the cartoon psychiatrist is still the Freudian, questioning the patient on the couch about his relationship with his mother, while Jungian analysts have no such visible public image. Academic psychology now has a strong component of experimental science in the tradition of B. F. Skinner and his rat mazes, something for which Jung never had any sympathy.

But despite being comparative outsiders in psychology and psychiatry, Jungians have made some striking contributions to modern life. These range from the ubiquitous Myers-Briggs personality test, which is explicitly based on Jung's theories, to a certain variety of affirmative-action rhetoric, which emphasizes the need to balance "male" and "female" perceptions and energies within the individual personality as well as in groups and institutions.

New Age & Old Occultism

Jung has been particularly popular in liberal religious settings and New Age circles because his psychological theories assume the critical importance of religion in human life, whereas Freud dismissed all religion as illusion. The recent Joseph Campbell New Age fad, for instance, has not taken much account of his essentially Jungian approach to mythology; Campbell in fact worked personally with Jung and published through the Bollingen Foundation, which was established and run by a coterie of Jung's clients and disciples with his active support.[3]

Now another book, Richard Noll's *The Jung Cult: Origins of a Charismatic*

Movement, confirms what some already had suspected: Jung's religiosity, which underpins crucial components of his psychological theories, is essentially a variant of Central European occultism, presented under a veneer of nineteenth-century scientific patter.[4]

Noll firmly locates Jung in the historical context of his formative years of training and initial practice (1895–1925). His upbringing, education, and early career took place almost entirely in the German-speaking parts of Switzerland, specifically Basel and Zurich. Both the time and the place shaped Jung's thought in decisive ways.

Jung took his training in medicine just as medical theories were going through a drastic change. The old "vitalistic" approach, best represented by Ernst Haeckel, maintained that evolution was guided by a sort of spiritual life-force that existed within all things. The newer theories, like those which are now dominant, were entirely materialistic and held that inheritance and evolution happened in a physical way, traceable through studies like genetics. Interestingly, Jung clung throughout his life to the older view, espousing a sort of pantheism that sought the life-energy itself within the processes of the natural world and the depths of the human soul.

Naturally, Jung's beliefs were informed by more than medical theories. Though Swiss, he had a strong identification with the larger German cultural heritage, bolstered no doubt by the family tradition that Jung's paternal grandfather had been the illegitimate son of the great Johann Wolfgang von Goethe. Goethe's *Faust* was an inescapable influence on anyone educated in German at this time. Jung, who first read it at his mother's suggestion, said later that it "poured into my soul like a miraculous balm" that "gave me an increased feeling of inner security and a sense of belonging to the human community." In contrast, he regarded the Christian teachings championed by his father as "fancy drivel . . . a specimen of uncommon stupidity whose sole aim was to obscure the truth."[5]

Jung, it is clear from some of his other remarks, had an immediate and lasting sense of identification with the demonic figure of Mephistopheles, whom he regarded as Faust's alter ego. Over against the academically inclined Dr. Faust, Jung considered Mephistopheles to represent "the true spirit of life as against the arid scholar,"[6] revealing words from someone who worked to influence the academic and medical establishments from the outside rather than the inside.

Friedrich Nietzsche was all the rage as Jung matured; his notion that spiritual regeneration could be won by throwing off artificial, civilized restraints on behavior seems to have appealed particularly to Jung.

The reworked Teutonic mythology of Richard Wagner, an equally towering figure of the time, could be seen in the same light. Noll remarks that Wagner "envisioned the operatic spectacles of his later decades as great Teutonic mystery-plays, and he sought to unite the soul of the German peoples through his music and Germanic mythological themes. . . . Wagner and his theater-temple performances became the center of a mystery cult with mystical overtones."[7]

In addition, German Switzerland and southern Germany comprised the homeland of the turn-of-the-century European counterculture, which Noll specifically compares to California of the 1960s. In this environment, vitalistic philosophies merged with nationalist and racialist speculation—many believed in things like a "folk-soul," which supposedly embraced the spirits of all the members of a national or racial group.

These systems of thought also drew heavily on occult sources like Spiritualism, Rosicrucianism, and Theosophy. Self-anointed sages like Guido von List and Jorg Lanz von Liebenfels went time-travelling in visionary trances, returning with descriptions of a utopian, prehistoric Aryan world. These reports were used to buttress calls for the purification and expansion of greater Germany.[8]

Some of Jung's maternal relatives were noted participants in occult activities; in fact, his doctoral thesis was based on seances performed by his own cousin, Helene Preiswerk. Inevitably, many of his later patients were steeped in these same ideas. These were among the people whose descriptions of their diseased fantasies gave Jung the raw material for his theories. The fact that Jung eventually managed to "confirm" many of his notions by sifting through the literary remains of Mithraism, gnosticism, and alchemy becomes much less surprising in light of the occult foundation on which he actually began.

Rebirth & the New Age

The roots of Jung's ideas in the general cultural context of his time are now much clearer than before, thanks partly to Noll's use of letters and lecture notes from Jung and his students, which have only recently become available. Jung's critics during this period castigated him as a cult leader who behaved as though he were God. The newly accessible material permits a stunning demonstration of the almost literal accuracy of these accusations.

In 1916 Jung undertook what amounts to a series of self-directed trance visions in which he experienced a spiritual "rebirth." He did not describe the key vision in any of his books; its contents are now known from notes taken at one of his seminars in 1925 and published in 1989.[9] He spoke of descending into the earth and meeting spirit guides known as Elijah (he later mutated into other figures named Philemon and Ka) and Salome. At the critical moment of the sequence, Salome addressed Jung as Christ, and he "saw" himself assume the posture of a victim of crucifixion, with a snake coiled around him, and his face transformed into a lion's visage. He interpreted the vision thus:

> One gets a peculiar feeling from being put through such an initiation. The important part that led up to the deification was the snake's encoiling of me. Salome's performance was deification. The animal face which I felt mine transformed into was the famous [Deus] Leontocephalus of the Mithraic mysteries. . . .[10]

From the details and his own comments about them, it is clear that he was combining some Christian ideas with themes from Mithraism, and that he saw himself as a combination of Christ and Mithra in this vision. Given his well-established pantheistic inclinations, Jung's resulting belief in his own self-deification is palpable in his description of the event.

This is the experience of regeneration that he then offered to the world through his form of psychotherapy. Difficult as it is to do justice to Jung's complicated theories, the basic idea behind Jungian analysis is the need for an individual to be guided through an exploration of the inner self, thus coming to recognize in full consciousness the various components or aspects of the personality.

In this lengthy process of "individuation," one learns that one's personality incorporates a series of polar opposites: rationality and irrationality, the "animal" and the "spiritual," masculinity and femininity, and so on. The goal of the exercise is the reconciliation of the opposites, bringing them all into a harmony that results in *self-actualization.* This term captures Jung's belief that the healthy individual does not pursue one side of a polarity at the expense of the other, but brings them all into balance, in a kind of psychological relativism.

To anyone acquainted with the European occult scene of the late nineteenth century, all of this sounds quite familiar. Noll properly emphasizes the turn-of-the-century south German fad for solar mysticism as the immediate source for much of Jung's system, but the broader context is informative too. Complex systems of corresponding polarities, and the quest to bring all opposites into complementary balance, were the stock in trade of magical "philosophers" like Eliphas Levi and his disciples in Rosicrucianism, the Ordo Templi Orientis, and the Hermetic Order of the Golden Dawn.[11] As Mary K. Greer notes in *Women of the Golden Dawn*, members of this English magical order, founded in 1888, pursued "spiritual harmony through self-examination" in order to "become one with their own divinity. . . . This involved a union of soul, mind, and body—necessitating correction of imbalances, combining of opposites, reclaiming what was lost, and surrender to dissolution and chaos."[12]

Behind Jung's partly Freudian, partly original terminology lies the standard occult goal of encountering "the god within," just as it appears in the writings of those who practiced ceremonial magic. Jung called the process used with his patients "active imagination," but from his description of his own experience with it, it resembles the visionary trances of the magical tradition much more closely than it does the therapy sessions conducted by his former colleagues in Freudianism.

All this serves to show Jung in his proper context and in a clear light: More than a shaper of scientific psychology, he is one of the major bridges from the nineteenth-century European occult revival to the modern New Age movement. His time with Freud did not define his life's work; it was more a temporary diversion from his lifelong interest in the magical and paranormal. It seems, then, that the study of Jung's thought belongs to the history of modern religion rather than to scientific psychology.

Noll, who argues precisely this conclusion in his book, has run into controversy as a result. He has been accused of breaching the confidence of another Jung researcher, although he has denied this in print, and his sensationalistic linking of Jung to the suicidal Order of the Solar Temple in a *New York Times* article apparently led Princeton University Press to cancel its plans to have Noll edit a collection of Jung's religious writings.[13]

But what of the substance of Noll's charge? In *National Review*, James Gardner's polemical review of *The Jung Cult* explains it away by suggesting that Jung is simply out of fashion now, like disco music, and may well return to favor. More to the point, he argues that Jung did not really mean what he said when he spoke of things like self-divinization. Noll took it all too literally, according to Gardner: "Once we remove this literalism, Noll's argument doesn't amount to much."[14]

Not so. For one thing, Noll has been a practicing clinical psychologist and presumably has grounds to know, as well as any outsider can, when Jung most likely meant what he said. Second, anyone who has more than a journalistic acquaintance with nineteenth-century European occultism can see how "literally" the serious magicians took the quest for self-divinization and how smoothly the central Jungian contentions slide into this framework. Moreover, it seems that Noll may actually have found the Achilles' heel in Jung's entire opus.

Fraudulent Offspring

Jung probably is most famous for his theory of the "collective unconscious" and its "archetypes." He asserted that our everyday conscious awareness and our personal subconscious are both shaped by our own day-to-day experiences. Deeper than these, however, are levels of consciousness shared by groups: families, nations, races, and ultimately the human species as a whole. The folk-soul lives on in Jungianism.

These deeper levels of consciousness, supposedly, have some specific contents. When people in different times and places develop similar symbols, such as using the sun to represent life and enlightenment, this is because they are drawing on the same archetype, a complex of ideas that exists within the collective unconscious.

The archetypes are the source of all religious symbols, and all religions are therefore "true" and, indeed, essentially identical. Myths from around the world arise from the same archetypes, and to that extent they all mean the same thing. Judaism and Christianity, however, are guilty of blocking people's access to the inner source of truth because of their devotion to an abstract, heavenly God. The collective unconscious is accessible in theory to all human beings, but only a few, like Jung himself, discover for themselves the way to experience it. The rest of us need their help.

Jung maintained later in his career that the linchpin in the development of his whole theory was the case that has been nicknamed "The Solar Phallus Man." This was a psychiatric patient who reported having visions in which he saw the sun with an "upright tail." Jung claimed to have analyzed this patient himself in 1906. Subsequently, in 1907 and 1910, two books were published that revealed that Mithraism had employed solar-phallic symbolism almost two thousand years ago. Upon reading these books (the first of which was written by the theosophist G. R. S. Mead), Jung supposedly realized that the ancient visionaries and the modern psychotic must have been perceiving the same psychic object, and his theory of archetypes and the collective unconscious was born.

Noll, however, presents information that appears to demolish Jung's claims.[15] First, it turns out that the Solar Phallus Man was treated at the Burgholzli Mental Hospital by another doctor, J. J. Honegger, after Jung himself had left the institution; Honegger committed suicide in 1911, leaving the way open for Jung to claim the case in later years. Second, the therapy actually took place in 1909, after the new information on Mithraism had already begun to circulate. Third, the solar phallus theme was not at all new. It was already well known through two other influential sources: Friedrich Creuzer's survey of ancient mythology (published in 1810–1812) and Johann Jakob Bachofen's *Mother-Right* (published in 1861).[16] Jung himself was thoroughly familiar with both Creuzer and Bachofen before the Solar Phallus Man was ever treated.

Medically, then, there was no need whatsoever to postulate the existence of archetypes or a collective unconscious to explain the content of the psychotic visions. Both patient and therapist could easily have known the solar phallus motif from books they had read or heard about. Jung's self-proclaimed linchpin case thus becomes his Achilles' heel: At best, it is a distortion in which the most obvious and reasonable explanations of the patient's symptoms were ignored in favor of a grand mystical theory; at worst, Jungianism may be founded on a fraud.

If this is the truth about Jung, whose heirs have prevented Noll from examining Honegger's surviving notes to clinch the argument, the possible ramifications are breathtaking in scope. How many personnel and policy decisions have been based on the Myers-Briggs test? How much affirmative-action and inclusive-language policy depends on Jungian definitions of masculinity and femininity? Campbell shared the Bollingen experience with the likes of Heinrich Zimmer and Mircea Eliade; how much established scholarship in mythology and the history of religion needs to be reconsidered?

To take one example, the importance of Jung to some forms of radical feminism is quite pronounced. Proponents of the fast-growing Goddess movement in feminist spirituality like to claim that the pre-literary cultures of Europe and the Near East were Goddess-worshipping, matriarchal utopias. Their citizens supposedly lived in peaceful, egalitarian, productive harmony with each other and with Nature herself, thus exemplifying "feminine" virtues as Jung defined them, until patriarchal barbarians overthrew them a few millennia ago.

When they are not ignoring the actual evidence (like the many weapons and injured skulls found in one of their "peaceful" prehistoric utopias, Catal Huyuk in modern Turkey) or making it up entirely (like the claim that Silbury Hill in southern England is the swollen womb in a huge earth-portrait of the Goddess), the Goddess devotees often use Jungian notions to harmonize ancient artifacts with their matriarchal ideology.[17] Marija Gimbutas, the late professor of archaeology at UCLA, included Jung and more than a half dozen of his noted disciples in the bibliographies to her books on the alleged matriarchies of the Balkans, *The Language of the Goddess* and *The Civilization of the Goddess*.[18]

In fact, Jung's own ideas were strongly influenced by the works of Bachofen, who first invented the theory of ancient matriarchies. Jung knew this unorthodox, independently wealthy scholar by sight during his childhood, since they both lived in Basel, and the close resemblance of Jung's characterizations of the "masculine" and the "feminine" to Bachofen's descriptions of matriarchy and patriarchy has been recognized for some time.[19]

Noll goes further, noting that Jung's own copy of Bachofen's *Mother-Right* still survives and suggesting, plausibly enough, that his interest in Bachofen was stimulated by the psychoanalyst cum sexual libertine cum anarchist cum drug addict Otto Gross, whom Jung was trying (unsuccessfully) to treat as early as 1908. The modern use of Jung as independent confirmation of the theories of Bachofen, then, is a classic case of circular reasoning—Jung got these ideas from Bachofen in the first place!

Bachofen had a shaky reputation among serious scholars; Noll aptly likens him to Erik von Daniken, of *Chariots of the Gods* fame. Rather than a follower of the Solar Temple group, I would liken Jung himself to the Maharishi Mahesh Yogi. Both Jung and the Maharishi began their careers with university degrees in science, and continued using scientific jargon and claiming scientific verification for their theories. Jungian analysis and Transcendental Meditation (along with its second-generation variant, Yogic Flying) involve trance techniques that are advertised as scientifically proven ways of promoting psychological well-being, but which also have specifically religious content.[20] Not content with science, both the Jungians and the Maharishi make quasi-messianic claims about the benefits that will come to society as a whole if enough individuals follow their lead.[21]

Each of the movements, however, despite its claims to scientific objectivity, consists of a hierarchy of specialists trained and certified exclusively within the movement itself, who constitute their own "apostolic succession" from the founder. And both require their followers to undergo long programs of extensive and expensive instruction, apart from standard medical accrediting agencies.

Jungian Modernism or Orthodoxy?

There is a serious side to the effects of Jungian influence today. Jung's therapeutic technique of "active imagination" is now revealed as a sanitized version of the sort of trance employed by spiritualistic mediums and Theosophical soul travelers, with whom Jung was personally familiar. There is, further, an uncomfortably close resemblance between these practices and the modern use of "guided imagination" that seems to lie at the root of so many cases of False Memory Syndrome and phony allegations of satanic ritual abuse.

As many reports have now shown, the questioning of witnesses and alleged participants in ritual abuse often takes the form of having them return in their imaginations to the scene of the supposed crime so that they can report what they "see." Especially when children are involved, investigators' questions and instructions can easily include suggestions ("Do you remember anything about a rope?").

When people are put through the procedure repeatedly, the suggestions can gradually work their way into the story. Both adults and children have been put through this exercise dozens of times; extensive use of guided imagination has even led people to "confess" to horrendous crimes they could not possibly have committed.[22] "Satanic panics" accompanied and followed the notorious McMartin day-care child-abuse trial in California, a similar case in Martinsville, Saskatchewan, and many others; vast amounts of time and money have been wasted in investigations, and there may be innocent people in jail. Is all this another part of Jung's legacy to the modern world?

The pervasiveness of Jungian notions in modern culture presents a multifaceted challenge to Christians who may encounter those notions in many different guises—sometimes from the pulpit. Jung and his devotees have been responding to a very real problem: the loss of meaning in contemporary society. Modernism, if we define it as the post-Enlightenment combination of pure rationalism, materialism, and secularism, has obviously done an effective job of damaging the public credibility of biblical religion.

As critics have noted for more than a century, however, modernism has failed to put a satisfying alternative to biblical religion in place. Technology we have in abundance, but we have been taught to think of ourselves as the accidental outcome of natural evolutionary processes: complicated descendants of pond scum. For those who are not completely distracted by the gadgets and the quest to get more of them, there is still something deeply unsatisfying about this.

For those who wish to be more than complicated pond scum, what could be better than a road map to godhood like Jungianism? Especially a map that, instead of proposing a pilgrimage of spiritual and moral discipline, tells you that you have already arrived, indeed you have always been there, if only you could see it clearly? Some follow this invitation into actual occultism or New Age activities, but many others settle for the superficial comfort of buying into these ideas without actually dabbling in magical practices. The modern, scientific veneer of Jungianism gives it tremendous advantage and appeal to the unsuspecting.

Orthodox Christians know the problems of modernism; we also know that there is no solution in pretending to be gods. When we let go of our belief in the one and only God, the Father Almighty, and in the one and unique Incarnation of his Son, we leave ourselves open to two great risks: allowing the illusion of our own godhood to lead us into limitless self-indulgence; or, if we cannot handle that, surrendering to the false godhood of some charismatic pseudo-messiah.

As Christians, we know that the truth will make us free. The emerging truth about Jung has its small part to play in the larger drama of our times.

Reprinted from Touchstone: A Journal of Ecumenical Orthodoxy, *Spring 1996, Volume 9, Number 2.*

ENDNOTES

1. E. Michael Jones, *Degenerate Moderns: Modernity as Rationalized Sexual Misbehavior* (San Francisco: Ignatius Press, 1993).
2. Jones, p. 194, quoting William McGuire, ed., *The Freud/Jung Letters: The Correspondence Between Sigmund Freud and C. G. Jung,* trans. Ralph Manheim and R. F. C. Hull (Cambridge, Massachusetts: Harvard University Press, 1988), p. 289.
3. William McGuire, *Bollingen: An Adventure in Collecting the Past* (Bollingen Series; Princeton: Princeton University Press, 1982).

4. Richard Noll, *The Jung Cult: Origins of a Charismatic Movement* (Princeton: Princeton University Press, 1994). This article is an expansion of my review of Noll's book, "'It sounds so strangely weird': The Occult Sources of Jungian Psychology," *Anglican Free Press* 12:3 (Michaelmas, 1995), pp. 15–17.

5. Jones, pp. 201–202.

6. Jones, p. 202.

7. Noll, p. 70.

8. Nicholas Goodrick-Clarke, *The Occult Roots of Nazism: The Ariosophists of Austria and Germany, 1890–1935* (Wellingborough, Northamptonshire, UK: Aquarian, 1985), pp. 33–122.

9. *Analytical Psychology: Notes of the Seminar Given in 1925 by C. G. Jung*, ed. William McGuire (Princeton: Princeton University Press, 1989); described in Noll, pp. 211–215, and in John Kerr, *A Most Dangerous Method: The Story of Jung, Freud, and Sabina Spielrein* (New York: Vintage, 1993), p. 469.

10. C. G. Jung, *Analytical Psychology: Notes of the Seminar Given in 1925* (Princeton: Princeton University Press, 1989), pp. 96, 98; quoted in Noll, p. 213.

11. Richard Cavendish, *The Magical Arts: Western Occultism and Occultists* (originally *The Black Arts;* London: Arkana, 1967), pp. 23–42.

12. Mary K. Greer, *Women of the Golden Dawn: Rebels and Priestesses* (Rochester, Vermont: Park Street Press, 1995), p. 57.

13. See Scott Heller, "Flare-Up over Jung," *Chronicle of Higher Education*, June 16, 1995, pp. A10 and A16; and Noll's reply in a letter to the editor, *Chronicle of Higher Education*, September 15, 1995, p. B6.

14. James Gardner, "Jung at Heart," *National Review*, July 10, 1995, pp. 60–63; quotation from p. 62.

15. Noll, pp. 181–184.

16. Friedrich Creuzer, *Symbolik und Mythologie der alten Völker, besonders der Griechen*, 4 vols. (Leipzig und Darmstadt: Leske, 1810–1812); Johann Jakob Bachofen, *Das Mütterrecht: Eine Untersuchung über die Gynaekokratie der alten Welt nach ihrer religiosen und rechtlichen Natur* (Stuttgart: Kreis und Hoffman, 1861).

17. For a brief critique of the historical claims made by the Goddess movement, see Philip G. Davis, "The Goddess and the Academy," *Academic Questions*, vol. 6, no. 4 (1993), pp. 49–66.

18. Marija Gimbutas, *The Language of the Goddess* (London: Thames & Hudson, 1989); *The Civilization of the Goddess* (San Francisco: Harper, 1991).

19. Henri F. Ellenberger, *The Discovery of the Unconscious: The History and Evolution of Dynamic Psychiatry* (London: Allen Lane, The Penguin Press, 1970), pp. 218–223.

20. J. Gordon Melton, *Encyclopedic Handbook of Cults in America* (New York and London: Garland, 1986), pp. 187–192.

21. Noll, pp. 188–190, citing McGuire, *The Freud/Jung Letters* (Princeton: Princeton University Press, 1974), p. 294 (letter 178 J), p. 346 (letter 206 J).

22. Lawrence Wright, "Remembering Satan—Part I," *The New Yorker*, May 17, 1993, pp. 60–81; "Remembering Satan—Part II," *The New Yorker*, May 24, 1993, pp. 54–76.

VIGEN GUROIAN

FAMILY & CHRISTIAN VIRTUE IN A POST-CHRISTIAN WORLD

*Reflections on the Ecclesial Vision
of John Chrysostom*

O F THE MANY quotable passages from the writings of St. John
Chrysostom, the most often cited is located in his twentieth homily
on Ephesians: "If we regulate our households [properly] . . . we will also
be fit to oversee the Church, for indeed the household is a little Church. Therefore,
it is possible for us to surpass all others in virtue by becoming good husbands and
wives."[1] Frequently, this passage has been cited as a text supporting high sacramental interpretations of marriage. Rarely has there occurred sustained discussion of
what might best be described as Chrysostom's ecclesial vision of the Christian
family and household. That is my task here. I also want to show how this vision
enables Christians to better understand what truly is at stake for the Church in the
contemporary debate about the family and its role in moral upbringing.

Chrysostom lived at a moment of genuine cultural crisis. The pagan culture
of antiquity was in decline, and Christianity had become a social force with which
to be reckoned. It was not yet clear, however, what shape a future Christian culture might take. Chrysostom was one of a minority of Christian apologists (St.
Basil was another) who voiced serious misgivings about the emerging Christian
order. Like Basil, he brought the spirit of monastic reform into his critique of

93

society. He inveighed against the moral laxity of self-professed Christians and their excessive preoccupation with material possession, power, and social status. This reform spirit drove Chrysostom's ecclesiology as he struggled to steer a course that would lead neither to an imperial church nor to a cake-frosting version of Christianity for the masses. His example is relevant all over again for churches today as they enter a definitively post-Christendom era marked by cultural deterioration and are faced with difficult choices about how to relate to the emerging hegemonic secularity.

Chrysostom might easily have succumbed to the temptation to promote the moral rehabilitation of the family as a means of securing societal stability. We hear repeatedly today from religious sources—Protestants, Roman Catholics, and Orthodox alike—that the family is of social value as a bulwark against social decay. Recent presidential campaigns have made the family an issue as we have heard from candidates how important strong and healthy families are to the American way of life. Less clear in the political rhetoric is what these family values actually amount to or what they are grounded in.

Chrysostom did not ignore the sociological dimension or function of the family. On one occasion he said, "When harmony prevails [in the household], the children are raised well, the household is kept in order, and neighbors, friends, and relatives praise the result. Great benefits, both for families and states, are thus produced."[2] He, however, subordinated this societal function of the family to its ecclesial role. Christian marriage and family are a vocation in the Church to build up the kingdom of God. In order to fulfill this vocation, the Christian family must practice a spiritual and moral discipline that resists the ways of the world. Chrysostom was clear about the proper source of family morality: Christ in his life and commandments.

Chrysostom's vision of the ecclesial family was radical when he preached it in the fourth century, and it is equally radical in our secular culture. Living after Christendom, we as spouses and parents can no longer assume that our children will be nurtured in biblical and Christian norms apart from the Church, because these standards of behavior and moral norms no longer govern in our culture. It should be obvious to Christian spouses and parents how truly radical their vocation as family is within contemporary society; we seem regrettably prone to forget what actually is entailed in being married "in the Lord." The printed and electronic media bombard us with powerful and seductive alternatives to the demanding, disciplined life to which the Christian family is called biblically and through the marital rites of the Church. It is easy to think of the Christian family as merely a church-going version of any number of comfortable and idealized sitcom families or, alternatively, to despair of traditional marriages and families altogether.

Chrysostom addresses us when he urges the churches to make strenuous and sustained efforts to cultivate and restore the vision of the family as an ecclesial entity and a mission of the kingdom of God. Sociologists tell us that for vast numbers of Americans, the family has lost its public meaning and outlook. It is being redefined as a haven of private living, consumption, and recreation. Civic-mindedness has been replaced with hunger for privacy. Personal sacrifice for children and community has been replaced by self-centeredness and hedonism. Chrysostom's ecclesial vision of the family speaks to this disintegration of community, but it does so in a fashion that can only look strange even to people who otherwise worry about the privatization and moral privation of the family. While sociologists and politicians contend that the family is in trouble because it is not contributing as it should to the formation of viable community and civic virtue, Chrysostom argues that the Christian family is a calling to community in service to God and his kingdom that spreads into the whole of society.

Chrysostom's teachings on marriage and family push us into a much larger debate that is at the center of contemporary Christian ethics—a debate over the prospects for the Christian faith and ethics generally within our secular order. As I have suggested, there are those who cling to the empty hope that some version of Christendom is still possible and, hence, that Christian ethics can still be done in old and familiar ways of correlating Christian truth with norms and institutions found within the culture. Others pin their hope on a more modest goal of designing a new public theology for a pluralistic order. Efforts in this direction go on in diverse and even opposing ideological camps, among neo-conservatives, mainline Protestants, and liberal as well as neo-Thomist Catholics. Still others are persuaded that Christendom has ended and that it never was a good idea in any case. Many of these have turned to alternative models of a confessing church, whose "main political task" lies "not in the personal transformation of individual hearts or the modification of society," but rather, as Stanley Hauerwas and William H. Willimon have put it, "in the congregation's determination to worship Christ in all things . . . and to build up an alternative polis"—that being the

Church.[3] The contending parties fling accusations back and forth at one another about whether their respective proposals for the Church are too accommodating towards the culture or too sectarian.

Chrysostom helps us to see that this perennial question about the appropriate relationship of the Church to the culture is reflected in microcosm within the Christian family. With respect to the contemporary debate, I want to demonstrate how Chrysostom's way of stating the relation of family to church and church to culture eludes some of the facile categories in which we have learned to pigeonhole other points of view. Chrysostom was neither sectarian, accommodationist, nor triumphalist. He resisted the Eusebian Christian imperialism of his day. He was not taken with the Constantinian-Theodosian theocratic synthesis of church and state that, as later codified by Justinian, provided the ideological framework for Byzantine theocracy. Nor did he propose that the Church retreat into the catacombs or hold the opinion that the only pure and true Christianity was restricted to the monastery. Rather, Chrysostom's idea of an evangelical and socially responsible Christian faith was bound up with the pastoral and moral theology he addressed to Christian parishioners and Christian rulers alike. In all that he said about the nature of the church-world relationship, Chrysostom returned again and again to the belief of the church fathers that salvation is accomplished from within the *ecclesia* through its process of making the kingdom of God present to an unbelieving world. And he viewed the family as an ecclesial entity that figured centrally in this salvific process.

The "Ecclesial" Household

As Gerhardt B. Ladner has observed, by the end of the fourth century, especially in the East, "the ascetic and mystic and the ruler shared between them as it were true kingship. Reformed in the royal image of God, they represented two different but equally high orders of mankind."[4] The Constantinian-Theodosian initiatives to establish a Christian commonwealth, formalized by the Emperor Justinian in the sixth century, tipped the balance away fom the ascetic and mystic toward the ruler. The emperors increasingly asserted a "quasi-sacerdotal position [for themselves] in the Church, and generally made it understood that the value of all acts of reform in the Church and empire flowed directly from the fact that they were put into effect by, or on the command of, the emperor."[5]

Early in his career Chrysostom resisted these trends toward imperial domination of the Church and society. He did so by championing monastic claims of true "kingship" over the Eusebian conception of the king-philosopher. This is a clear aim of his short treatise, "A Comparison Between a King and a Monk" (ca. 380). As Ladner puts it: "There was one great exception to the eastern development of [the] Basileia ideology: the thought and life of St. John Chrysostom."[6] The truly significant turn in Chrysostom's thought came, however, as he struggled with his pastoral and homiletic duties at Antioch and later in Constantinople. In these settings, Chrysostom became convinced "that, apart from the privilege of marriage, the Christian who lived in the world had the same obligations as the monk."[7] While expounding a churchly interpretation of the Christian household as a mission of the kingdom of God in the world, he also anticipated and answered the later Byzantine alternatives of (1) envisioning the Church as the sacramental organism that whispers in the emperor's ear and sacralizes an imperial order, and (2) endorsing the view that the monks are the only true representatives of holiness in a compromised and sinful world.

At the close of his Antiochene ministry, Chrysostom wrote the "Address on Vainglory and the Right Way for Parents to Bring Up Their Children" (ca. 386–387). There he spoke "of a child's soul as of a city in which the King of the universe intends to dwell, and God's earthly representative in this city is not the emperor, but the child's father." "Nothing," concludes Ladner, "could be less 'Eusebian' than this conception of the Kingdom of God on earth, and it is not surprising that John Chrysostom perished as a martyr for Christian ethical principles in resistance"[8] to the emerging and solidifying ideology of a Christian empire.

From this point on, Chrysostom sought to "reform the 'Polis' within the 'Basileia'."[9] He increasingly identified the proleptic presence of the kingdom of God not primarily with empire or the cloistered monastery but with the near and familiar Christian household. The cardinal "marks" of the kingdom, Chrysostom insisted, are compassion, love of neighbor, and hospitality toward friends and strangers alike. The Christian household, he maintained, is an exact image of the *ecclesia* when it puts into practice the gospel teaching about our behavior toward one another and toward God.[10]

Chrysostom thought of the Abrahamic household as the ancient biblical type of the Christian "ecclesial" household. He maintained that the Abrahamic household kept and practiced in an exemplary fashion those virtues of the kingdom of

God that should belong to the people of God in order that they may receive the Messiah when he comes. In his homily on Acts 20:32, Chrysostom says:

> Make yourself a guest-chamber in your own house; set up a bed there, set up a table there and a candlestick. For is it not absurd, that whereas, if soldiers should come, you have rooms set apart for them, and show much care for them, and furnish them with everything, because they keep off from you the visible war of this world, yet strangers have no place where they may abide? Gain a victory over [prevail over] the Church. . . . Surpass us in liberality: have a room to which Christ may come; say, "This is Christ's cell; this building is set apart for Him. . . . Abraham received the strangers in the place where he abode himself; his wife stood in the place of a servant, the guests in the place of masters. He knew not that he was receiving Christ; knew not that he was receiving Angels; so that had he known it, he would have lavished his whole substance. But we, who know that we receive Christ, show not even so much zeal as he did who thought that he was receiving men. . . . Let our house be Christ's general receptacle."[11]

Clearly Chrysostom has in mind something even more concrete than the actual network of human family or household relations. The physical dwelling itself is realized as "Christ's general receptacle." Abraham's tent is the Old Testament type of Christian dwelling, which has become the house of God. When the members of the household provide for guests and greet them in their home, the dwelling itself serves as the body of the Lord.

Elsewhere in his homilies on the Book of Acts, Chrysostom filled this metaphor of the house of God with its members and their relations. "Let the house be a Church, consisting of men and women. . . . 'For where two,' He saith, 'are gathered together in My Name, there am I in the midst of them.'"[12] Hospitality was such an important virtue for Chrysostom that he held that it should figure in the selection of one's spouse. Abraham sent his servant to his own country to find a wife for his son Isaac, and the servant determined through prayer that he should choose the woman who offered him water not only for himself but also for his camels (Gen. 24:11–14). The servant was sent looking for such a bride for Isaac, writes Chrysostom, because "everything good" that happened to the household "came because of hospitality. . . . Let us not see only the fact that he asked for water, but let us consider that it shows a truly generous soul not only to give what is asked but to provide more than is requested."[13] This sort of cultivation of a righteous household, he concludes, is a means of seeking and receiving the kingdom of heaven. "'Thou who receivedst Me,' He saith, 'into thy lodging, I will receive thee into the Kingdom of My Father; thou tookest away My hunger, I take away thy sins; thou sawest Me a stranger, I make thee a citizen of heaven; thou gavest Me bread, I give thee an entire Kingdom, that thou mayest inherit and possess.'"[14]

Chrysostom cites the home of Aquila and Priscilla as a quintessential New Testament example of an "ecclesial" household. These two workers in the Lord unselfishly opened their home to St. Paul and other disciples of Christ. "It was no small excellency, that they had made their very house a Church. . . ." And Paul exhorted the Corinthian Christians to greet one another "with the holy kiss . . . as a means of union: for this unites, and produces one body."[15] As Gus Christo has summarized, Chrysostom held that "a Christian home's transformation into the Church . . . or a church, happens when its occupants salute each other with the holy kiss . . . are hospitable to people and remain free of deceit and hypocrisy."[16] Such a home or church becomes a site from which Christ draws the rest of the public world into his kingdom. This in turn is described as a liturgical and sacramental action. "Charity," Chrysostom once exclaimed, is "a sacrament. . . . For our sacraments are above all God's charity and love."[17]

The Christian Family as Mission of the Kingdom of God

In order to emphasize the larger ordained purposes and calling of the Christian family, Chrysostom repeatedly returned to the stories of the Abrahamic household, even Abraham's willingness to follow God's command and offer his only son in sacrifice. Yet the Old Testament story of Hannah and her son Samuel is the one he most often invoked to illumine the unselfish and heroic qualities required by God of those who assume the office of parenthood. Chrysostom's use of the story shifted over the years, however, from an early defense of monasticism to a later focus on the responsibility of Christian parents to attend consciously to raising their children as true Christians, and not just nominal ones.

In his early work, *Against the Opponents of the Monastic Life,* Chrysostom called on parents to raise their children unselfishly to be fit inheritors of the kingdom of heaven. This entailed especially, though not exclusively, preparing them

for the monastic life. Chrysostom described Hannah as an exemplar of such responsible and unselfish parenthood. She "gave birth to one child and did not
expect to have another. Indeed, she had scarcely given birth to him, and this after
many tears, for she was sterile. . . . When he no longer needed to be nursed, she
immediately took him and offered him up to God, and she ordered him to return
to his father's house no longer, but to live continually in the temple of God."[18]
Thus it was that Hannah fulfilled the community's office of a parent, by dedicating her son to God and to the well-being of his people. For "when God had
turned away from the race of the Hebrews because of their profuse wickedness . . .
[Samuel] won back God's favor through his virtue and persuaded him to supply
what had been given previously. . . . Such," concluded Chrysostom, "is always
the reward for giving our possessions to God . . . not only possessions and things,
but our children."[19]

More than a decade after he wrote these words, during his ministry in Antioch,
or perhaps even later during his episcopacy at Constantinople, Chrysostom returned to the very same story in his homily on Ephesians 6:1–3. In the context of
instructing parents on how to raise their children, he grants that it is not necessary to raise them as monks; it is enough that they be raised as good Christians.[20]
Still, of "the holy men and women of old," he cites Hannah as the example to
imitate. "Look at what she did. She brought Samuel, her only son, to the temple,
when he was only an infant!"[21] Chrysostom uses the story to emphasize the importance of raising children on Scripture. "Don't say, 'Bible reading is for monks;
am I turning my child into a monk?' . . . It is necessary for everyone to know
Scriptural teachings, and this is especially true for children."[22]

This instruction that parents should raise their children not to become monks
but just to be good Christians is not at all inconsistent with Chrysostom's earlier
use of the Hannah and Samuel story in *Against the Opponents of the Monastic Life*.
The cardinal obligation and task of Christian parenthood remains the same: to
prepare the child for service to God and his people. Hannah "gave Samuel to
God, and with God she left him, and thus her marriage was blessed more than
ever, because her first concern was for spiritual things."[23]

In an ancient prayer of the Armenian rite of matrimony, the priest beseeches
God to plant the couple "as a fruitful olive tree, in the House of God, so that
living in righteousness, in purity, and in godliness, according to the pleasure of
Thy beneficent will, they may see the children of their children and they may

be a people unto Thee."[24] This liturgical prayer emphasizes the ecclesial nature of Christian marriage and family. This is to seek the kingdom of God. To raise children in virtue and righteousness renders them "a people unto" God. In *Against the Opponents of the Monastic Life,* Chrysostom quotes 1 Timothy 2:15: "'They will be saved through bearing children, if they remain in faith and love and holiness, with modesty.'"[25] Hannah's "wisdom" was a matter of comprehending through faith that by dedicating to God "the first-fruits of her womb" she might "obtain many more children in return."[26] Her attention to spiritual things was not a retreat into the private self or family; it was an affirmation of the existence of a community of faith to which she belonged and in which she held the divinely commissioned office of parent. God in turn bestowed upon her the growing company of that community.

Ephesians 5 & the Ecclesial Marriage

John Chrysostom's strongest statements about the ecclesial calling of Christian husbands and wives, fathers and mothers, comes, not surprisingly, in his homily on Ephesians 5:22–23: "Wives, be subject to your husbands, as to the Lord. For the husband is the head of the wife just as Christ is the head of the church, the body of which he is the Savior." Feminist theologians have regarded this passage as a central piece of what they characterize as the theologization of antiquity's structures of domination.[27] Other theologians have maintained that there is more Christianizing of the marital relationship than the critics admit in this and other *Haustafeln* passages. John Howard Yoder, for example, argues that submission here assumes the character of a revolutionary subordination through the Pauline theology of *agape* and freedom in Christ.[28]

Virtually all who write on this passage, however, agree that it reflects the Pauline author's strong interest in ecclesiology. As Elisabeth Schüssler Fiorenza conjectures at one point in her analysis of Ephesians 5, "The reason for . . . [its] theological shortcomings might be the author's interest in clarifying the relationship between Christ and the Church, whose unity is his primary concern in the rest of the letter."[29] Chrysostom's interpretation of this passage is strongly ecclesiological. He believes that it establishes a sacramental and even ontological relationship between the institution of marriage and the Church. God's economy is channeled first of all through the Body of Christ, the Church; the peace of the world is guaranteed by the peace of that Body. And the peace of the Church is a discipline and task of the Christian family; and the peace of the Church is strengthened by the harmony and good order of a godly household. Thus, reasons Chrysostom, the wife does not obey the husband ultimately for "her husband's sake," but "primarily for the Lord's sake."[30] Just as the husband loves his wife "not so much for her own sake, but for Christ's sake."[31]

After discussing the proper attitude of the wife toward her husband, Chrysostom considers the proper attitude of the husband toward his wife. Keeping in mind St. Paul's analogy of the husband as the head of the wife, Chrysostom works together Christic and ecclesial metaphors, exhorting each husband to

> be responsible for the same providential care of . . . [your wife], as Christ is for the Church. And even if it becomes necessary for you to give your life for her, yes, and even to endure and undergo suffering of any kind, do not refuse. Even though you undergo all this, you will never have done anything equal to what Christ has done. You are sacrificing yourself for someone to whom you are already joined, but He offered Himself up for one who turned her back on Him and hated Him.[32]

Both husband and wife must imitate the Lord, but the greater burden is on the husband, precisely because he is in the position of greater power. He who would view himself as master is called upon to be servant in the likeness of Christ, who is the head of the Church. "What sort of satisfaction could a husband himself have, if he lives with his wife as if she were a slave, and not a woman of her own free will," asks Chrysostom. "Suffer anything for her sake, but never disgrace her, for Christ never did this with the Church."[33] In his condescending and sacrificial relationship to the Church, Christ becomes the example husbands must follow in their relationship to their wives: "Imitate the Bridegroom of the Church."[34] Christ condescended to take the Church as his bride even though "the Church was not pure. She had blemishes, she was ugly and cheap. Whatever kind of wife you marry, you will never take a bride like Christ did . . . you will never marry any one estranged from you as the Church was from Christ. Despite all this, he did not abhor or hate her for her extraordinary corruption."[35] Rather, Christ loved the Church, in order that she might be sanctified (Eph. 5:25–27). The ecclesial metaphor reigns throughout Chrysostom's strong advice about spousal

attitudes and conduct within the marital relationship. The nature of the Church
and the nature of marriage illumine each other.

In this theology, the Christian family figures as the primal and sacramental
human community in which kenotic and agapic love are learned and rehearsed.
Husband and wife share this love within the conjugal relationship, and in turn,
they communicate this love to the children through their parental care. Further-
more, the Christian family, rehearsed in and equipped with the right virtues, is an
arena of ascetic combat with the demons of personal and public life. This *askesis*
not only perfects persons but also deepens community.

The Virtues of the Christian Family

Chrysostom admired the historic virtues of classical culture. Yet he was not to be
counted in the company of those Christian writers who thought that the classical
and Christian virtues were identical, always complementary, or easily correlated
with one another. When Chrysostom looked out at the culture, he saw that
Christians were captives to its human-centered standards of success and happiness,
and he pleaded with Christian parents to foster another kind of character in their
children.

> If a child learns a trade, or is highly educated for a lucrative profession, all this
> is nothing compared to the art of detachment from riches; if you want to make
> your child rich, teach him this. He is truly rich who does not desire great pos-
> sessions, or surrounds himself with wealth, but who requires nothing. . . . Don't
> worry about giving him an influential reputation for worldly wisdom, but pon-
> der deeply how you can teach him to think lightly of this life's passing glories;
> thus he will become truly renowned and glorious. . . . Don't strive to make him
> a clever orator, but teach him to love true wisdom. He will not suffer if he lacks
> clever words, but if he lacks wisdom, all the rhetoric in the world can't help
> him. A pattern of life is what is needed, not empty speeches; character, not
> cleverness; deeds, not words. These things secure the Kingdom and bestow God's
> blessings.[36]

Stoic influences alone cannot account for this passage. The Beatitudes, which
Chrysostom described as the very constitution of the kingdom of God, lie very

near to its surface, together with a biblically founded eschatological hope.

The Bible, said Chrysostom, is the basic primer and lesson book for the virtues of the kingdom that God charges parents to teach their children. Scripture provides the narratives of the lives of patriarchs and matriarchs, parents and siblings, who struggled in God's presence to maintain a way of life distinct though not necessarily separate from the world. In *Address on Vainglory and the Right Way for Parents to Bring Up Their Children,* Chrysostom pioneered what might be regarded as one of the first Christian curriculums for children's Bible study. The responsibility for such education, however, resides first with the parents. Chrysostom commended especially the stories of Cain and Abel, Jacob and Esau, Joseph and his brothers, Hannah and Samuel, and the like. His method is worth observing.

Much of Chrysostom's discussion is concerned with identifying biblical models for relations between parents and children and of siblings with each other. For example, he encourages parents to juxtapose the stories of Cain and Abel and of Jacob and Esau in the manner of a diptych, drawing out the distinct lessons of each story as well as the common themes within both narratives of sibling rivalry, envy, and fratricide. He urges parents to tell the stories of Cain and Abel and Jacob and Esau, not once, but repeatedly. Then they should say to the child:

> "Tell me the story of those two brothers." And if he begins to relate the story of
> Cain and Abel, stop him and say: "It is not that one that I want, but the one of
> the other two brothers, in which the father gave his blessing." Give him hints
> but do not as yet tell him their names. When he has told you all, spin the sequel
> of the yarn, and say: "Hear what occurred afterwards. Once again the elder
> brother, like in the former story, was minded to slay his brother. . . ."[37]

In his twenty-first homily on Ephesians, Chrysostom gave his rationale for such instruction and pleaded its importance for Christian living.

> Don't think that only monks need to learn the Bible; children about to go into
> the world stand in greater need of Scriptural knowledge. A man who never
> travels by sea doesn't need to know how to equip a ship, or where to find a pilot
> or a crew, but a sailor has to know all these things. The same applies to the
> monk and the man of this world. The monk lives an untroubled life in a calm

harbor, removed from every storm, while the worldly man is always sailing the ocean, battling innumerable tempests.[38]

From the perspective of Chrysostom's vision of Christian family and virtue, strategies for the revitalization of the family and preservation of society based on the Constantinian model are theologically misdirected. Once one defines Christian existence and tradition in merely sociological terms, a certain kind of ecclesiology and definition of the Christian family emerges. The family is a training ground for virtues that first have to do with the well-functioning of the secular polity—a worthy enough goal, but not what lies at the heart of the vocation of Christian parenthood and family. Nor in these post-Christendom times is it helpful to seek to counteract the privatism in the American family with social ministry, as liberal Protestants and liberal Roman Catholics seem to think.[39] The Christian family, weakened and secularized by powerful cultural forces of privatism, narcissism, and consumerism, is scarcely the agent of social change in any case.

There is a necessary interim step missing in such calls to commit the Christian family to social transformation. The Christian family can receive a public vocation only after it has first engaged in the struggle for the kingdom of God. The jargon of the Christian activists: "intimacy," "shared decision making," "peacemaking," "cooperative projects," and the like, is hardly distinctive; nor is it in advance of the other kinds of progressivism in the culture that fail to provide a transcendent imperative for ethical behavior. Chrysostom insists on another course:

> When we teach our children to be gentle, to be forgiving, to be generous, to love their fellow men . . . we instill virtue in their souls and reveal the image of God within them. This then is our task: to educate both ourselves and our children in godliness; otherwise what answer will we have before Christ's judgment seat? . . . How [else] can we be worthy of the kingdom of heaven?[40]

Reclaiming the Vision

There exists a great need in the Christian churches today for ecclesial formation, for they stand to become increasingly dissipated if they continue to depend for strength upon cultural supports of Christian faith that are in fact no longer present. The churches must seek ecclesial formation not for their own sake but to prepare believers to greet the Bridegroom when he returns. If Chrysostom was right about the Christian family as a vocation of the kingdom and about the Christian household as a little church, then we would do well in this time and place to reclaim that vision. We must work to make the Christian family once again a training ground in which, by becoming good husbands and wives, fathers and mothers and children, we become "fit to oversee the Church" and good "house-keepers" of God's now and future kingdom.

We also need to join Chrysostom in regarding the Church as a body related in various ways to the larger society and reject all notions of the Church as an elite group concerned solely with so-called spiritual matters and appropriately heedless of worldly things. Then we will begin to appreciate anew the special value of Chrysostom's vision of the "ecclesial" family for the re-formation of the Church and the introduction of a new discipline into its life for the salvation of the world.

Reprinted from Touchstone: A Journal of Ecumenical Orthodoxy, *Spring 1993, Volume 6, Number 2. Another version of this article appeared as a chapter in* Ethics After Christendom: Toward an Ecclesial Christian Ethic *(Eerdmans, 1994).*

ENDNOTES

1. John Chrysostom, *St. John Chrysostom on Marriage and Family Life,* trans. Catherine P. Roth and David Anderson (Crestwood, New York: St. Vladimir's Seminary Press, 1986), p. 57.
2. Ibid., p. 44.
3. Stanley Hauerwas and William H. Willimon, *Resident Aliens: Life in the Christian Colony* (Nashville, Tennessee: Abingdon Press, 1990), pp. 45–46.
4. Gerhardt B. Ladner, *The Idea of Reform* (New York: Harper and Row, Publishers, 1967), p. 125.
5. Ibid., p. 126.
6. Ibid., pp. 125–126.
7. Ibid., p. 127.
8. Ibid., p. 129.
9. Ibid.
10. I have learned much about this from Gus George Christo's dissertation, "The Church's Identity Established Through Images According to St. John Chrysostom" (Ph.D. dissertation, University of Durham, 1990). Christo's work has alerted me to a number of passages that I cite from Chrysostom below.
11. John Chrysostom, *The Homilies of St. John Chrysostom on the Acts of the Apostles,* in *A Select Library of Nicene and Post-Nicene Fathers of the Christian Church,* First Series, vol. 11 (Grand Rapids, Michigan: Wm. B. Eerdmans Publishing Co., 1956), p. 277 (homily 26).

12. Ibid., p. 127 (homily 26).

13. Chrysostom, *Chrysostom on Marriage*, pp. 103–104.

14. Chrysostom, *Homilies on Acts*, p. 276 (homily 45).

15. John Chrysostom, "First Epistle of St. Paul the Apostle to the Corinthians," in *The Homilies of St. John Chrysostom*, Part II (Oxford and London: John Henry Parker, J. G. F. and J. Rivington, 1839), p. 620.

16. Christo, "Church's Identity," p. 386.

17. I have used Emilianos Timiadis's translation of this passage as it appears in his "Restoration and Liberation in and by the Community," *Greek Orthodox Theological Review*, vol. 19, no. 2 (Autumn 1974), p. 54. See also John Chrysostom, *Homilies on the Gospel of St. Matthew*, in *A Select Library of Nicene and Post-Nicene Fathers of the Christian Church*, vol. 10 (Grand Rapids, Michigan: Wm. B. Eerdmans Publishing Co., 1956), pp. 434–435 (homily 71).

18. John Chrysostom, *A Comparison Between a King and a Monk/Against the Opponents of the Monastic Life*, trans. David G. Hunter (Lewiston, New York: The Edwin Mellon Press, 1988), p. 171 (book 3).

19. Ibid., pp. 171–172.

20. Chrysostom, *Chrysostom on Marriage*, p. 67.

21. Ibid., p. 68.

22. Ibid.

23. Ibid.

24. *The Blessing of Marriage or The Canon of the Rite of Holy Matrimony According to the Usage of the Armenian Apostolic Orthodox Church* (New York: Armenian Church Publications, 1953), p. 56.

25. Chrysostom, *Opponents of Monastic Life*, p. 172.

26. Chrysostom, *Chrysostom on Marriage*, p. 68.

27. Elizabeth Schüssler Fiorenza, *In Memory of Her* (New York: The Crossroad Publishing Co., 1988), esp. pp. 266–270.

28. John H. Yoder, *The Politics of Jesus* (Grand Rapids, Michigan: Wm. B. Eerdmans Publishing Co., 1972), esp. pp. 174–175, 180–181, 190–192.

29. Fiorenza, *Memory*, p. 270.

30. Chrysostom, *Chrysostom on Marriage*, p. 45.

31. Ibid., p. 58.

32. Ibid., p. 46.

33. Ibid., p. 47.

34. Ibid., p. 48.

35. Ibid., p. 47.

36. Chrysostom, *Chrysostom on Marriage*, p. 69.

37. Chrysostom, *An Address on Vainglory and the Right Way for Parents to Bring Up Their Children*, appended to L. W. Laistner, *Christianity and Pagan Culture* (Ithaca, New York: Cornell University Press, 1951), pp. 106–107.

38. Chrysostom, *Chrysostom on Marriage*, p. 69.

39. See, for example, James and Kathleen McGinnis, "The Social Mission of the Family," in *Faith and Families*, ed. Lindell Sawyers (Philadelphia: The Geneva Press, 1986), pp. 89–113.

40. Chrysostom, *Chrysostom on Marriage*, p. 71.

JAMES L. SAUER

AN EVERLASTING LIFE

Remembering Mary Denise Sauer:
July 12, 1995 – August 26, 1995

IN THE SUMMER OF 1995, my wife Paula gave birth to a little girl we named Mary. Mary was not a normal child. Her genes were all mixed up. Mary was doomed from day one to die.

We had no hint that there would be any trouble. The ultrasound had picked up nothing amiss. We had prepared her crib and painted the room. All was ready for the normal joys of a newborn child. But then Mary came and she was not the kind of child we were expecting at all.

Dr. B. looked troubled that day in the delivery room. Things were not going right. Delivery was too slow. He kept feeling what he thought were the irregularities of a face wrongly positioned in the birth canal. But Mary was not face forward. It was the irregularity of human deformity. And when our daughter's head crested from the womb, there was a hole the size of a silver dollar that exposed the rough membrane of her brain and a mouth that opened wide into the cavity of the nose. Dr. Evans, the neonatalogist, was rushed in to pronounce the death sentence. Prognosis: short term. What was that prognosis—long term? "No, short term," she reiterated. This was the baby that God had sent us. This was his gift. This was the child we received with gratitude.

We sent out this announcement to my work community a week after her birth in an effort to explain our strangely mixed feelings:

BIRTH ANNOUNCEMENT

We are happy to announce that on July 12th, Mary Denise Sauer, 8 lb. 15 oz., was born at Chester County Hospital.

Mary is a special child created by God for his unique purposes. Mary was born with an extra 13th chromosome (Patau syndrome). On the exterior, she has a cleft palate and a scalp lesion. On the interior, a hole in her heart and neurological malformations, which will result in a short life of a few weeks or even months.

The Psalmist says: "Children are a blessing from the Lord." And Mary is a blessing to us. She has already been the focus of prayers, tears, gifts, calls, and acts of charity. Her presence in the world is advancing Christ's kingdom. (Something that, unfortunately, cannot always be said of everyone.)

Mary reminds us of our own helpless, short life; and God's inexpressible love for us in the humanity of Jesus Christ our Savior, God's incarnate Son, "who was conceived by the Holy Spirit . . . and suffered under Pontius Pilate."

We rejoice that Mary has come to be with us a short time.

I believe in God the Father Almighty, Maker of Heaven and Earth . . .
Life strikes me as very odd at times. Shakespeare compared it to players, walking shadows, strutting and fretting, tales told by idiots. And it is very much like a story. Very seldom is it heroic; mostly it is idiotic. Vanity upon vanity; trivia upon trivia. Repetitious events strung out. Work, work, work. Lost hours. Things break down. The basement is backed up with sewage. Didn't get the raise. Sisyphian tasks that lead nowhere. Many times it's tragic. Tragi-comic. Death is always at the door. Bills to pay. The checkbook doesn't add up. Yet somehow, we know it has meaning. Life is a gift. When we hold a baby in our hands we are looking at a miracle. We are created beings, fearfully and wonderfully made. God is in charge. There is a Maker who is making sense out of all the senselessness. There is an Author who is writing the history of man's suffering and man's redemption. And yet our baby is dead. And I can't give a nice theological reason for it. All I can do is weep as I drive home from work alone in my car. I believe, Lord, help my unbelief.

. . . And in Jesus Christ His Only Son, Our Lord; Who was conceived by the Holy Ghost . . .

I don't think we consider enough what it means to have had God become one of us. The Incarnation is a miracle of incredible proportions. Humanity is generally so self-centered that we don't realize what petty insects we must appear to angels, let alone God. Yet he loves us. Yes, it is amazing that humanity has produced people like J. S. Bach or St. Francis; but we also produced some nasty slugs like Heinrich Himmler and Idi Amin. We may be the crown of creation, but we are animals nevertheless. And not just animals, but savage sinners. We eat. We excrete. We smell. We copulate. Good stuff. But we also fornicate. We blaspheme. We hate. We steal. We disobey our parents. We murder. We are helplessly dependent and wickedly miserable creatures. Since Adam every one of us, as our little Mary, has been born deformed, perhaps not physically, but certainly morally. The miracle is that we are not all physically deformed; the amazing thing is the relative uniformity of creation. Into this mess the Creator took on the form of a baby. God was made man at conception. Helpless in the womb, as we are helpless, he came forth as one of us.

. . . Born of the Virgin Mary, suffered under Pontius Pilate, was crucified, dead, and buried . . .

Our Mary suffered a little. Perhaps we suffered more than she. Why must we suffer? That's the way it is. It's not a normal world. Why must babies be born with extra chromosomes? Because it's a broken world. And yet the Lord God of the universe, the Creator of heaven and earth, is still in charge. It's not a mistake. It's not chance. He allows it. We are born for his purposes. He chooses it. We suffer from pain and stupidity. History goes on. Pilate, Caesar, Mr. President. We are stuck under leaders whom God has allowed who are as sinful and as stupid as we are—but with more opportunity to do evil. We get taxed and taxed some more. They lie to us, and tax even more. Death and taxes. And what do I do? I cite our little dead baby on my 1040 Form as a tax exemption for the short time she was here. I mark down her social security number so that some bureaucrat is happy. "And a decree went out from Caesar Augustus that all the world should be taxed." The tax rolls are the Goat's Book of Death. Then we buried our baby.

. . . He descended into hell . . .

Some people have known hell. Dachau. Buchanwald. Treblinka. Kampuchea. The Armenian Genocide. The Gulag. Sometimes I get a flat tire, get a tooth filled, have a check that bounces, or get a sinus infection. I suppose that's a kind of suffering. And I do sit through academic committee meetings—that's a kind of hell. Ever the pessimist, I sometimes feel as if society is falling apart, that hell is about to break out around us. What's holding it back? God. His Spirit. His Church. "And the gates of hell shall not prevail. . . ." It was hard having a baby who was going to die. But when Mary was born, it wasn't hell; in fact, it was more like a taste of the Cross, of heaven and hell mixed together—to be drunk down, bitter and sweet at the same time. Can you drink from the same cup as I drink? Yes, we can, Lord. How, I don't know. For it was he who descended into hell, not us; and it was he who bore our sins; and it was he who bore the brokenness of all the broken babies. "Suffer the little children to come unto me." I went through our personal hell in a kind of daze. Paula, on the other hand, was constantly working as nurse and mother. She would get up every night and, like the Statue of Liberty, she'd hold above her head a small container of formula connected to a feeding tube shoved down Mary's little throat. The baby fed and resting, Paula would cry each night as she held her dying baby. I slept on, the self-centered, oblivious husband.

. . . the third day He rose again from the dead . . .
If Christ is not risen, we are fools. Life is just a series of meaningless, suffering events. If we are just evolved animals, then we are just suffering the process of evolution. Be content, you are advancing randomness to the glory of nothing! Babies come, babies die. Vanity of vanities, saith the Preacher.

. . . He ascended into heaven, and sitteth on the right hand of God the Father Almighty. From thence He shall come to judge the quick and the dead.
I am not a good man. People think I'm good. (My wife knows better.) People think I'm a happy intellectual joker. But I'm a miserable sinner. Without Christ interceding for me, I am lost. Without Christ dying for me, I am doomed. Lust. Greed. Anger. Pride. Despair. More lust. These are a few of my favorite sins. And yet he is returning in triumph. And because of his merit I will stand before my Maker. When he returns, I want to be on the side of God. I want to be on the side of the babies. This is why abortion is such a horrible thing. Kill a little baby like Mary because she is deformed? Why, you're killing the image of Christ among us! We have very few opportunities to serve truly helpless people. "But when did we torture you, Lord, when did we suck your brains out, when did we cut you apart

limb from limb?" "Whenever you did it to the least of these, you have done it unto me." Thank you, Lord, for letting us have Mary; otherwise, we could not have served you.

. . . I believe in the Holy Ghost; the Holy Catholic Church . . .

Mary was an ecumenical baby. When her head popped out of her mother's womb, I'm not exactly sure what the doctor and nurses felt. In the birthing room everyone was quiet, there was nothing much to say. Sadness reigned. But from the moment she came, the Spirit began to move. Choked with emotion, I prayed with my wife and gave thanks for Mary, the hospital staff standing with us as witnesses. Later I called our pastor, Wayne Brauning, and our friends, Tom and Becky Albrecht; they came, and with the hospital staff again as a drafted congregation, we prayed and baptized the baby.

Weeks later when Mary died, we held the memorial service at the First Baptist Church in Downingtown, Pennsylvania, pastored by Chuck Vuolo. Both Wayne and Chuck took part in the service attended by over 200 people. The gospel was preached. We sang "Away in a Manger" and all four verses of "Jesus Loves Me" (I didn't even know it had other verses!). Perhaps the most startling thing was that a pro-choice woman attending Mary's memorial service became pro-life. How the little people defeat the strong! The pebble drops in the pool and it becomes a great wave. "And you shall call his name Jesus, for he shall save his people from their sins."

Seeing how much the First Baptist folk had done, some people asked us, "Is this your church?" We answered yes and no. No, we don't attend here; but yes, yes, this is our Church, we are part of their body, and they are part of Mary's body, and we are all part of Christ's Body.

. . . the Communion of Saints . . .

One of the things that the short life of our daughter Mary taught us was the doctrine of the "communion of saints," the vital interrelation of the Body of Christ. Our own church, Immanuel Presbyterian, rallied round us, as did scores of others. During her frail life, Mary was the focus of notes, meals, visits, prayers, gifts, and acts of kindness—all done in the name of Christ. People all around the country were praying for us—from Chicago, Idaho, Texas, Buffalo, not to mention our own area. Later I found out that people were praying for her on the other side of the world in Africa. We were adopted as a Christian mission by the youth group of a local Baptist church who came to work at our house. Three Catholic ladies brought us special holy water that had been blessed by their bishop.

And we also know that prayers were given by Presbyterians, Baptists, Plymouth Brethren, Independents, Eastern Orthodox, Episcopalians, and Roman Catholics. Ecumenical Mary had brought unity in a way that ecumenical councils could not.

. . . the forgiveness of sins . . .

Death makes many people bitter. They can't forgive God for exercising his divine prerogatives. They didn't ask to be born. It was a gift. And the potter can do what he wants with the clay. I read that somewhere. (Who says Presbyterians can't write anything without mentioning predestination?)

Oh, I suppose I could write one of those nice "how-to" pieces with the 10 steps to take when you have a baby that's deformed and dying; but honestly, life isn't always neatly wrapped up. "And they wrapped him in swaddling cloths and laid him in a manger." From the moment he was born they were preparing for his funeral.

I said earlier that Mary was born to die. But then, I was born to die. Paula was born to die. You were born to die. And thank the Lord that Jesus was born to die. "For without the shedding of blood there is no remission of sins." Strange logic from the Divine Mind—but without it we are doomed.

. . . the resurrection of the body . . .

Mary was always half here and half in the next world. The first night she spent in the hospital she turned blue. She forgot to breathe at times. The signals from her brain were like two sets of computer software running simultaneously. Three times in the weeks we had her with us she choked and forgot to breathe. Three times we administered resuscitation and she returned to us. Once after church, she stopped breathing and we stopped our car and tried to bring her back to life on the hood. The children in the car didn't know what to do—they just cried. I told the truth: "Their tears were prayers to God." He heard them, and gave Mary back to us.

It was not so at the end. She would stop breathing, look at heaven, return, resume breathing. Stop breathing, look again, return. Stop breathing, look again, and then look again, and stay. We were blessed to have our Mary for the few days she was given. I do not know whether she will be a child or a grown-up in heaven. I do not know whether a cleft palate is a badge of glory in heaven the way pierced hands are. I believe I do know at the Last Day I will see her. She will meet me in the clouds with him.

DEATH ANNOUNCEMENT

Date: August 28, 1995

From: Jim and Paula Sauer

On August 26th, our daughter Mary Denise went home to be with the Lord. She was 45 days old. She was a little broken baby greatly used by God to advance his work and glory. "God chose the weak things of the world to shame the strong."

We want to thank all God's people, friends and family, for their gracious support, wishes, notes, cards, flowers, meals, groceries, gifts, visits, and prayers. Mary not only taught us about serving the helpless, she also taught us about the unity of Christ's body, "the communion of the saints." You helped us through this hard time.

Mary will be buried early this week. A memorial service, open to all, will be held at First Baptist Church of Downingtown, 11 A.M., on Saturday, September 2nd.

In lieu of flowers, gifts will be accepted at the memorial service for the Bible placement work of the Gideons; and also for Chester County Women's Services, a group that gives practical pro-life services to women tempted to abort babies just like Mary.

Jesus said: "Let the little children come unto me, for of such is the kingdom of heaven."

On September 8, 1996, a little over a year later, Paula gave birth to another baby, Martha, our eighth child, our seventh surviving child, our fourth girl, our third surviving girl, sister of Jacob, Adam, Joseph, Ariel, Isaac, Abigail, and sister of Mary, who is in the hands of God, as we all are.

. . . *And the life everlasting.* Amen.

Reprinted from Touchstone: A Journal of Mere Christianity, *Winter 1997, Volume 10, Number 1.*

RECOGNIZING THE CHURCH

*A Personal Pilgrimage & the Discovery
of Five Marks of the Church*

I WAS BROUGHT UP in an Evangelical household. To say this is to say something good. My father was a layman, not a preacher; but he was a devoted and
assiduous daily student of the Bible. He and my mother exist to this day in my
imagination as the very icons of the godly man and woman. It was a wonderful
thing—that sage, earnest, transparent, Bible-centered faith. I owe the fact that I am
a believer today, and that my whole pilgrimage, steep and tortuous as it has been
sometimes, has been towards the center, not away from it, to the faith and prayers
and example of my father and mother.

I believe that I and my five brothers and sisters, all of whom, now, in our
sixties, are Christians who want to follow the Lord wholly, would all testify to this
godly influence of our parents. The household was a household suffused with the
Bible. We sang hymns—daily—hundreds of them over the years, so that probably
all six of us know scores of hymns by heart. We had family prayers twice a day, after
breakfast and after supper. Our parents prayed with us at our bedside, the last
thing at night. We all went to Sunday school and church regularly.

There is only one agenda in a fundamentalist Sunday school: the Bible. The
Bible day in and day out, year in and year out. Flannelgraph lessons, sword drills,

Scripture memory: Everything was focused directly on the Bible itself. I am grateful for every minute of this, now, 50 years later. Because of this, the whole of Scripture, from Genesis to Revelation, is ringing in my ears all the time. Hundreds of verses, in the language of the King James Version, are there, intact, in my memory. I hope that, if my memory fails and I lose my wits in my old age, perhaps these verses, from so long ago, will remain there and bring me solace.

The Christian believers among whom I grew up were very forthcoming about the faith. They spoke easily and informally about the Lord. When you were among them, you knew that you were among people of "like precious faith," as St. Peter phrases it. Many of the guests in our household had been overseas missionaries, some of them interned in concentration camps by the Japanese during World War II. Our ears were full of stories of how God had been faithful in all sorts of human extremities. It would be hard to find a better ambiance, I think, than this good and trusty Evangelicalism of my youth.

The Pilgrimage Begins

But I speak as one whose pilgrimage has led him from the world of Protestant Evangelicalism to the Roman Catholic Church. One way or another, all of us whose nurture has been in one of the sectors of Protestantism where the Bible is honored, where the gospel is preached without dissimulation, and where Jesus Christ is worshipped as God and Savior—all of us desire to be faithful to the ancient faith that we profess, and to be found obedient to the will of God. Certainly such fidelity and obedience have motivated us so far, and we want to be able to give an accounting of ourselves when it comes to our turn at the Divine Tribunal, for we must all appear before the judgment seat of Christ.

Why then, would anyone want to leave such a world? Was not that a rendering of the ancient faith almost without equal? Surely to leave it would be to go from great plenty out to famine and penury?

Of my own case, I would have to say that I did not want to leave it. Certainly I was restless as a young man, like all young men, and any grass across any fence tended to look very green. I did, out of mere curiosity, draw back from the little church of my parents and my childhood when I returned to my hometown after having graduated from college and put in my time in the army. I visited the local Presbyterian church, and the Methodist and the Lutheran and the Episcopalian.

Only this last one held any great attraction for me—I think it was a matter of aesthetics more than any other single factor. The Episcopal liturgy is the most elegant thing in the world, and this is to be attributed to their Prayer Book, which has since been supplanted by a modern translation, but which in 1960 was still the old *Book of Common Prayer,* with its matchless Shakespearean prose. Episcopal churches tend to be gothic, with stained glass and cool, dark interiors. Episcopal hymnody is virtually the best in the world, if we are speaking of a rich treasury of hymns drawn from the era of Isaac Watts and Charles Wesley, as well as from ancient Christendom. I was attracted by all of this. There was also a strange note of nostalgia in it, since I knew that my mother had been "saved" *out* of Episcopalianism *into* fundamentalism in about 1915, but that she still retained an undying love for Episcopal hymns and liturgy. Somehow that nostalgia had communicated itself to me.

The next step in my pilgrimage was made easy. I found myself teaching at a boys' school in England, so this put me in the neighborhood of the Church of England. There is a robust Evangelical wing in this old church, so I did not have to "leave" anything. I could have all this and heaven too, so to speak. I was received into the Church of England in 1962 and found myself among the best crowd of all, I thought: Evangelicals who took the liturgy, and the atmosphere of Anglicanism, for granted. I loved it.

When I returned to the United States and married, my wife, who was a wise and holy woman, was fairly quickly received into the Episcopal Church—or the Anglican Church, as many prefer to call it—and our two children were raised as Anglicans. Fortunately, we found ourselves, both in New York in the early years of our marriage and then in Massachusetts, in parishes where the Scriptures were honored and the gospel was preached and sturdy fellowship was central.

Liberalism & Worship

Two questions, I think, spring into the minds of people when they hear of someone opting into Anglicanism. First, what about the liberalism in these big Protestant denominations? And second, doesn't one have to settle into worship that is dull and lifeless since it is all canned and rote, leaving behind the wonderful spontaneity and freshness that marks the worship in the Evangelical and Pentecostal churches?

On the first question, there is only one answer, and that is yes, one does have to learn to live in a denomination that has very largely given itself over to an extremely liberal interpretation of Scripture and now, alas, of sexual morality. The good and faithful souls in these Protestant denominations suffer over this, of course, and will tell you that they are trying to bear witness *in* the situation, and that the Church historically has been plagued always with heresy and sin, and that we can't keep splitting and splitting, as we Evangelicals have done, in the interest of doctrinal or moral purity. You end up with an ecclesiastical flea market that way, such people might urge.

On the second question, about canned and rote worship, we come to an immense issue. What is at stake here is the rock-bottom question as to what worship *is* and how you do it. Put briefly, the question comes to this: Worship is *the* thing that we were created for—to know God and, knowing him, to bless him and adore him forever. This is what the seraphim and the cherubim and all the angelic hierarchy do ceaselessly. This is what the creation is doing: The Psalms call upon winds and mountains and seas and frost and hail and sun and stars to worship the Most High. We believe that in some very literal sense the entire creation does, each part of it after its own unique mode, "worship" him. But you and I belong to the species whose dignity entails *leading* the praises of our world.

To worship God is to ascribe worth to him. It is an activity distinct from teaching, and from fellowship, and from witnessing, and from sharing. It is an act, not an experience. We come to church primarily to *do* something, not to receive something, although of course in the ancient worship of the Church we do indeed receive God himself, under the sacramental species of Bread and Wine. But our task in worship is to offer the oblation of ourselves and our adoration at the Sapphire Throne.

Obviously this is a daunting and an august task. Fortunately we are not left to our own resources, nor to the whim of the moment, nor even to our own experience. The faithful have been worshipping God since the beginning, and there is help for us. All of us, even those of us who come from the so-called free churches where spontaneity is supposed to be the rule, are accustomed to borrowing secondhand, canned words to assist us in worship. I am speaking of hymns. When we sing "Amazing Grace" or "O, For a Thousand Tongues to Sing," we are borrowing John Newton's and Charles Wesley's words. And we discover that, far from cramping or restricting our worship, these secondhand words bring us up to a level quite unattainable by our own spontaneous efforts. They take us away from ourselves.

That is another crucial point in ritual worship: People who are fellowshipping with each other, and sharing, are, characteristically, facing each other. People who are worshipping are, all together, facing something else, namely the Sapphire Throne. The liturgy of the Church brings us into these precincts. Our Lord Jesus Christ was accustomed to this kind of worship—indeed, when he joined his parents and fellow Jews in weekly worship, he entered into the ritual. No one had ever heard of spontaneous public worship. The early Church, in great wisdom, realized that this is a principle that goes to the root of the mystery of our being. Spontaneity is a good and precious thing. The Lord loves any lisping, stammering, broken, and halting words we can offer to him, as he loves the buzzing of bumblebees and the braying of donkeys. But when we come together for the particular *act* of offering our corporate, regular, recurring adoration to him, then we need a form.

The Question of the Church

During my 23 years as an Anglican, I discovered, and gradually became at home in, the world of liturgy, and of sacrament, and of the church year. But also as I read in theology and church history and in the tradition of Christian spirituality, I found myself increasingly acutely conscious of a question: But what is the Church?

Every Sunday at the Anglican liturgy I found myself repeating, "I believe in one, holy, catholic, and apostolic church." These are words from an era that all of us—Roman, Orthodox, Anglican, Protestant, and unaffiliated—must take seriously, since all of us, whether we are pleased to admit it or not, are the direct beneficiaries of the work of the men who hammered out those words. You and I may think, in some of our less reflective moments, that all we need is the Bible and our own wits. *Sola Scriptura*. Just me and my Bible. But that is an impertinent notion. Every Christian in every assembly of believers in this world is incalculably in the debt of the men who succeeded the apostles. For they are the ones who, during those early centuries when the Church was moving from the morning of Pentecost out into the long haul of history, fought and thought and worked and wrote and died, so that "the faith once for all delivered to the saints" might indeed be handed on. Heresiarchs popped up out of the weeds left, right, and center, and all of them believed in the "verbal inspiration" of Scripture. It was the Church, in her bishops and councils, that preserved the faith from the errors of the heresiarchs and other zealots, and that shepherded the faithful along in the Way, as it was called.

You and I, insofar as we are familiar with modern Protestantism and, *a fortiori*, with Evangelicalism and Pentecostalism, are familiar with a state of affairs that would have been unimaginable to our Fathers in the faith in those early days. I am referring to the oddity that, even though we all say we believe in the final and fixed truth of divine revelation, we are nevertheless all at odds when it comes to deciding just what that truth is.

Oh, to be sure, we all agree on the so-called fundamentals of the gospel—but of course those fundamentals have been articulated and distilled for us by the Church that wrote the creeds. The Mormons and the Jehovah's Witnesses and the modernists all toil away at the pages of the Bible, but you and I would say they are not getting the right things out of that Bible. Why do we say that? Because, whether we acknowledge it or not, our "orthodox" understanding of the Bible has been articulated for us *by the Church*. All sorts of notions, for example, have cropped up about the Trinity, about the mystery of Our Lord's divine and human natures, and so forth. The reason you and I are not Nestorians or Eutychians or Apollinarians or Docetists or Arians or Montanists is that *the Church* guarded and interpreted and taught the Bible, and we, the faithful, have had a reliable and apostolic voice in the Church that says, "*This* is what Holy Scripture is to be understood as teaching, and *that* which you hear Eutychius or Sabellius teaching from the Bible is not to be believed."

But I was speaking of the question that began to force its way into my mind during those years: What is the Church? What may have appeared as a digression just now, when I referred to the men who worked so hard to preserve the faith, and the bishops and councils who settled upon the right understanding of revelation, was not a digression at all. When I heard myself repeating the words from the Nicene Creed at the liturgy, "I believe in one, holy, catholic, and apostolic church," I was, of course, saying words that are not directly from any one text in the Bible and yet that have been spoken in all of Christendom for a millennium and a half now and in some sense constitute a plumbline for us.

The creed is not Scripture; that is true. But then all of us, whether we come from groups that repeat the creed or not, would agree, "Oh yes, indeed; that is the faith which we all profess." Some would add, "But of course, we get it straight out of the Bible. We don't need any creed." The great difficulty here is that Eutychius and Sabellius and Arius got *their* notions straight out of the Bible as well. Who will arbitrate these things for us? Who will speak with authority to us faithful, all of us rushing about flapping the pages of our well-thumbed New Testaments, locked in shrill contests over the two natures of Christ, or baptism, or the Lord's Supper, or the mystery of predestination?

This question formed itself in the following way for me, a twentieth-century Christian: Who will arbitrate for us between Luther and Calvin? Or between Luther and Zwingli, both appealing loudly to Scripture, and each with a view of the Lord's Table that categorically excludes the other's view? And who will arbitrate for us between John Wesley and George Whitefield—that is, between Arminius and Calvin? Or between J. N. Darby (he thought he had found *the* biblical pattern for Christian gathering, and the Plymouth Brethren to this day adhere to his teaching) and all the denominations? Or between the dispensationalists and the Calvinists on the question of eschatology?

A piquant version of this situation presented itself to us loosely affiliated Evangelicals, with all of our independent seminaries and Grace chapels and Moody churches, and so forth. When a crucial issue arises—say, what we should teach about sexuality—who will speak to us with a finally authoritative voice? The best we can do is to get *Christianity Today* to run a symposium, with one article by J. I. Packer plumping for traditional morality, and one article by one of our lesbian feminist Evangelicals (there are some) showing that we have all been wrong for the entire 3,500 years since Sinai, and that what the Bible really teaches is that indeed homosexuals may enjoy a fully expressed sexual life. The trouble here is that J. I. Packer has no more authority than our lesbian friend, so the message to the faithful is, "Take your pick."

This is not, whatever else we wish to say about it, a picture of things that would be recognizable to the apostles, or to the generations that followed them. The faithful, in those early centuries, were certainly aware of a great babel of voices among the Christians, teaching this and teaching that, on every conceivable point of revelation. But the faithful were also aware that there was a body that could speak into the chaos, and declare, with serene and final authority, what the faith that had been taught by the apostles was. Clearly, we Evangelicals have been living in a scheme of things altogether unrecognizable to the apostles and the Fathers of the Church.

"I believe in one, holy, catholic, and apostolic Church," I found myself saying in the creed. What Church? What is the Church? What was the Church in the minds of the men who framed that creed? Clearly it was not the donnybrook that the world sees nowadays, with literally thousands of groups, big and small, all clamoring, and all claiming to be, in some sense, the Church.

Five Recognizable Marks of the Church

As an Anglican I became aware that I, as an individual believer, stood in a very long and august lineage of the faithful, stretching back to the apostles and fathers. The picture had changed for me: It was no longer primarily me, my Bible, and Jesus (although heaven knows that is not altogether a bad picture: the only question is, is it the whole picture?). Looming for me, as an Anglican, was "the faith," ancient, serene, undimmed, true. And that faith somehow could not be split apart from "the Church." But then, what was the Church?

I realized that, one way or another, I had to come to terms with the Church in all of its antiquity, its authority, its unity, its liturgy, and its sacraments. Those five marks, or aspects, of the Church are matters that all of us, I think, would find to be eluding us in the free churches. I speak as a Roman Catholic, for that is where my own pilgrimage has brought me in my quest for this Church in all of its antiquity, authority, unity, liturgy, and sacraments. Let me touch on each of these briefly.

ANTIQUITY

First, the *antiquity* of the Church confronts me. As an Evangelical, I discovered while I was in college that it was possible to dismiss the entire Church as having gone off the rails by about A.D. 95. That is, we, with our open Bibles, knew better than old Ignatius or Polycarp or Clement, who had been taught by the apostles themselves—we knew better than they just what the Church is and what it should look like. Never mind that our worship services would have been unrecognizable to them, or that our church government would have been equally unrecognizable, or that the vocabulary in which we spoke of the Christian life would have been equally unrecognizable. We were right, and the Fathers were wrong. That settled the matter.

The trouble here was that what these wrong-headed men wrote—about God, about our Lord Jesus Christ, about his Church, about the Christian's walk and warfare—was so titanic, and so rich, and so luminous, that their error seemed infinitely truer and more glorious than my truth. I gradually felt that it was I, not they, who was under surveillance. The "glorious company of the apostles, the noble army of martyrs, and the holy Church throughout all the world" (to quote the ancient hymn, the Te Deum) judge me, not I them. Ignatius, Polycarp, Clement, Justin, Irenaeus, Cyprian, Cyril, Basil, the Gregorys, Augustine, Ambrose, Hilary, Benedict—it is under the gaze of this senate that I find myself standing. Alas. How tawdry, how otiose, how flimsy, how embarrassing, seem the arguments that I had been prepared, so gaily, to put forward against the crushing radiance of their confession. The Church is here, in all of its antiquity, judging me.

AUTHORITY

Second, the Church in its *authority* confronts me. That strange authority to bind and to loose that our Lord bestowed on his disciples has not evaporated from the Church—or so the Church has believed from the beginning. If you will read the story of those decades that followed Pentecost, and especially that followed upon the death of the apostles, you will discover that the unction to teach and to preside in the Church that passed from the apostles to the bishops was understood to be an apostolic unction. I, for example, could not start up out of the bulrushes and say, "Hi, everybody! The Lord has led me to be a bishop! I'm starting me a church over here." The whole Christian community—bishops, presbyters, deacons, and laity—would have looked solemnly at me and gone about their business.

The Holy Spirit, in those days, did not carry on private transactions with isolated souls, and then announce to the Church that so-and-so had been anointed for this or that ministry. The unction of the Holy Spirit, and the authority of the Church to ordain for ministry, were not two random enterprises. The Holy Spirit worked in, and through, the Church's ministry and voice. To be sure, he could do what he wanted to do, as he had always done, being God. Under the Old Covenant, we could say that he worked in and through Israel; but of course you find these extra characters like Job and Jethro and the Magi, coming across the stage from outside the Covenant, yet nonetheless undeniably having been in touch with God. God can do what he wants, of course.

But the Church understands herself to be the appointed vessel for God's working, just as the Incarnation was. Her authority is not her own. She arrogates nothing to herself. Her bishops and patriarchs are the merest custodians, the merest passers-on, we might say, of the deposit of faith. As a Roman Catholic, I am, of course, acutely conscious of this. When someone objects to me, "But who does the Catholic Church think she is, taking this high and mighty line" (about abortion or about sexual morality or about who may or may not come to the Lord's Table), the answer is, "She doesn't think she's anything particular, if you mean that she has set herself up among the wares in the flea market as somehow the best. She has her given task to do—to pass on the teaching given by the apostles, and she has no warrant to change that. She is not taking her cues from the Nielsen ratings, or from a poll, or even from a sociological survey as to what people feel comfortable with nowadays. She didn't start the Church, and it's not her Church."

As a free-church Christian, one can, of course, make up one's mind about lots of things. Shall I fast or not? Well, that's for me to decide. Shall I give alms? Again—a matter for my own judgment. Must I go to church? That, certainly, is my own affair. Need I observe this or that feast day in the church year? I'll make up my own mind. Piety and devotion are matters of one's own tailoring: No one may peer over my shoulder and tell me what to do.

Indeed, no one may do anything of the sort—*if* we are speaking of ourselves as Americans who have constitutional rights. But if we are speaking of ourselves as Christian believers, then there is a touchstone other than the Constitution by which our choices must be tested.

Our Christian ancestors knew nothing of this sprightly individualism when it came to the disciplines of the spiritual life. They fasted on Fridays, and they went to church on Sundays. Some Roman pope did not make these things up. They took shape in the Church very early, and nobody dreamed of cobbling up a private spirituality. And likewise with all sorts of questions. Shall women be ordained as priests? It is, eventually, not a matter of job description, or of politics, or even of common sense or public justice. The question is settled by what the Church understands the priesthood to be—with cogent reasoning given, to be sure. It is not a question to be left interminably open to the public forum for decade after decade of hot debate.

The Church is here, in all of its authority, judging us.

UNITY

Third, the Church in its *unity* confronts me. This is the most difficult and daunting matter. But one thing eventually became clear: My happy Evangelical view of the church's unity as being nothing more than the worldwide clutter that we had under our general umbrella was, for good or ill, not what the ancient Church had understood by the word *unity*. As an Evangelical, I could pick which source of things appealed most to me: Dallas Seminary; Fuller Seminary; John Wimber; Azusa Street; the Peninsula Bible Church; Hudson Taylor; the deeper life as taught at Keswick; Virginia Mollenkott; John Stott; or Sam Shoemaker. And in one sense, variety is doubtless a sign of vigorous life in the Church. But in another sense, of course, it is a disaster. It is disastrous if I invest any of the above with the authority that belongs alone to the Church. But then who shall guide my choices?

Once again, we come back to the picture that we have in the ancient Church. Whatever varieties of expression there may have been—in Alexandria as over against Lyons or in Antioch as over against Rome—nevertheless, when it came to the faith itself, and also to order and discipline and piety in the Church, no one was left groping or mulling over the choices in the flea market.

Where we Protestants were pleased to live with a muddle—even with stark contradiction (as in the case of Luther versus Zwingli, for example)—the Church of antiquity was united. No one needed to remain in doubt for long as to what the Christian Church might be, or where it might be found. The Montanists were certainly zealous and earnest, and had much to commend them; the difficulty, finally, was that they were *not the Church*. Likewise with the Donatists. God bless them for their fidelity and ardor and purity, but they were *not the Church*. As protracted and difficult as the Arian controversy was, no one needed to remain forever in doubt as to what the Church had settled upon: Athanasius was fighting for the apostolic faith, *against heresy*. It did not remain an open question forever.

There was one Church and the Church was one. And this was a discernible, visible, embodied unity, not a loose aggregate of vaguely like-minded believers with their various task forces all across the globe. The bishop of Antioch was not analogous to the general secretary of the World Evangelical Fellowship or the head of the National Association of Evangelicals. He could speak with the full authority of the Church behind him; these latter gentlemen can only speak for their own organization. He was not even analogous to the stated clerk of the Presbyterian Church or the presiding bishop of the Episcopalians, neither of whom is understood by his clientele to be speaking in matters of doctrine and morality with an undoubted apostolic authority.

This line of thought could bring us quickly to the point at which various voices today might start bidding for our attention, each one of them with "Hey—*ours* is the apostolic voice—over here!" That is not my task here. I only would want to urge you to test your own understanding of the Church against the Church's ancient understanding of itself as united, as one. What is that unity? It is a matter that has perhaps been answered too superficially and frivolously for the last two hundred years in American Protestantism. The Church in its unity is here, judging us.

LITURGY

Fourth, the *liturgy* of the Church confronts and judges me. That seems like an odd way of putting it: In what sense can anyone say that the liturgy "judges" me? Certainly it does not condemn me or pass any sort of explicit judgment on me. But if only by virtue of its extreme antiquity and universality, it constitutes some sort of touchstone for the whole topic of Christian worship.

Often the topic is approached as though it were a matter of taste: John likes fancy worship—smells and bells—and Bill likes simplicity and spontaneity and informality. There's the end of the discussion. And certainly, as I mentioned before, God receives any efforts, however halting and homespun, which anyone offers as worship, just as any father or mother will receive the offering of a limp fistful of dandelions as a bouquet from a tiny child. On the other hand, two considerations might be put forward at this point.

First, what did the Church, from the beginning, understand by worship— that is, by its corporate, regular act of worship? The Book of Acts gives us little light on the precise shape or content of the Christians' gatherings: The apostles' doctrine, fellowship, the breaking of bread, and the prayers are mentioned. St. Paul's Epistles do not spell out what is to be done. We have to look to other early writings if we are curious about the apostolic church's worship. And what we find when we do so is the Eucharistic liturgy. This, apparently, was what they did as worship. If we think we have improved on that pattern, we may wish to submit our innovations for scrutiny to the early Church in order to discover whether our innovations have in fact been improvements.

Which brings us to the second consideration: the content of the Eucharistic liturgy. From the beginning, the Church seems to have followed a given sequence: readings from Scripture (including the letters from Paul and Peter and John), then prayers, and then the so-called *anaphora*—the "offering," or, as it was also called, the Great Thanksgiving. This was the great Eucharistic Prayer, which took on a fairly exact shape at the outset, and which you may still hear if you listen to the liturgy in any of the ancient churches. Psalmody, canticles, and hymns also came to be included, and certain acclamations like the "Kyrie, eleison!" The whole presents a shape of such rich perfection that one wonders what exactly is the task of the "coordinators of worship" on the staff of various churches. The worship of the ancient Church is far from being a matter of endless tinkering, experimenting, and innovating. The entire mystery of revelation and redemption is unfurled for us in the church's liturgy. That liturgy is here in all of its plentitude, majesty, and magnificence, judging us.

SACRAMENTS

Fifth and finally, the *sacraments* of the Church confront me. The word *sacrament* is the Latin word for the Greek *mysterion,* mystery. Indeed, we are in the presence of mystery here, for the sacraments, like the Incarnation itself, constitute physical points at which the eternal touches time, or the unseen touches the seen, or grace touches nature. It is the Gnostics and Manichaeans who want a purely disembodied religion.

Judaism, and its fulfillment, Christianity, are heavy with matter. First, at creation itself, where solid matter was spoken into existence by the Word of God. Then redemption, beginning not with the wave of a spiritual wand, nor with mere edicts pronounced from the sky, but rather with skins and blood—the pelts of animals slaughtered by the Lord God to cover our guilty nakedness. Stone altars, blood, fat, scapegoats, incense, gold, acacia wood—the Old Covenant is heavily physical.

Then the New Covenant: We now escape into the purely spiritual and leave the physical behind, right? Wrong. First a pregnancy, then a birth. Obstetrics and gynecology, right at the center of redemption. Fasting in the wilderness, water to wine, a crown of thorns, splinters and nails and blood—our eternal salvation carried out in grotesquely physical terms. Then pure spirituality, right? Wrong. A corpse resuscitated. And not only that—a human body taken up into the midmost mysteries of the eternal Trinity. And Bread and Wine, Body and Blood, pledged and given to the Church, for as long as history lasts. Who has relegated this great gift to the margins of Christian worship and consciousness? By what warrant did men, 1,500 years after the Lord's gift of his Body and Blood, decide that this was a mere detail, somewhat embarrassing, and certainly nothing central or crucial—a show-and-tell device at best? O tragedy! O sacrilege! What impoverishment for the faithful!

May God grant, in these latter days, a gigantic ingathering, as it were, when Christians who have loved and served him according to patterns and disciplines and notions quite remote from those of the ancient Church find themselves taking their places once again in the great Eucharistic mystery of his one, holy, catholic, and apostolic Church.

Reprinted from Touchstone: A Journal of Ecumenical Orthodoxy, *Summer 1993, Volume 6, Number 3. Adapted from a lecture given in 1993 to the Fellowship of St. Barnabas in Oklahoma City.*

LEON J. PODLES

ALL THAT SEPARATES
MUST CONVERGE

The Fragmentation of Christianity
& the Unity of Faith

OPE JOHN PAUL II HAS SPECULATED in his recent bestselling book,
Crossing the Threshold of Hope, that the division of the churches may have
a purpose in the ways of Divine Providence. He put his thoughts in the
form of a question in answer to a question about why God has allowed so many
divisions in the Church. The pope asks, "Could it not be that these divisions have
also been a path continually leading the Church to discover the untold wealth
contained in Christ's gospel and in the redemption accomplished by Christ?
Perhaps all this wealth would not have come to light otherwise. . . ." Generalizing
from the human tendency to develop insights separately before integrating them
into a higher unity, the pope concludes, "It is necessary for humanity to achieve
unity through plurality, to learn to come together in the one Church, even while
presenting a plurality of ways of thinking and acting, of cultures and civilizations."

This dialectic of division and unity is therefore, although sometimes made
painful by human sin, essential to understanding the fullness of the gospel. The
great division between East and West, between Rome and the Orthodox Churches,
and the multiplying divisions in Western Christianity can serve God's purpose, if
they are eventually, if not exactly overcome, but rather transcended by a higher

synthesis that preserves the valid although partial perceptions of the truth that each church has developed in isolation from the others.

Although trying to discover the purposes of Providence is always a chancy affair, it is possible to hazard a guess at what might be the beneficial results of the division of the churches. I speak as a Roman Catholic who accepts the primacy of the bishop of Rome and for whom the importance of visible church unity always is great. The bishop of Rome himself, however, is more than willing to discuss the weaknesses of his church and its serious errors over the centuries.

The greatest division is the one between the East and West; but it is not total. There are some Eastern churches in communion with the bishop of Rome, but the vast bulk of Eastern Christianity is not in communion with Rome, to the point that, for almost everyone in the world, *Roman Catholic* equals the Latin or Western Church. Many Roman Catholics, including priests, as late as the 1950s did not even recognize Maronite or Ukrainian Rite Catholics as Catholics, and denied them Communion. But the Uniate churches and the small Western Rite Ortho-dox movement do not change the overall picture much: There is a vast gulf be-tween East and West.

A Lamentable Split

What would have been the result for Christianity if the Eastern and Western churches had not divided? Would the Western church have been influenced by the Eastern, or the Eastern by the Western? It would have been a tragedy, as the pope himself would admit, if the Western church, as it developed after the split, had influenced the Eastern church to follow the same path of development as the West.

The development of the Western church has been, if not disastrous, at least a source of endless trouble. It is not clear whether the West took the course it did because it split from the East, or whether it would have taken that course and drawn the East along with it. The characteristic genius (or fault) of the West is to take aspects of Christianity and to develop them as far as possible, even if this develop-ment isolates them from the fullness of Christian life. The characteristic genius of the East is to maintain all the elements of Christianity in the original synthesis, even if this means that certain aspects remain undeveloped. The West fragmented the white light of revelation in order to see the colors clearly; the East has maintained the purity of the original light, but does not always distinguish the colors.

In the West, theology split into academic theology and spirituality. The theologian was no longer one who engaged in prayer, in a dialogue with God, after the model of both the Eastern and Western Fathers, but someone who "did theology" in an academic setting. The results of academic theology are impressive. St. Thomas Aquinas's achievements are undeniable. But already in Aquinas something is missing. The note of prayerful devotion is absent from his theology; it is present in his hymns, but these were already distinct from his theology. In lesser and less saintly figures, the split became total. Roman Catholic theology sometimes almost totally prescinds from belief. Theologians feel no obligation to church unity and orthodoxy, and the diversity of theologies they espouse is not one of diverse insights into the one faith handed down from the apostles, but new faiths constructed from such rags of Christianity as can be made to appear compatible with current fads and academic preoccupations. Theology can be done by unbelievers as well as by believers, and is consciously designed to be noncommitted, so that it can be academically respectable.

This split has been lamented by Roman Catholic writers of the *ressourcement* (the attempt to recover the scriptural and patristic wisdom that antedated the Scholastics) who sought to go back to the patristic union of theology and spirituality. Louis Bouyer and Jean Leclerq in their *History of Christian Spirituality* (1963) diagnose the situation at the end of the Middle Ages, a situation that has continued to the present: "The theologian became a specialist in an autonomous field of knowledge, which he could enter by the use of a technique independent of the witness of his own life, of its personal holiness or sinfulness. The spiritual man, on the other hand, became a *dévot* who cared nothing for theology, one for whom his own experience ultimately became an end in itself." This split between theology and devotion allowed each to develop largely in isolation. This development produced impressive specialized products, but at the cost of a living unity of Christian life and thought.

In dogmatic and doctrinal development the magisterium of the Church, which has until very recently been attuned almost totally to Western modes of thought, has continued to isolate and develop individual truths, at the cost of extracting them to some extent from the whole context in which they are intelligible. The proclamations of the Immaculate Conception and of papal infallibility are two examples of this. They are the ones most often cited by the Orthodox and Anglicans as unwarranted additions to the deposit of faith.

The doctrine of the Immaculate Conception seems to be clearly implied in the Orthodox liturgy, where Mary is addressed as "All Holy," *Panagia*. The new *Catechism of the Catholic Church* seems to say that these are equivalent statements, in two modes, one dogmatic, one liturgical. Why is this doctrine seen as a stumbling block? There are two reasons, one related to differing theologies and the other to church government.

Theology & Governance

The first is that the East and West do not differ in simply having different liturgical traditions, but also in having different theologies, and even in the role that theology plays in the life of the churches. In the West theology is isolated from spirituality and liturgy; in the East, theology is incarnated in the liturgy. In the West, the emphasis on law colored the development of the doctrine of original sin. In the East, the lesser stress on law led to an underdevelopment (if one may call it that) of the separate doctrine of original sin. In the East the stress was on death rather than guilt as the consequence of sin, and consequently on the Resurrection as the delivery from the death mankind suffers because of Adam's sin. Without the legal emphasis of the West, the doctrine of the Immaculate Conception does not make much sense. The doctrine of the Assumption, on the other hand, is shared by both East and West, because it is clearly a consequence, a firstfruits, of Christ's Resurrection.

Different conceptions of church government underlay much of the discontent with these dogmas. Even though the substance of these Marian dogmas may not be offensive to the Orthodox, Rome's decision unilaterally to define the dogmas of the Immaculate Conception and the Assumption provoked discontent among the Orthodox, who hold that only an ecumenical council can define dogmas. But is the age of the councils over? Was it a passing phase in the Church, or are there organs in the Church that still have the authority to define doctrine infallibly, as the first seven councils did? My understanding is that the Orthodox believe that a council of Orthodox bishops from the various churches would be a true ecumenical council and have the same authority as the first ecumenical councils. It is just that the Church has not had occasion to call one since the patristic era.

Rome, of course, holds that the councils held in the West were ecumenical (they had little, if any, Eastern representation, but the early councils had as little

Western representation). Rome also holds that solemn declarations of the pope are infallible, and that the ordinary magisterum of the Church (*quod semper et ubique et ab omnibus*) is also infallible. What is causing discontent in the West is not the handful of solemn papal definitions of dogma, but the Vatican's attempt to maintain "mere Christianity" in the churches of the West, especially in matters of moral theology. Papal reassertion of traditional morality is the cause for attacks on papal authority. Without that authority, the moral teaching of the Roman Catholic Church would be a shambles.

Isolation & Divergences

But to go back to the split between East and West. The West was allowed to develop largely in isolation from the East, and spun out increasing specialized manifestations of its religious life. In the East, there is one form of religious life, that of the monks. In the West, there are hundreds, perhaps thousands, of religious orders and congregations, many of them devoted to a specialized purpose: education, health care, missionary work. These specialized orders do their individual tasks better than the monks of the East could, but at the price often of forgetting the context of Christian life, of liturgy and spirituality, in which these tasks should be carried out.

More importantly, the emphasis on law in the West has led to what the Orthodox perceive as papal authoritarianism. As I understand the current state of Orthodox-Roman relationships, the real problem is not dogmatic formulations or even the guidance the pope receives from the Holy Spirit when he infallibly proclaims dogmas of the Church. The real problem is one of jurisdiction, the canonical claims of the papacy to interfere in the internal affairs of the various churches.

There are two things to be said about the role of the papacy. First, there are the problems the stress on jurisdiction has created in the West, and second, there are the benefits papal jurisdiction might have, even for the Orthodox churches.

The West has been obsessed with law, and for centuries bishops have been appointed, whether by cathedral chapters or secular rulers or the Vatican, because they are good canon lawyers and administrators. Learning and piety are considered to be desirable qualities for a bishop, but what Rome wants, and gets, is good administrative skill.

Rome has indeed gotten what it wants, although it is beginning to realize that administration is not the foremost gift of the Holy Spirit. The Vatican is not really populated by papal bureaucrats who want to run the lives of every Christian and the affairs of every local church. However, the Vatican feels it has an ultimate responsibility to handle serious problems that the local church is unable or unwilling to handle. The affair of Matthew Fox (formerly of the Dominicans, and now an Episcopal priest) is characteristic. Fox, the guru of creation spirituality, was involved with witches and preached the goodness of homosexuality. Why were the American bishops and the authorities of his own order totally unable to deal with him? Why did the American bishops allow Charles Curran to contradict the moral teaching of the Roman Catholic Church from a position in a papally chartered university paid for by the American bishops? Why are feminist nuns given charge of dioceses? Why is elementary knowledge of Catholic life missing even among the clergy? In one major archdiocese, the priest in charge of religious education for the whole archdiocese for almost 20 years did not know how to say the Rosary, did not know who St. Maximilian Kolbe, the martyr of Auschwitz was, and mispronounced Eusebius' name as e-su-bi-us, because he had never heard it pronounced, which meant that he had never had a class in patristics. This priest, when he left his office, was made a papal monsignor as a reward for his services, and has ambitions to be made a bishop.

This stress on administration means that Catholics see the visible organizational unity as the true mark of the Church. Doctrine and liturgy are of less importance. As long as things are well administered, the bishops and Rome are largely satisfied. The officially approved changes in liturgical practice since Vatican II largely have destroyed faith in the Eucharist. However, since the changes are approved and their implementation is being carried out, Rome seems to be happy, whatever the effects on the faith.

These changes show a possible pitfall in any attempt simply to revive patristic practices that have been preserved in the East. The Orthodox Church believes in transubstantiation (although it does not use that term) and the belief in the Real Presence of Christ in the Eucharist is widespread and does not seem to be controversial. The Orthodox Church has never developed separate Eucharistic devotions the way the West has. Instead, following the tendency of Orthodox life, the Eucharist remains firmly embedded in the Liturgy. In the West, Eucharistic theology and devotion have developed in a specialized manner, as all things in the West tend to.

Religious art became largely detached from the Liturgy, as simply an aid to devotion, but there is still a thirst to see Christ among the faithful. In the East the icon enhypostasizes Christ—that is, the icon bears the likeness of Jesus Christ, and by gazing at the icon, the worshipper truly sees the likeness of the face of Jesus Christ, the Second Person of the Trinity. The iconoclasts claimed that the Eucharist was the best icon of Christ, and in the West the consecrated bread was exposed during the elevation at Mass, in benediction, and during periods of adoration. These Eucharistic devotions, and various practices during Mass, such as genuflections before the tabernacle and kneeling during the Canon and Communion, presented the faith of the people in the Real Presence. When these later accretions were done away with and older practices, such as standing for the Eucharistic prayer and the reception of Communion, were restored, faith among Roman Catholics in the Real Presence largely disappeared. A Gallup poll showed that more Lutherans than Roman Catholics chose a strong statement of the Real Presence as representing their faith. Roman Catholics tend toward Zwinglianism and believe in a more symbolic presence.

The tendency of the West to focus on individual aspects of the faith, doctrines, and practices, and to develop them in isolation from the integrated whole of the Christian life, was given even further expression in the Reformation. Wycliffe criticized the Catholic orders because they called themselves Dominicans and Franciscans and Augustinians rather than Christians. What would he have made of Lutherans and Calvinists? The protests focused upon doctrines or insights that had been neglected by the Western church, and emphasized them to such an extent that the integrity of Christian life was distorted or compromised. Luther correctly saw that the practices of the Roman Church, by encouraging Christians to focus on secondary matters such as indulgences rather than primary matters such as faith, were betraying the gospel. But did Lutheranism manage to escape its own distortions, with its opposition of law and gospel? Or did Calvinism escape, which in emphasizing the sovereignty of God slighted the reality of human freedom? The reactions within Protestantism itself followed the same pattern. Anglicanism became dominated by the dry manners of the upper classes; Wesley's followers emphasized proletarian emotionalism. Protestants generally tended to say the age of miracles was past; Pentecostals proclaimed the full gospel, including the miracles, but forgetting the Liturgy, church government, and other aspects of the gospel that are present in Acts itself.

Insights & Convergence

So, with each split, individual truths and insights were developed, even if at the expense of the symphonic unity of truth, in Hans Urs von Balthasar's phrase. But if the splits had not occurred, the insights might have been lost, and the Church as a whole impoverished. As it is, there is a holy competition going on. Roman Catholics have been forced to look at the necessity for individual conversion, while Protestants have been forced to take a look at the Liturgy and the sacraments and religious life.

While from my point of view the Orthodox broke with Rome rather than the other way around, it would have been harmful to the Church as a whole if they had not. Roman centralization and scholasticism, especially since the Western countries had the advantage of freedom from the Turks and the prosperity brought by the Industrial Revolution, would have led to a massive infiltration of Western ways into the East and a loss of patristic theology and practices. The churches of the East would have been opened fully to the damaging rationalism and infidelity that have ravaged the Western churches. The separation allowed the East to preserve as a touchstone the way of life of the patristic church, and so to become, to the Western eye, somewhat immobilist, but at the same time escaping the distortions of the West.

However, the separation was only for a time, and I (and the pope) hope that it is rapidly drawing to an end. Papal leadership might offer the Eastern churches a way out of the nettlesome problem of establishing new churches outside of the ancient homelands. It might also, as in the West, offer a partial antidote to extreme nationalism, which the Orthodox churches recognize is a danger, although they seem to be still tempted by it (as in Serbia). But what the East has to offer the West is infinitely more important. The Western church, including the Roman Catholic Church, is in real danger of ceasing to be a Christian body. Neither St. Augustine nor St. John Chrysostom would recognize as Christian much of what goes on in Roman Catholic parishes. A quiet advocacy of homosexuality goes on unimpeded by rebukes from the Vatican. Belief in the sacraments is rapidly evaporating. Confirmation and confession are almost totally neglected. Feminism is the reigning ideology, and bishops promote it as much as they can without provoking direct action from Rome. Reports of concelebrations by laywomen are increasing, and the archdiocese of Chicago plans to put women in charge of dozens of its parishes.

Feminism is the chief challenge to the Church today. It is as dangerous as gnosticism, to which it bears a strong resemblance in its internal incoherence and its resentment of the natural order. It is more dangerous than even grave doctrinal errors, such as the unitarianism of the Second Person propounded by a handful of Pentecostal groups, because it appeals to a sociological situation in the Western church. Women dominate, sometimes by large ratios, the congregations of the West, and Western church life has been profoundly affected by this sociological fact. The Western churches perhaps for this reason are unable to deal with feminism because they fear to alienate the last group in society that goes to church: women. I have my fears that the Orthodox also may succumb. Although the spiritual significance of gender is prominent in Scripture, it is not treated by the Fathers, who adopted the Greek attitude to the body, that, if it was not evil, it was certainly not important, especially in its gendered and sexual aspect. Carl Jung, the main channel for the revival of gnosticism in the Church, is all too appealing to Christians who think that his system can be used to elucidate Christianity to modern man. Even such an excellent thinker as Paul Evdokimov (although he wrote and died before the dangers of feminism became clear) shows an aversion to Christ's masculinity as a theological fact, and instead tends to see him as the supreme androgyne. The novel challenge of feminism is probably beyond the internal resources of Orthodoxy; it also requires both careful rational analysis and new delving into the resources of Scripture, specialized tactics that are more the province of the West.

Both to meet the challenges of modern life and to fulfill Christ's prayer that they may all be one, it is necessary for all Christians to join in a visible union. Each church may properly maintain its identity and traditions, not in isolation, but in fruitful communion with other churches with divergent traditions. It is hard to see what other institution than the papacy could provide visible unity. The popes, especially the current one, regard their office not as an opportunity to lord it over other Christians, but as a grave burden of responsibility. As in a marriage, authority is based upon self-sacrifice. A wife might question a husband's authority over her. After all, the man is equal to her, and who is he to exercise authority over an equal? But if the husband shows his willingness to die for his wife, his exercise of authority becomes not a means of self-aggrandizement, but an act of love.

The pope, too, is the first among equals, and knows that his authority has to be validated by self-sacrifice. Pope John Paul II has worked tirelessly in the service of Catholics, Christians, and indeed all men. His endless travels and extensive writings try to bring the gospel to all. He knows that his actions provoke the wrath of God's enemies, and he has shed his blood at their hands. His greatest desire is for reunion with the Orthodox, a union that would revivify the Church, allowing it to breathe with both lungs, and that would lead eventually to the reunion of all Christians, not in an institutional consolidation, but in a *communio* that reflected the *communio* of the Three Persons of the Trinity, eternally distinct yet eternally one in love.

Reprinted from Touchstone: A Journal of Ecumenical Orthodoxy, *Summer 1995 Volume 8, Number 3.*

DAVID MILLS

THE BIBLE TELLS ME SO

Everything You Need to Know
About Morality & the Bible

A COLLEAGUE ONCE attacked me in a meeting, then cut off my response by turning to our supervisor, thrusting his fist into the air, and declaring, "I'm not interested in the past, I care about the future!" In one move he managed to insult me, prevent me from responding, and portray himself as (in contrast to me) both forgiving and idealistic. This sort of linguistic terrorism leaves most of us stumbling over our own feet, while our opponents trot smugly over the finish line.

One feels much the same when engaged in arguments, especially arguments over sexual morality, with our liberals. Liberal or skeptical Christians have been inventing and field-testing ways of getting around biblical teaching for a very long time, and they have gotten very good at it. They are now so sophisticated that average Christians, who are called to pursuits other than biblical scholarship and theology, can give no convincing answers to their exotic proposals for revising the Christian faith.

I will take sexual morality as an example, not because (as our liberals keep hinting) orthodox Christians are afraid of sex, but because it is where the debate on biblical teaching has been most clearly joined.

Unlike the modernists of old, our liberals are usually quite happy to let us believe in the Virgin Birth or the bodily Resurrection, or for that matter praying in tongues, presumably on the assumption that it keeps us occupied and out of their way. They only object when we dare to argue for moral limitations and ideals they have long ago abandoned. They will tolerate the most extravagant supernaturalism, as long as it is not assumed that the supernatural makes binding statements about human sexual behavior.

Orthodox Christians (with the embarrassing exception of groups trying to raise money) actually talk far less about sex than the representatives of liberalism. Some Christians on both sides are rather unhealthily concerned with sex. They have sex on the brain, which, as someone remarked, is an odd place to have it.

But if we tend to talk a lot about sex, we do so because it is the aspect of the inherited Christian moral teaching most directly challenged by our culture and, sadly, by powerful and vocal movements in our own churches. The use of sex is the question of the hour. To accuse orthodox Christians of being obsessed with sex is somewhat like accusing firemen in a city victimized by arsonists of thinking too often about fires.

The Authority of Scripture

The question of what the Bible really says is a problem because, when members of the major churches discuss moral questions, surprisingly enough they are all still talking about the Bible. Even the most radical Christian still appeals to the authority of Scripture, or to be more precise, to Scripture as an authority. Whatever limitations he wants to put upon that authority, or other authorities he wants to add, he still looks for what support he can find in the Bible.

In *Living in Sin?*, for example, Bishop John Spong attempted to ground his moral innovations in the Bible. He argued that though we should ignore the Bible's prohibition of sex outside marriage because "science" tells us that some people are not made for marriage and current social practices tell us that many want sex without marriage, we should endorse its belief in monogamy.

You may remember Spong's shock several years ago when one of his priests— whom the bishop had ordained with great publicity because of his open practice of homosexuality—denigrated monogamy as "unnatural" and said Mother Teresa would be a more effective minister if she were sexually experienced. The bishop removed his license to function as a priest, though, as several commentators noted at the time, the priest was only being faithful to the bishop's own assumptions about the superiority of cultural practices to biblical injunctions. But despite his rather confused approach to the Bible, Bishop Spong still tries to get its support whenever he can.

In a book called *Dirt, Greed, and Sex,* a professor at an Episcopal seminary based his entire moral teaching on the one verse that Jesus "made all things clean." (He reads that verse, contrary to established Anglican principle, to contradict other verses, not least the first chapters of Genesis.) What we call biblical morality, he argued, is unfaithful to the Bible. He contended that the Old Testament prohibition of homosexual acts expressed a "purity ethic" no longer needed now that all things have been made clean. This led him to the extraordinary conclusion—one among several—that "among the young and those in temporary isolation, bestiality should not occasion too much concern." It might not occasion him too much concern, but one does wonder what the sheep are thinking, grazing nervously whenever an Episcopalian walks by.

I am told this sort of thing happens in other churches as well—except for Orthodoxy, which is spared (for the moment) the subtleties of liberalism—and that, if anything, the Bible is newly fashionable in liberal circles. We all still take Scripture as an authority of some sort, but it hasn't gotten us very far.

A few examples from the current movement to legitimize homosexual relationships show the problems we face in discerning the true biblical teaching. The movement's answers and questions make our own amateur responses look terribly inadequate.

For example, if we quote the verses condemning homosexual acts, we are told that scholars have shown that these verses did not condemn what we now call "loving, committed, monogamous relationships" but promiscuous, predatory sex. Or we are told that scholars have shown that it applies not to those of *homosexual* orientation but only to *heterosexual* men and women committing homosexual acts contrary to their orientations. If we argue that the Church has never approved homosexual relationships, we are told that scholars have found that the Church blessed homosexual marriages long before it blessed heterosexual ones.

We are told that the Bible is hopelessly biased, or our reading is hopelessly biased, by "heterosexism" or "homophobia." We are promised that if we could read it without these prejudices we would find that "loving, committed, and monogamous relationships" are in fact good and holy. We are asked to find the Bible's true meaning—and condemned for not having done so already—which our liberals see and we don't. Thus, an Episcopal organization dedicated to legitimizing homosexuality can run an ad claiming to represent the true "tradition-alists" and to rescue the Bible and Tradition from people like us.

I don't know, off the top of my head, how to refute these claims, much less any new ones they think up—and I have the advantage over most Christians of being professionally involved in church issues and of having theological colleagues to ask and a theological library to use. So what are we to do? How shall we hear God's word about morality in the Bible?

In short, we ought to do three simple but not easy things. These won't make us able to successfully counter new interpretations of Scripture, but they will give us a confidence in biblical teaching that will sustain us even when we can't answer an objection. They will give us a serene certainty that may well prove more effective in changing others' hearts and lives than any amount of knowledge or skill in debate. The three things are: first, read and study the Bible; second, interpret it from within the Church and her Tradition; and third, allow yourselves to be formed more and more into the image of Christ by his Word in his Body, the Church.

These three actions depend, of course, on the assumption that the Bible is true. Not just that it tells the truth on this or that matter, if we are discerning enough to separate the wheat from the chaff, but that everything in it tells the truth about God and man. We should only put ourselves in the right place to hear God speaking if he is actually speaking. If he isn't, the liberals are right, because, to revise Dostoevsky's remark, if God is not speaking in the Bible, then everything is permitted.

Read & Study the Bible

First, read and study the Bible. This means daily, for a significant amount of time, using accurate translations and trustworthy commentaries. It means mastering the ancient art of meditating upon the Scriptures, reading and thinking about them in such a way that you encounter the Lord in them. It means listening to God where he's widely known to be speaking. You are reading this because you had good reason to think you'd read something you wanted or needed to hear. How much more eagerly should you go where the Lord God himself is speaking?

To put it bluntly, you must read the Bible because the Bible is the source of biblical moral teaching. It is just no good taking a stand for biblical moral teaching when what you mean are the ideas everyone I know believes in, and that I remember from my parents and my old Sunday school teacher and a few sermons from the pastor when I was a kid. That is idolatry: putting in the place of God's Word the false assumptions, the exaggerated notions, the blind spots, the self-serving ideas of one's time or culture or class or upbringing.

Above all things, you must read the Bible. When the serpent slithered up to Eve in the Garden, he asked her, "Hath God said, 'Ye shall not eat of every tree of the Garden?'" The very first temptation in the Bible was the temptation to forget, not to deny, the Word of God. The serpent surely had exceptional insight into human nature. If *he* thought that the temptation to forget was the most likely to work, it undoubtedly is. And we are, if anything, far more susceptible to this temptation than Eve.

We protect ourselves from this temptation by following the example of Eve's counterpart, the Blessed Virgin. As St. Luke's Gospel says, "And all they that heard it [the shepherds' testimony to the Christ Child] wondered at those things which were told them by the shepherds. But Mary pondered them in her heart" (Luke 2:18–19). Had the serpent asked her, "Hath God said?" she would have been able to say, "Yes. Now get thee behind me." All I am asking you to do, in this first part, is to imitate Mary and to ponder the Word in your heart.

However, reading the Bible is not quite as easy as it sounds. It is not just a matter of disciplining our time, but of disciplining our souls. If we are to hear the message of the Bible with any accuracy, we must come to it with more humility than most of us like or have. We must remember that we read the Bible as utter moral failures, men and women whose goodness is "as filthy rags" (Isaiah 64:6)—which is, among other reasons, why it should be read in the context of a prayer that includes confession.

The Bible convicts you and me as thoroughly as anyone else on earth. As G. K. Chesterton said, the fall is the only empirically provable Christian doctrine. Even St. Paul, who was much, much farther advanced in sanctity than most of us, called himself the worst of sinners. With typical and currently unfashionable realism, the confession in all the historic liturgies is to be said by all people without exception—by Mother Teresa as well as by Joseph Stalin. In the words of the traditional Anglican confession, everyone must daily "acknowledge and bewail our manifold sins and wickedness, which we, from time to time, most grievously have committed, by thought, word, and deed, against thy Divine Majesty, provoking most justly thy wrath and indignation against us."

When we're feeling good about our apparent superiority to some others we could name, we must remember that each of us faces some temptations and not others. We are tempted according to our situation in life. We are all oriented toward particular sins. Whatever its source—defective genes, a dysfunctional family, poor potty training—an "orientation" is merely a recurring temptation, not, as the homosexual lobby claims, an excuse to act in a certain way or evidence of God's intention for one's life.

The story of the rich young ruler and the parable of the camel and the needle's eye show that wealth brings with it peculiar temptations (or orientations) quite difficult to resist. To our Lord's sorrow, the rich young ruler did not resist these temptations. But in response to him Jesus did not—as some church leaders would now have us do—relax the entrance requirements to bring him into the group. Our Lord did not think it compassionate or inclusive to tell him that God approved whatever he wanted to do. (Misuse of wealth, by the way, sometimes seems the only sin identified in the New Testament many church leaders still recognize.)

We have all sinned and, from God's point of view, are not a pretty sight. To think ourselves better than others because we haven't committed their particular sin is like a town boasting that it has the prettiest toxic waste dump.

A Clear & Coherent Pattern

When you read and study the Bible with a redeemed heart you will find that its teachings are, by and large, clear. And you will find also that its teachings are, by and large, coherent and consistent. If God is its author, this is to be expected. The Bible is the owner's manual for our life, written by someone who was—unlike most VCR companies—quite careful to write it so that we could understand it. A divinely inspired owner's manual will be clear and coherent and consistent to those who read it carefully with humility and trust. We should take our Lord at his word when he said, "Seek and ye shall find. Ask and it shall be given to you."

Of course, some people will refuse to read the Bible and try to figure things out themselves, or only read the easier parts, or skim it for the high points, or refuse to believe what they read, or take someone else's word for it, or forget it the next day. Having given them free will, the Author can't do much about them. Once you buy a car, the dealer can't help it if you use leaded gasoline and ruin the engine.

Unfortunately, the laity often think that the Bible is just too hard to understand. The laity see scholars fighting over its interpretation and assume, quite reasonably, that the rest of us shouldn't even bother. Or they are assured by the clergy that the Bible is a difficult and deceptive document that really doesn't say what it seems to say, and that only those with seminary training should try to penetrate its mysteries.

Fortunately, however, though the Bible is sometimes difficult to understand, it isn't *too* difficult to understand. All the most important truths the Bible teaches really are clear. The Bible is an owner's manual written by someone who wants you to understand it. If you read it with humility, no matter how little you know, you're like a builder who can put up the walls and put in the furnace but cannot do the finish work, cannot put in the kitchen cabinets and the bookshelves, and so on. Even if your house isn't pretty, and you have to pile the cans and books on the floor and order take-out food, it will keep you warm and dry. It will do what a house is supposed to do, even if it will never be featured in *Architectural Digest.* If you read the Bible with a humble and contrite heart, you will know what you are supposed to know, even if you will never qualify as a scholar and will never be able to defeat the clever arguments of its enemies.

The Bible's moral teaching, for example, is clear. The Bible both forbids us to do certain things and commands us to do others, and when there are two holy states of life, such as being married or single, it gives us instructions for both.

The Bible is quite clear that sex outside marriage and homosexual behavior are not allowed and that marriage is good, as indicated by our Lord's contribution to the festivities of the marriage at Cana and his declaration that God himself has joined together husband and wife (Matthew 19:6).[1] We know that celibacy is also a good thing, by our Lord's own example. And Jesus and St. Paul imply it is a better state than marriage.

If you know your Bible, you will begin to see the pattern in the biblical cloth. You will know that any particular error doesn't fit the pattern, is a blotch on the tartan or a tear in the tweed. You will know it doesn't feel biblical, even if you can't refute it. If you read a story set in a place where you've lived, you know with some certainty whether the author really knew the place. He might have made some error in description. Or he might have gotten all the details right and still not described the place itself, so that though you can't point to any particular error, you can still say "No, that isn't my home." So with the Bible. If you live in it, wander down its streets, play in its parks, you will easily detect the frauds and imitations.

If you want to know a true Rembrandt from a forgery, you study true Rembrandts.[2] You learn to distinguish an authentic painting from a very good fraud by studying with excruciating care paintings known to be authentic. (Their authenticity, by the way, you have to take on reliable authority, as most of us must take the authenticity of the biblical books on reliable authority, in which we're as justified as the student who accepts the consensus of Rembrandt scholars.)

You use a magnifying glass to study Rembrandt's brushwork, and you stare at his paintings for hours to learn how he composed his pictures and how he used color, and so on. You'll never know Rembrandt if you don't spend a lot of time with Rembrandt. But if you won't learn his methods with scientific reliability, you won't ever be able to say with mathematical certainty that this or that painting is authentic. But you will have trained your eye to recognize Rembrandt. If you think this an unreliable way of judging things, just remember that prudent people spend millions and millions of dollars on paintings on just such recommendations.

Knowing the biblical pattern helps us discern its teaching on controverted questions. If someone says that self-fulfillment is more important than continued faithfulness to his wife or that St. Paul condemns only promiscuous homosexuality but would have approved "loving, committed, monogamous relationships," and he produces a wealth of scholarship to support his claim, you will be able to say that it simply doesn't fit the pattern. If you know the pattern, you will be able to say that every time the Bible mentions homosexuality, it condemns it, and that nowhere does the Bible commend or approve such acts, as you would expect if they were sometimes permissible, because otherwise God had failed to tell us something important. You could add that the biblical ideal is either chastity or faithfulness between husband and wife, and that this is understood to be the source of joy and happiness and contentment, and that unfaithfulness is understood to be a source of sorrow and pain and tragedy.

Further, if you know the pattern, you will know how intimately God has tied together the body and behavior. It will be clear that the fact that men and women have complimentary sexual organs, and that the combination of those organs produces fruit, means that they are meant for each other and that to use them in any other way is a perversion. You will know that becoming "one flesh" through sexual intercourse is not a metaphor for "growing closer" but a natural and supernatural reality.

And you will sense the many more profound and subtle meanings, even if only the wisest men and women are able to make them explicit. Since the deepest truths are the truths most easily denied by the liberals' simple and rational (or rationalist) criticisms, it is thus important that you actually sense them yourself rather than take them on someone else's authority, if you don't want to wander into deeper darkness. It is easy to believe things seen in the distance are actually mirages or illusions when they are only far away, and can be reached if you keep walking.

Thus, there are sometimes no conclusive *answers* to questions about biblical teaching—answers, that is, that will win arguments and convince skeptics—but there is a conclusive *pattern,* which convinces despite our inevitable ignorance on one point or another. This pattern of answers will convince and sustain you despite your ignorance, much as a net with a hole or two will still catch enough fish to feed your family.

The better you know the Bible, the better you will know the pattern, and the better you will understand even the difficult parts that scholars dispute among themselves. Reading the Bible daily is like living with a family. After a while, you know what they are going to say almost before they say it, and you know what they mean even when they don't make any sense. Actions you couldn't understand when you were first married make perfect sense when you've been married five or ten or twenty years.

Read the Bible Within the Church

So, read and study the Bible. That is absolutely necessary, and you won't get anywhere if you don't start there. But still more is required. The second thing to do is to read the Bible within the Church and her teaching Tradition, for otherwise you will go wrong. This may seem to contradict my claim that the Bible is astonishingly clear and coherent and consistent, but it really doesn't because the man or woman committed to hearing the Word of the Lord will want to hear it within his Body. If you don't want to hear it within his Body, it's likely that you really don't want to hear it. You aren't really a friend of the Lord if you don't care what his other friends think.

Only within Christ's Body, the Church, will you find guidance and direction, the answers to obscurities, and the encouragement to accept the (to worldly minds) unlikely and (to sinful hearts) unappealing. There, in the line of believers going back to the apostles, you will find the insights and discoveries, the accumulated wisdom, the experiments and theories successful and unsuccessful, to balance and correct your own weaknesses and most grievous faults.

We are in grave danger without the Church. Because we sin we will misread the Bible in our favor. It is all too easy to use the pages of the Bible to paper over all the mirrors in our house so that we never see ourselves as we really are.

Look again at Eve. She erred only when she strayed from her "interpretive community," to use the current jargon: from those (in her case, Adam) who could have identified the serpent's lines as lies, and whose love would have encouraged her to resist. When she set out on her own to interpret God's words, she inevitably fell into sin. (Adam's sin was in failing to be a faithful and authoritative interpretive community, which has obvious implications for our clergy.)

It has to be noted that to read the Bible within the Church and her Tradition is necessary to keep from reading the Bible within the increasing rejection of Tradition now practiced by many in the churches, including their elders. Error and heresy are as likely to come from the elders and official bodies of the churches as from anywhere else. We need the Church, the Church of the ages, to protect us from the wrongful teachings of some in our churches.

The Church's guidance is not just intellectual but spiritual and moral. The fellowship and counsel of other believers sustain us, while we are restrained by their censure and scrutiny. Holy Communion nourishes us and gives us strength to act rightly, and confession forces us to admit that we act wrongly. Most of us would be much worse without "the goodly fellowship of all faithful people," as the traditional Anglican liturgy puts it. It is often much easier to offend the Lord than the people in your parish.

Christian moral teaching goes wrong—very quickly becomes narrow and twisted and legalistic—when it is separated from the Church and her Tradition. Years ago, in some circles "temperance" had come to mean "not drinking," which is not even a Christian idea. It had lost its meaning of doing all things as they ought to be done, in moderation. The Church would have protected these people from such a narrow and unbiblical interpretation, and at the same time taught them the profound and life-giving wisdom carried in the idea of temperance.

Without the traditional understanding of the Church, they inflicted upon the country a prohibition that, among other things, led to the growth of organized crime and taught many people disrespect for the law.

Without the Church, one person's or one group's or one society's or one age's eccentricities and tastes and hates and loves become identified with Christian morality, which leads at best to absurdity, but usually to tragedy and squalor. Many sincerely religious Victorians justified the oppression of the poor by quoting "the poor ye shall have with you always." But those Anglican priests nurtured by the Oxford Movement's rediscovery of Christian tradition and the authority of the historic Church gave up promising careers to serve the poor in the slum parishes and worked to change the hearts and minds and laws of their countrymen to abolish the horrors of the Victorian slums and factories.[3]

The Image of Christ

So, read and study the Bible, and read and study it within the Church and her Tradition. But there is yet one more thing to do, and it is the most difficult. You must give yourselves to be formed more and more into the image of Christ by his Word in his Body the Church, of which he is the Source and Author.

In the beautiful words of the Anglican prayer of consecration, we ought to live so that we may "be filled with thy grace and heavenly benediction, and be made one body with him, that he may dwell in us, and we in him." You will only begin to truly understand the moral teaching of the Bible when you become like its Author, when he dwells in you, and you in him. The Risen Christ spent the time before his Ascension opening the Scriptures to his disciples. The Lord dwells with us to open his Word to us.

We tend to think that we can go to the Bible and find out what it says, and then obey it or not as we wish. This belief is the product of an entirely modern way of thinking often called "positivism." Positivism wrongly applies the objective methods of scientific observation—which aren't, as philosophers have been saying for some time, quite so objective after all—to moral and spiritual things. It assumes that anyone can discern God's law as easily as he can observe the law of gravity.

Modern liberalism or skepticism, born from the great advance in the scientific study of the Bible in the last century, began with this assumption. When, after decades of confidently announcing "the assured results of biblical criticism" (which tended to contradict the previously assured results), liberal scholars found that the Bible could not be quite so reliably understood with the methods of science, they generally abandoned not the assumption but any belief that the Bible had a coherent message. Such is the reason, I think, for the current vogue of movements like "deconstructionism," "postmodernism," and "reader response criticism," which deny that "the text" can carry truth from the author (who is definitely not the Author) to the reader.

Positivism fails in spiritual things because it leaves out the human heart. The heart is the instrument through which we see and measure spiritual things. If your heart is corrupt and unredeemed, you won't be able to see with it—or rather more worrisomely, its subtle flaws will make you see wrongly while thinking you see rightly.

The commandment "Thou shalt not kill" seems absolutely clear. It means *"Don't kill."* Even those who believe it allows for war or capital punishment know that it forbids the killing of innocent people. But today certain ideologues in the mainline churches believe it doesn't apply to unborn children. I suspect that the ideologues' interpretation is often distorted by their lust for power and control. However "sincere" the abortionists' reading of Scripture might be, innocent people still die.

You cannot come to the Bible as a scientist observing a physical phenomenon. You can't read the Bible and then decide whether or not to believe and obey it. You are the instrument for interpreting Scripture, and how you live your life determines how accurate and sensitive an instrument you will be. What you say to God in the way you live your life determines whether you can hear him speaking in the Bible. You have to believe it and guide your life by it, have to read it with a humble and a contrite heart, or you'll never know with assurance what it says—or, worse, will think it says something to your comfort when it announces your damnation.

The only way to avoid this is to be formed into the image of Christ, by cooperating with the work of the Holy Spirit. And this means making, with what light you have at the moment, the choice God would have you make. "Every time you make a choice you are turning the central part of you, the part of you that chooses, into something a little different from what it was before," C. S. Lewis wrote in *Mere Christianity*.

And taking your life as a whole, with all your innumerable choices, all your life long you are slowly turning this central thing either into a heavenly creature or into a hellish creature: either into a creature that is in harmony with God, and with other creatures, and with itself, or else into one that is in a state of war and hatred with God, and with its fellow creatures, and with itself.

To be the first is heaven, he concludes:

To be the one kind of creature is heaven: that is, it is joy and peace and knowledge and power. To be the other means madness, horror, idiocy, rage, impotence, and eternal loneliness. Each of us at each moment is progressing to the one state or the other.

Part of heaven, notice, is knowledge; part of hell, idiocy. Goodness and knowledge are all mixed up together. To know the Lord of heaven is to know the truths he gave in his Scriptures; not to know him is to believe the lies and nonsense of hell. As Chesterton said, when men stop believing in God, they don't believe in nothing, they'll believe in anything—a truth the tragedy and buffoonery of our age's pursuit of answers, from Communist utopias to uninhibited sex to crystal pyramids, should make clear to anyone.

"When a man is getting better, he understands more and more clearly the evil that is still left in him," Lewis continued.

When a man is getting worse, he understands his own badness less and less. A moderately bad man knows he is not very good: a thoroughly bad man thinks he is all right.

This is just common sense, Lewis continues.

You understand sleep when you are awake, not while you are sleeping. You can see mistakes in arithmetic when your mind is working properly: while you are making them you cannot see them. You can understand the nature of drunkenness when you are sober, not when you are drunk. Good people know about both good and evil: bad people do not know about either.

In other words, if you want to know what is good, become good. If you want to know what the Bible teaches about morality, you must not only read and study it, and not only read and study it within the Church, but you must become conformed to the image of its Author.

This will convince us of the truth of the Bible's moral teaching and protect us from the subtle and seductive arguments of its enemies. But what of those to whom we speak? How can we convince them when we still don't know all the answers? As we each become more like our Lord, we will find that our witness for biblical morality will increase. People are rarely convinced by arguments but often transformed by love.

We ought not to rest satisfied with our knowledge of biblical morality, nor with our spotless orthodoxy, nor with our painfully acquired ability to explain every doctrine and refute every objection. Even the devils believe. Biblical morality is not a possession or accomplishment of our own, to be used when needed and then put away. It is the life we live in Christ, who came that we might have life, and have it more abundantly.

Reprinted from Touchstone: A Journal of Ecumenical Orthodoxy, *Summer 1992, Volume 5, Number 3.*

ENDNOTES

1. See also Matt. 5:31; 22:23–30; Mark 10:2–12; 12:19–25; Luke 16:18; 20:27–35; Rom. 7:1–4; 1 Cor. 6:16–18; 7:1f; Eph. 5:22–23; Col. 3:18–19; 1 Tim. 5:9–16; Heb. 13:4; 1 Peter 3:1–8.
2. I am grateful for this illustration to Fr. Kenneth Hunter of St. James Church in Newport Beach, California.
3. The truth of biblical morality is somewhat demonstrated in purely worldly terms. See, for example, C. S. Lewis's *Mere Christianity,* Book 3, and G. K. Chesterton's *Orthodoxy,* especially chapter 7. For an explanation of the intimate relation of church doctrine and morality, see Gertrude Himmelfarb's brilliant essay, "From Clapham to Bloomsbury: A Genealogy of Morals," in *Marriage and Morals Among the Victorians* (New York: Vintage Books, 1986).

PATRICK HENRY REARDON

CHRISTOLOGY & THE PSALTER

The Church's Christian Prayer Book

THE LOVELY TITLE of a recent book summarizes my simple thesis in the following reflections. It is called *Psalter for the Christian People,* a name suggesting that the Psalms have a necessary and important place in Christian thought and worship. Indeed, such has been the persuasion of the Church from the very beginning. The New Testament tells us to address one another with psalms (Eph. 5:19), to teach and admonish one another with them (Col. 3:16), and to sing them (James 5:13). After the Lord's Ascension, the believers turned immediately to the Book of Psalms for guidance. The Church's first canonical act, choosing a replacement for Judas, was explicitly based on a text from the Book of Psalms (cf. Acts 1:20). Again, two psalms were quoted and interpreted in that first sermon on Pentecost (cf. Acts 2:25–35). The Psalter is the Old Testament book most frequently cited in the New Testament.

The history of Christian prayer also bears witness to the distinct dominance of the Psalms. For example, in prescribing that a monastic community is to pray its way through the full Psalter each week, chapter 18 of the *Rule of St. Benedict,* in the sixth century, recalls that the monks at an earlier and more devout period had accomplished that task every day. Simplifying the daily office for the layman at a still later date, Archbishop Cranmer continued to maintain a major place for the Psalms in the *Book of Common Prayer.*[1]

But why the Psalms? Why should Christians not simply stick with what seem to be more explicitly Christian prayers, such as the various canticles of the New Testament and other primitive Christian literature? To what purpose should we Christians burden our worship with so many culturally strange images and themes from the Psalter, such as kingship, city walls, blowing ram's horns, blood sacrifice, bows of bronze, cries for vengeance, harp music, sword battles, and oil dripping down on somebody's robe? Doesn't this sort of thing tend to make our prayer a bit unreal?

The Christological Theme

The origins of this Christian attachment to the Book of Psalms go far back. It was the Risen Lord who taught the first Christians to discover "in the Law of Moses and in the Prophets and in the Psalms" the Spirit-given references to himself (Luke 24:44). It was in that very first gathering on Easter that the Christian Church began to discern the significance and the importance of the Psalms in its thought and worship. Put simply, the Psalter is a book of Christology; it is Christology in prayer form. This is the reason why, if Christians are to engage in truly Christian prayer—prayer "in Christ"—then the Psalms must be an integral and important element of that prayer. Thus, in what appears to be our first extant example of the use of a psalm in Christian worship, one observes that its impulse and interest are entirely Christological (cf. Acts 4:24–30, quoting Ps. 2). Prayer "in the name of Jesus" (cf. Acts 4:30 again) readily takes the form of psalmody. So has it been from the beginning.[2]

It is truly remarkable to note how this steady theme of Christology in the Psalms was shared by Christian authors who were otherwise so diverse: Eustathius of Antioch, Ambrose of Milan, John Chrysostom, Cyril of Alexandria, Augustine of Hippo, Gerohus of Reichersberg, Bernard of Clairvaux, and Martin Luther. Just to limit ourselves, for now, to the last name on that list, we observe that Luther so consistently interpreted the Psalms in the light of the New Testament and Christian theology that sometimes this approach even determined how he translated them into German. He insisted on reading the Psalms precisely as a

Christian and not following some "misleading Jewish slant."[3] All the other writers on that list would have agreed with him.

Although all of the Psalter refers to Christ and is properly to be prayed within the context of that reference, certain passages of the Psalms have from the beginning enjoyed a special prominence. A ready example is the opening line of Psalm 109 (Hebrew 110): "The Lord said unto my Lord: Sit thou at my right hand." In the traditions reflected in the synoptic Gospels, Christians remembered that Jesus had cited that verse in controversy with some of his rabbinic opponents (cf. Matt. 22:44; Mark 12:36; Luke 20:42) and that the context of his citation was the decisive and great kerygmatic question, the question of the Lord's identity: "What think ye of the Christ? Whose son is he?" In those few words of the Psalter, "the Lord said unto my Lord," Christians learned that Jesus is not only David's descendent but also his pre-existing Lord. He is the son not only of David, but also of God.[4]

Having mysteriously addressed the identity of Christ, that same line of the psalm then goes on to speak of his triumphal enthronement. Scarcely any words of any psalm were more beloved of the first Christians than "Sit thou at my right hand." They were quoted in the first sermon of Pentecost (cf. Acts 2:34) and became the foundation of some of the most important Christological and soteriological statements of the New Testament (cf. Mark 16:19; Rom. 8:34; Eph. 1:20; Col. 3:1; Heb. 1:13; 8:1; 10:12; 12:2).

Then, that same verse of the psalm goes on to refer to those who oppose the victory of Christ: "Until I make thine enemies thy footstool." Once again, those few words were to lay the basis for important dimensions of eschatology in the New Testament (cf. Acts 2:35f; 1 Cor. 15:25; Eph. 1:22; Heb. 10:12f; and perhaps 1 Pet. 3:22).

The remaining lines of this same psalm speak of still other grand dimensions of Christian doctrine. Most specifically, this is the psalm that identifies Jesus as "a priest forever according to the order of Melchizedek," and this identification is made the major theme of the Epistle to the Hebrews, our psalm cited repeatedly throughout the development.

With so much Christian theology concentrated in a single psalm, and so much of it in the very first line of that psalm, it is no wonder that Psalm 109, the *Dixit Dominus*, rather quickly assumed a notable place in Christian worship, particularly on the Lord's Day. The use of this psalm as the solemn opening of

Sunday vespers, a feature still prevalent in the Western Church, seems to have its roots in the third century.[5]

Christ in His Mysteries

To treat adequately the place of the Psalms in Christian prayer would be the work of several lifetimes, one suspects. It would involve, for example, a lengthy discussion of the Psalms in Christian meditation on the Passion of the Lord. Jesus himself died with words of the Psalter on his lips (cf. Mark 15:34, quoting Ps. 21:2; Luke 23:46, quoting Ps. 30:6) and was imitated in this respect by the Church's first martyr (cf. Acts 7:59). Images and even whole lines from the Book of Psalms are found within the Gospel accounts of the Lord's sufferings. The Psalter speaks of the vinegar and gall (Matt. 27:34, from Ps. 68:22), the dividing of Jesus' garments (Matt. 27:35 and John 19:24, citing Ps. 21:19), the distance of his friends (Mark 15:40, from Ps. 37:12), and the blasphemies of his enemies (Matt. 27:39–44, citing Pss. 21:8f; 108:25). Since the believer's daily routine of prayer tended almost universally to be related to the various events comprising the Passion of the Lord,[6] it is not surprising that psalmody early became the daily bread of Christian piety.

The Tradition of the Church also associated various psalms to the sacraments. Of particular importance in this regard was the Good Shepherd Psalm, 22 in the traditional Psalter but popularly known now as Psalm 23. Ancient Christian use and exposition of this psalm found in it references to the initiatory sacraments of baptism ("He leadeth me beside the still waters; He restoreth my soul"), chrismation ("Thou anointest my head with oil"), and the Eucharist ("Thou preparest a table before me. . . . My cup runneth over"). It was employed extensively in the patristic catechesis associated with those rites. Indeed, words and images from this psalm found their way into the rites themselves.[7]

The Christocentricity of the Psalter is not simply a matter of identifying certain select passages as "messianic." Rather, the Tradition of the Church regards Christology as the proper key to the whole Psalter. This appropriate Christian attitude toward the Book of Psalms is the fruit of daily praying those Psalms within the Church's worship, centered around the sacraments. Praying the Psalms as Christians means praying them with the "mind of Christ" and illumined by the Christian mysteries. Correct ("orthodox") understanding of the Psalms (or, indeed, any other part of the Bible), then, always involves Christ. Thus, whether interpreting

all or only part of the Book of Psalms the older Christian commentators spontaneously looked at each psalm through the lens of the "life in Christ." It is no
accident, then, that those exegetes who were not disposed to adopt a sustained
Christological interest in the Psalms, such as Theodore of Mopsuestia and Theodoret
of Cyrus, were ultimately judged to have a defective Christology.

The Anthropology of the Incarnation

Among those who speak and write about the Book of Psalms, it has become a
commonplace to mention the great range of human emotions and conditions that
are expressed there. In this respect the Psalms lend themselves to a definite
anthropological interest. Indeed, such comments about the Psalter, which are
undoubtedly valid, were also made occasionally by the Fathers of the Church,
notably St. Athanasius.

A certain anthropological preoccupation in the Book of Psalms would seem
to be established from its opening line: "Blessed is the man." This "man" appears
repeatedly throughout the Psalter, and it would seem important to identify just
who he is. Christian Tradition does not regard him as just anyone but as a very
specific man. As we have seen, the proper key to the understanding of the Psalter
is Christ. So St. Augustine, in his *Enarrationes* on the Psalms, commenting on
those opening words of Psalm 1—"Blessed is the man"—said simply and directly:
"This is to be understood of our Lord Jesus Christ." Augustine then went on to
pursue this theme through the rest of his magnificent work on the Psalter. The
only valid anthropology for Christians is . . . well, Christian anthropology, and
Christian anthropology begins with Christ, of whom the Nicene Creed says: "who
for us men and for our salvation . . . became man."

The question "what is man?" is asked in the Psalter itself, specifically in Psalm
8: "What is man that thou art mindful of him? Or the son of man that thou
visitest him? Thou hast made him a little lower than the angels, and hast crowned
him with glory and honor. Thou madest him to have dominion over the works of
thy hands; thou hast put all things under his feet."

Just what man is the psalmist talking about here? The earliest extant Christian
commentary on these lines leaves no doubt. The Epistle to the Hebrews quotes
these very verses of the psalm and sees them as descriptive of the person and work
of Christ: "For in that he put all in subjection under him, he left nothing that is not

put under him. But now we do not yet see all things put under him. But we do see Jesus, who was made for a little while lower than the angels for the suffering of death, crowned with glory and honor, that he by the grace of God should taste death for every man" (Heb. 2:6–9).

For the Epistle to the Hebrews, the Incarnation of God's Son (cf. ch. 1 passim) is the source of Christian anthropology. In assuming our humanity and experiencing the depths of its mortality, the Son of God shares his life with us. This is the burden of the second chapter of Hebrews, which was to be one of the major doctrinal texts for the Christological developments of the fourth and fifth centuries. Citing yet another psalm, the author of this work continues to speak of Christ's solidarity with us by reason of the Incarnation: "I will declare thy name unto my brethren; in the midst of the Church I will sing praise unto thee" (Heb. 2:12 and Ps. 21:23). Taking our nature (Heb. 2:16), becoming a partaker of our flesh and blood (2:14), sharing our temptations (2:18), and tasting our death (2:14f.), Jesus is made our High Priest and reconciles us to God (2:17). That is the only New Testament answer to the anthropological question "what is man?"

The Present Impiety

Necessarily brief, I hope my comments have nonetheless demonstrated my initial thesis: The Psalms are Christology in prayer form and the reason we Christians pray them is that they speak of Christ and are a Spirit-given means of praying "in Christ." It appears to me that the authoritative Tradition of the Church speaks on this matter with one voice.

I began these reflections by citing the lovely title of a recent book: *Psalter for the Christian People.*[8] It is now my sad responsibility to say that the only thing lovely about that book is its title. Motivated explicitly in the interests of gender-inclusiveness (another crippled offspring of contemporary feminism), it is the most recent of modern translations that seem as though systematically and of set purpose to destroy any semblance of Christology in the Psalter. That is to say, they render the Psalms, in varying degrees, unfit for Christian prayer.

Emulating the anemic Psalter in that version of the *Book of Common Prayer* used by the Episcopal Church since 1976, these new translations (a word very loosely used here) differ among themselves only in detail.[9] Whether by the elimination of nouns like *man*[10] and masculine pronouns generally,[11] or by the insertion of female names to provide "balance"; whether by making the word *lord* optional,[12] or by exiling it completely, or by doing most of these things simultaneously,[13] such efforts uniformly produce translations that would be unrecognizable to any New Testament author, father of the Church, or Protestant Reformer.

By way of briefly demonstrating the systematic exclusion of Christology from these recent translations, I will limit my remarks to Psalm 8 which, as we have seen, was a major, formative text in Hebrews 2 and in the whole history of Christological and soteriological development: "What is man that thou art mindful of him, or the son of man that thou visitest him?"

In *Psalms Anew* of 1984, this line of Psalm 8 became: "Who are we that you should be mindful of us, that you should care for us?" The next year saw the publication of the now popular *New Jerusalem Bible*,[14] in which this same verse was rendered: "What are human beings that you spare a thought for them, or the child of Adam that you care for him?" Then, in the so-called *Grail Psalter* of 1986[15] it was phrased: "What are we that you should keep us in mind, men and women that you care for us?" And most recently the *Psalter for the Christian People* gives the verse as: "What are human beings that you should be mindful of them? mortals that you should seek them out?"

Now we are dealing with a line of the Psalms of which the Christian meaning is not in doubt, because it is specifically and explicitly interpreted in the New Testament. But in each of the translations just given, one observes that the choice of words has been determined by considerations of "political correctness," with no reference to a Christ-centered reading of the text.

Quite simply, the psalm in question is not being presented in a Christian way because Christ has been eliminated in the interests of an alien ideological agenda. The Arians learned this lesson early: if you want to change Christian doctrine, to alter the thinking and religious experience of Christians, to vary or avert their vision, just tamper with the wording of their prayers. Now, to corrupt the prayers of Christian people, to remove Christ from those prayers, is an evil thing to do.

Besides this, however, a loving reverence for the institutions that have traditionally served the prayer life of the Church renders it extremely painful to read the copyright inscription of this new *Psalter for the Christian People*. It says, "The Order of St. Benedict."

Reprinted from Touchstone: A Journal of Ecumenical Orthodoxy, *Spring 1994, Volume 7, Number 2.*

ENDNOTES

1. A brief but useful discussion of psalmody in primitive Christian worship can be found in Josef Jungmann, *The Early Liturgy* (South Bend, Indiana: University of Notre Dame Press, 1959), pp. 167f, 278–287. In the present article, I will follow the Church's ancient custom of citing the Psalms according to their numbering in the Septuagint and Vulgate versions, which is most often one digit lower than in the rabbinic text and its various translations.

2. Notwithstanding a grateful reverence for my fascinating professor of yesteryear, I must dissent from Fr. Norbert Lohfink's view that "In Christian worship the Psalms were first used at the end of the second century" ("The Psalter and Christian Meditation," *Theology Digest*, vol. 40, no. 2 [Summer 1993], p. 134). His conclusion rests solely on the relative silence of the scanty evidence, but Acts 4 is a clear testimony to the contrary. Fr. Lohfink is also impressed by the fact that the Psalter saw very little use in the public worship of Judaism at that time, but surely the Christological themes perceived in the Psalms by the early Christians would have given them a special reason for adopting psalmody in their worship very early. Indeed, this curious inattention to Christology is the real problem I have with Fr. Lohfink's otherwise helpful article.

3. Cf. his 1531 "Defense of the Translation of the Psalms," *Luther's Works*, vol. 35 (Philadelphia: Fortress, 1960), pp. 209–223, more specifically p. 219; cf. also his 1545 "Preface to the Psalter," ibid., pp. 253–257.

4. Cf. Demetrios Trakatellis, *Authority and Passion: Christological Aspects of the Gospel According to Mark* (Brookline, Massachusetts: Holy Cross Orthodox Press, 1987), pp. 80–82, 198f.

5. Cf. Jungmann, vol. cit., p. 107.

6. Virtually from the beginning Christians paused during the day to pray at certain fixed times associated with specific events of the Lord's Passion. This discipline is spoken of in Hippolytus, *Apostolic Tradition* 36; Tertullian, *On Fasting* 10.7f; Cyprian, *On the Lord's Prayer* 34; *The Apostolic Constitutions* 8.34; Basil, *Greater Rules* 37; John Cassian, *Institutes* 3.3. I have long suspected that the Markan Gospel, which ancient Christian testimony universally assigns to Rome, is already a quiet witness to that practice. Like Hippolytus, another writer of the Church at Rome, but unlike the literary tradition as a whole, Mark fixes the Crucifixion of Jesus at the third hour or 9 A.M., thus dividing the drama of the Passion into sections that are easily recognized as nocturns (Mark 14:32–42), matins (15:1), tierce (15:25), sext (15:33), none (15:34), and vespers (15:42). It would seem, then, that Mark, about A.D. 66, is our earliest witness to what are later called the "canonical hours" of the daily office. If this is so, it is a striking example of how the New Testament Scriptures had their origin, and thus find their proper context, in Christian worship.

7. To be convinced of this, one may read a truly inspiring section of Jean Danielou, *The Bible and the Liturgy* (South Bend, Indiana: University of Notre Dame Press, 1956), pp. 177–190.

8. Collegeville, Minnesota: The Liturgical Press, 1993.

9. A favorable evaluation of six such translations of the Psalms was made by Sr. Eileen Schuller, "Inclusive Language Psalters," *The Bible Today*, vol. 36 (1988), pp. 173–179.

10. Gary Chamberlain, *The Psalms: A New Translation for Prayer and Worship* (Nashville, Tennessee: The Upper Room, 1984). A Methodist pastor's contribution.

11. *Psalms for All Seasons: From the ICEL Liturgical Project* (Portland, Oregon: Pastoral Press, 1987).

12. *An Inclusive-Language Lectionary* (New York: Pilgrim Press, 1987). An effort of the National Council of the Churches of Christ in the U.S.

13. Sr. Maureen Leach and Sr. Nancy Schreck, *Psalms Anew: A Non-Sexist Edition* (Winona, Minnesota: St. Mary's Press, 1984). This is the most extreme distortion of the Psalms known to me.

14. *The New Jerusalem Bible* (Garden City, New York: Doubleday, 1985).

15. *The Psalms: An Inclusive Language Version Based on the Grail Translation from the Hebrew* (Chicago: G.I.A. Publications, 1986). (Note that this is *not* the real *Grail Psalter* of 1963.) This particular "inclusive" version has come precariously close to being adopted by the Roman Catholic bishops of the United States for liturgical use in this country. On December 15, 1993, it was announced to the Catholic News Service that 150 bishops voted in favor of it and 98 opposed it, so that it failed to receive the two-thirds majority necessary for approval. That three-fifths of those bishops did approve it, however, is truly alarming.

S. M. HUTCHENS

THE PROFESSOR & THE UNICORN

Reality, Revelation & the Seductions of Abstract Thought

I
N A RECENT SERIES of *Touchstone* articles and editorials Patrick Henry
Reardon and I were called upon to respond to arguments, historical and
theological, for the accession of women to church offices traditionally held
only by men (see *Touchstone,* Fall 1992, Winter and Spring 1993). For those who
are as weary of this topic as we are, let me say at the outset that this article is not
about women's ordination, but the way of thinking that makes this institution and
many others conceivable. One might say it concerns the line between reality and
imagination, which, translated into the language of theology, has to do with the
difference between revelation and speculation. It is a very old problem that needs
to be reconsidered by every generation.

It seemed to Fr. Reardon and me that we were tilting with the unicorn—
writing against things conceivable but imaginary. He was dealing mostly with
imagined history, and I was speaking against a contrived theology, but we were
both speaking to minds abstracted from the reality of the Christian faith as described in its apostolic constitution and lived by the Church. Reardon was con-
fronted with a history of Christian priestesses having so little evidential substance

that no reasonable person could consider it anything but a creature of imagination—and yet the imagined idea was strong enough to blind an intellectual giant to church history as it apparently was, and draw a bishopess (surely kin to the unicorness) out of the catacombs. I faced a theological argument that advanced from Christian premises to non-Christian conclusions on the strength of a concept of equality that defeated history, tradition, and St. Paul's explicit directives for the role of women in the churches.

We are disposed to shape the world to our desire by elevating notions over verity. This is a corruption of the gift that made *homo faber* in the image of God. Man who was made to imagine and create within the defined infinity of Truth now makes images of what cannot be. The world is full of his idols, weighted to their own destruction by their inability to answer to reality as it comes from the hand of God. The religious feminist, in the spirit of Antiochus and Pompey, invades the sanctuary and there—aided by the homosexual who also profits from the trivialization of gender distinctions—sets up her egalitarian idea. Those who bow before it finally find themselves in a war against God and nature they cannot win. The same elevation of idea over reality happens when the scientist distorts or ignores the book of nature in favor of his theory, or a nation is molested by political idealists and social architects.

My own experience as a student of theology, in conservative and liberal schools, among Protestants and Catholics, has largely been that of studying ideas about God, his word and will for mankind. The basic material in all cases, even among the most vehement modernists, has been extracted from the biblical mine. But very quickly the idea, separated from the context meant to limit and control it, takes root and grows on its own. One truth hypertrophies, others atrophy in response, and the school or the sect is born, each with its characteristic preoccupation and error. One segment of Christendom becomes controlled by the idea of bringing the kingdom of God to earth. In others, attributes of God, such as his sovereignty or kindness, or some aspect of the person of Jesus or his Mother, become ground-principles that control the vision of those who adopt them. Distended over the boundaries of revelation and traditon, these ideas are eventually used to attack their own source and essence. The phenomenon is the same in all instances—an idea, a generality, not in itself wrong, but given undue license, overcomes the particularity of the Given and conforms everything in its path to its own shape, leaving confusion and schism in its wake.

Conditions on the Western Front

Eastern Orthodox friends tell me that Western theology's proclivity to err comes from this habit of mind. The difference, they say, between Western theology, shared by Protestants and Catholics, and their own is that here we begin our thinking about God in terms of one of these preoccupations of which I have spoken: an ancient, but non-Judeo-Christian concept of God as Pure or Absolute Being, reflected in the *filioque* of the Western version of the Nicene Creed and enshrined in our theology by Thomas Aquinas and Protestant Scholasticism. In Eastern Christendom, they tell me, God is contemplated in the revealed mystery of his personhood, of the relation of the Persons of the Holy Trinity to each other and to creation. Once this alleged difference didn't matter very much to me, since I could not regard the Western theological conversation I had been privy to, considered as a whole, consistent enough to be controlled by any idea or method, faulty or otherwise. As as result of my controversy with feminism, however, I have been forced to consider the charge more carefully.

My conclusion is that the Orthodox cannot be blamed too much for generalizing as they do about our understanding of God in the West, but there is something about the inner life of the Catholic and Protestant churches I would like them to appreciate more. It is not true that Christians in the West have devoted themselves to a divine abstraction, that our conception of God is ultimately that of numinous being—and hence a malleable idea—instead of a revealed person. This, rather, has been a driving tendency of our scholastic tradition to which many countercurrents have answered. The history of theology in the West is that of a battleground between the abstract and particular God, the God of Judeo-Christian revelation and the God of speculative reconceptualization. It can be analyzed in terms of *ideas* of God, set forth in academies that arose as the churches divided—academies that have always been religious, especially when they claim to be secular—answered by personalistic antitheses that find most of their support beyond their walls.

If we use an analogy derived from C. S. Lewis's *The Abolition of Man*, a book with a voice far older than that of its author, we could say we are speaking here of the invidious tendency of the head, abetted by the pride and prejudice of the schools it has created, to rebel against the heart—which has reasons, as Pascal said, of which the head does not know. If the heart is where reason and affection are combined by the superior and ultimately mysterious agency of the person himself, we are speaking of a case where the Western head has a history of identifying the heart as mere belly to discredit it and assert control. Visceral faith is present here in force, but not every reaction against the sin of the intellect is a descent into enthusiasm. Sometimes it is the healthy soul's insistence, which is also found here in the West, that the abstractive, ratiocinative faculty is not qualified to rule the man and must itself be brought under a higher authority in the service of truth.

Those whose studies concentrate on theological literature rather than the actual life of the churches are apt to see the history of Western theology through the eyes of academic theologians, historians of dogma, and the church offices they influence, an ascendancy from which there has been a continuous and powerful revolt. This revolt is against the tendency of an abstractive and formalizing school theology to make clerics by training them in religious philosophy and to make God the property of this clerical caste, with the theological faculty firmly on top. Perhaps the place this is most evident these days is the attempt of Catholic academics to define Catholic faith in defiance of the bishop of Rome, who above all the popes of recent history combines devotion and intellectual power in a heart that has control of both. The pope's struggle is an old one, fought by many others on a variety of fronts.

The correspondence of Karl Barth and Adolf von Harnack is a fascinating example of this phenomenon. Barth tweaks the nose of the German theological academy on behalf of the Church's faith. Harnack loftily accuses him of enthusiasm and anti-intellectualism, and in the end doesn't see how they can carry on an intelligent conversation. The reason Harnack hadn't the slightest feeling for the Church as a theological authority to which he as a professing Christian is bound is because he was a professor, and therefore not in the slightest measure subject to it. This illustrates the strange end of a long process. What is called theology here in the West has been the province of specialists who have insisted on the privilege of defining the Christian faith with an ever-higher measure of independence from the spiritual life of the Church. What began as special privilege for discussion of doctrine within the universities has grown by our times into almost complete spiritual alienation of imperial theological faculties from the living Church. (My opinion as to why the churches seem nevertheless to welcome, or at least tolerate, the tyranny of the schools, and thus drink their own death, is that the school theologians buy their church salaries and endowments by telling people what they want to hear rather than what the historical faith teaches. Resistance to this morbid cycle rarely comes from the faculties. Often it is spearheaded by a conspicuous traitor from these ranks, like Wycliffe, Barth, or John Paul II, who makes his appeal to the people directly or through pastors who have the courage to swim against the stream.)

I do not blame the Orthodox for reading Western theology and identifying tendencies, but one should distinguish sharply between Church and academy and understand that the life of the Church in the West to a large degree has been preserved by people who are willing to oppose its schools, and so be identified as enthusiasts and anti-intellectuals, no matter how sober and learned they might actually be.

Where Orthodoxy and the Western resistance meet and agree most intensely is at seeing the heart of the faith in the sacraments, conversion to Christ, the reading of Scripture, prayer, devotional exercise, mystical or pentecostal experience, a *mysterium relationis* in which our primary and controlling understanding of who God is (as in the relationship of child and parent) comes from the ineffable mystery of communion with a Person, not from reflection on a religious concept. Here popular Christianity and an occasional deserter from the religious intelligentsia place themselves on the side of Eastern Orthodoxy, and yes, even of the pagans who had the notion that the gods were "personal." They could be propitiated, influenced, even bribed, but not reconceptualized. "Reconceptualization," they realized, required the invention of another god.

Aristotle, no great friend to popular religion, attempted to cleanse Hellenic theology with philosophy, resiling from pagan personalism by treating God at the level of pure being. Given the disreputabilty of the pantheon, it was a noble undertaking, and doubtless well meant. He and his Christian intellectual heirs honor God by speaking of him in terms of the highest and purest possible conceptualization to which the human mind can attain. In doing so, however, they frequently indulge a strong natural disposition to purge theology at its highest level of anthropomorphic associations. This is to avoid one temptation, that of confusing God with creation, while succumbing to another, that of setting him apart from creation in ways that he in fact is not. As Christians we believe that the unsurpassably perfect revelation of God is an Anthropomorph whose actual members we must be to be saved, and that the farther one is removed from this particular vision and relation, the farther one is removed from the one true God. When one speaks of God in terms of being, he must first speak of the particular being of this particular Revelation. Our address of God, in prayer, in thought, in every sacramental act, is "in Jesus' name," not to God as the highest being conceivable.

I came to this understanding by meditating on religious feminism, which has a strong natural interest in two paths of theological conceptualization: along that of Western theology's tendency to regard God in abstract, non-personal terms, apart therefore also from the infection of gender, and in terms of the mystical (apophatic) theology common to both East and West that teaches God negates every human category. Feminism will not get very far with the second, since, logically speaking, apophaticism is infinitely regressive, teaching that God as negation also is the negation of negation, so that the way of negation is also the way of hyper-affirmation. Ultimately one cannot de-Christify, de-paternalize, or de-hierarchialize Christianity with apophaticism—and that, of course, is what feminism must have. One can do much better with a concept of Absolute Being by which it can be said that God is beyond gender categories, something quite different than apophaticism, but easily confused with it. That way Christ can be, in fact must be, as a mere man, regarded as an inferior revelation of God, since he is no longer in fact consubstantial with Absolute Being, but adulterated by the addition of the human and, beyond that, the particularity of gender. He is removed from anything that can be called God by being (1) material creation, (2) human, and (3) male. This is a recrudescence of gnosticism and deeply anti-Christian.

While theological feminism might wish to regard itself as one of those personalistic revolts from an abstractive school theology, in fact it cannot be. That is because so far as it personalizes God, it does so in full retreat from *Christian* personalization—God as the *Father* of our *Lord*, the *Man* Jesus Christ—and invariably ends in neo-paganism, with goddesses, divine hermaphroditism (following its penchant for confusion of the sexes), and the like. To the degree that feminism's god is personal, it is also pagan. Its only plausible argument from within what passes for Christian theology comes from elevation of God beyond gender, a depersonalization in accordance with the abstracting tendencies of the schools and the doctrine of God as fundamental Being.

St. Thomas & the Antichrist

At this point I can almost see my Orthodox friends rubbing their hands and saying, "This is what we have been trying to tell you Western believers all along. The abstractive disease that makes God Absolute Being instead of *himself* is deep in your bones. 'Christian' feminism is the legitimate heir of Aristotle, Thomas Aquinas, and the whole scholastic tradition, Catholic and Protestant. Beza with his supralapsarian God, radically un-free against the determining force of his own decrees, Hegel's *Geist*, Whitehead's process deity, Tillich with his Ultimate Concern, the revivalists and superstitious Catholics who think 'God' can be manipulated with slogans, formulas, and sacred magic—all from the same addled family, just with different tastes in idolatry."

I painfully admit the point is well taken, but other observations need to be made here with some force, for the question of speaking of God in terms of his Being continues to reassert itself as legitimate. It cannot be, as the "early Barth" is accused of teaching by those who don't understand him, that God is so Wholly Other it is impossible to connect him in being or thought to what is not God, since if that were true we could have no relation to him and no valid thoughts of him at all. (The early Barth was not stupid.) There must be some relation, some connection, some way of speaking about him and being related to him. If there is, then what could be wrong with saying that the reason for this is that we share the quality of "being"? For surely God "is" and we "are"—we are connected by "being-ness" at the most fundamental level.

The problem here, of course, is that according to the Hebrew and Christian Scriptures God is radically different from his creation. What he made did not emanate from his essence, but was called out of nothing at his Word. Our ability to think abstractly about God ends at the infinite chasm between the Creator and the creation that calls any *analogia entis*—a relation of God and man on the basis of a common being—into question. Yet we *are* related, and on the level of being, too. St. Paul cites Aratus approvingly: "We are his offspring." Surely a relationship of this kind, in fact a relationship of any kind, is inconceivable apart from the idea of a community of being.

Thomas Aquinas dealt with this problem in a way that makes sense. He began by making the observation that if a certain property is rightly attributed to two different things, then those two things can be considered together in a single field of knowledge. If "being" is attributed to two entities, then there must be a science of being that treats them both to the extent they have being in common. Since faith finds it unthinkable to consider either God or the creature apart from their existence, which Scripture also attributes to them both, the predicate of being is properly applied to both. The distance between them cannot stand in the way of either a science of being that speaks of God and creation, or of some kind of community of being between them.

St. Thomas is careful to say that this does not mean when we speak of God's being and the being of his creation we are using the word in the same way. God's being is peculiar to him as ours is to us. But still, this doesn't mean there is no likeness of being between God and the creature, for if there were not, not only would the creature be unable to know God, but also God would not be able to know the creature, which is again unthinkable. Rather we speak of the being of God and of the creature in terms of their analogy, or their likeness in dissimilarity, in terms of an *analogia entis*—an analogy of being.

In the preface to *Church Dogmatics* Karl Barth calls the *analogia entis* the invention of Antichrist. It is important to understand that he did not make this accusation because he denied the relation between God and creation, but because he was convinced this concept connected them in an illegitimate way. That relationship, he later made clear, is through Christ alone, and must therefore always be seen through Christological lenses. To connect us through a general doctrine of being is diabolical because it bypasses the Incarnation—the place where the being of God and that of his creation are perfectly and comprehensively related, which contains all other such relations, and by which they are to be defined.

Let me say here, however, that it is unadvisable to try to understand Barth's meaning in terms of what St. Thomas says at the foundations of his metaphysics, for it is not at all plain that there St. Thomas is doing anything wrong. He is wrestling as a Christian with a difficult problem using conceptual tools borrowed from Aristotle, and comes to a conclusion that preserves, as it must to remain orthodox, both the radical difference and radical similarity between God and man, laying the foundations of a Christology in which Jesus Christ, the perfect and complete revelation of God, is both very God of very God and very man of very man. If there are problems with the analogy of being as St. Thomas uses it, that is, if it offends orthodox Christology, they would not become evident until one goes further into his thought. Here I only see him translating a Christian doctrine into the language of philosophy. As long as this is done accurately, and can be translated back when necessary, there is nothing erroneous or deceptive about it.

The difficulty Barth had with the analogy of being was more practical than theoretical. He recognized it has a spotted history that includes a strong, almost irresistible, tendency to draw in its train a general ontology that treats both God, where it is interested in him, and creation in terms of equivalent conceptualizations (which, it appears, St. Thomas would not have approved as consistent with his understanding of analogy). General sciences of being, even general sciences of being with something called God at the top of the essential heap, have nothing distinctively Christian about them. They have a long pre-Christian and post-Christian history, a very abundant and independent philosophical life of their own that is in no obvious way beholden to the first and final revelation of the Truth of God in Christ Jesus, by whom Christians insist that all other putative truth is to be measured, and to whom all being and thought are to be made subject. I would argue, and here I think von Balthasar would agree, that Barth disapproved of the analogy of being less because of what it said when you isolated it in the sphere of Christian doctrine than because of the bad company it keeps when it gets out on its own.

The Sovereignty of the Infinite Particular

Still, fundamental to the main stream of Western philosophy is a doctrine of being that is separable from and independent of a theology based on revelation—God's self-disclosure—to which Jews and Christians point as the starting place for all reflection on God and his creation. It is no coincidence that Martin Buber was a Jew. The understanding that all true theology begins not in ratiocination but in grace, in personal communion, and in doxology is an essential part of our common heritage. This also means that the theology of Christians and Jews is bound with a short chain (but which is also infinitely long) within the precincts of God's self-revelation. Its understanding of being—its conception of what *is*—has a particularity to it that a general doctrine of being cannot have, and this particularity is frequently in conflict with ideas of God generated in and through doctrines of being founded on *concepts* of God and driven thereafter not by information from God, but by a logic that rises from within the concepts themselves.

In the Christian faith we begin and end our thinking about who God is with revelation—with a specially vouchsafed disclosure of his reality, not simply an intelligent theory—with "the tether and pang of the particular" (C. S. Lewis). Eve became the first philosopher-theologian as well as the first human idolater when she allowed herself to step outside the bounds of the revealed by adopting the serpent's conceptual God: An *idea* of God was made available to her with which to defeat the Particular with whom she was coming into controversy. The serpent provided her with a re-formed God who was different from the Person she actually knew. The known reality became abstracted to a concept subject to free ratiocination. The personal, particular God who had spoken to her could now be bypassed by theologizing, that is, by philosophizing about "God." The first step in the process of temptation always is that of offering to the mind an abstracted essence—what God must be in accordance with a supervenient Idea apart from his actual and known Self. A doctrine of God's being—mere being, that is, shorn of the particularity of his revelation—thus becomes clay for idolatry, for it can be shaped by the vermiculate will where the self-revealed God cannot be.

This tendency to reach beyond what may be known on the impulse of an idea of God is at the base of much religion. It is very natural for the high-minded to move from the idea of an incomparable Creator-God, to that of his absolute Purity of Being. While it is true that he may be accurately spoken of in that way, the concepts of the being and purity of God must be able to bear the weight of an immanence in which God becomes flesh and bears human sin. Aristotle would have had trouble with Christianity. The next logical step from attribution of Pure Being in a theology uninformed by Judeo-Christian revelation is to his separation from all that is inferior to that Being. This idea of separation is also, in a sense, true, but now more heavily weighted toward falsity, since those who believe it are going to have even greater difficulty with the Incarnation, as we have seen among Gnostics and Muslims. Reality, as Pascal and Kierkegaard so forcibly reminded us, and the revelation that tells us its nature and history, is full of surprises that mere logic cannot predict, even when it begins from formally correct premises.

Revelation & the Logic of Ideas

Revelation conveys in accurate symbolic depiction the reality that mere conceptualization cannot predicate with confidence or authority. It gives us the shape of things as they truly are, and to which therefore our logic must conform. An illustration of ideation apart from revelation would be the study of human anatomy pursued apart from thorough examination of the body—the very sort of trap into which medieval science, with its lack of empiricism and dependence upon classical authorities, typically fell. The body is, to external view, bilaterally symmetrical. A logic of mere conceptualization would assume, and not without reason, that its interior reflected its exterior: two eyes, two ears, two arms, one side of the forehead the mirror image of the other, therefore, two lungs, two brain lobes, two hearts, and each side of the liver the image of the other. In this case the original idea, which conceptualizing reason followed out, did not bring it to complete untruth with regard to the invisible world of the body's interior. There are, after all, two lungs, two kidneys, and a symmetrical bladder. But to know the actual truth of the body, one must rely on the anatomical equivalent of revelation. A surgeon whose understanding of anatomy was based on mere logic and not on the way the body actually is would kill, not all, but many, of his patients. The decisiveness of empirical discovery over speculation in the natural sciences is analogous to the ultimacy of a theology of revelation over that based on a general doctrine of being.

The history of philosophy, which is the story of ideas about being and the logic contained in those ideas that flesh them out into metaphysical systems or anti-systems, is likewise not a story of complete error when it comes to thinking about God any more than a science of anatomy based upon mere logic would be. It appears to me, for example, that Hegel's *Science of Logic* contains a great many "hits" when placed up against Christian revelation, and therefore can be useful, at the places where the philosopher's insight is deep, for understanding what Christians believe. Its power, as Kierkegaard told us, is in its ability to reflect the reality in which we believe, its error in the pretense of a relation to that reality that no abstract system can have. Hegel made the mistake of falling in love with a photograph, in forgetting that the story of Pygmalion and Galatea is a myth, or rather, is true only in a particular case that he does not recognize. Similar things can be said of the work of many thinkers who are not Christians, whose writings are often rich conceptual mines for the believer who knows what he believes and can understand it better with the aid of those who make pictures of it, even if the artists don't understand the subject of their art. Some truths, as a matter of fact, stand out with the starkest clarity in people who are, or believe themselves to be, hostile to Christianity.

But always, revelation, being the representation of reality given by God himself—and which in its origin and perfection is Christ—rules our conceptualizations of God and his creation. This is so that the simplest Christian believer with the most rudimentary insight into this revelation has the necessary experience to be more thoroughly right about God than the most sophisticated theological systematician, whose work may consist largely of conceptualization imperfectly related to revelation, all too often flawed by faulty methods and prolegomena, and correct only where inconsistent with its first principles. This is why I, even though trained in school theology, do not hesitate to cite St. Paul's restrictions on the activities of women in the Church against contrary opinions based upon a theory of God determined not by what the Church has tradition-ally believed to be revelation on these matters, but by an egalitarian idea that construes the reality of Christian doctrine in the same way as our concept-driven anatomist conceives the human body. This is not to say that revelation is illogical, only that where it is given it tells us what something we might call the prime logic is. To this prime logic we must submit, even when we have otherwise reasonable arguments to place against it.

The great problem for Christian thinkers (I first encountered this among Calvinists and then later, with even greater force, among Roman Catholics) is in telling where revelation leaves off and speculation—that is, the pursuit of logic into revelation—begins. I do not believe it is always wrong to speculate, but it is always risky—like assuming the correspondence of the external logic of the hu-man body to the internal. If it is done, those who do it are responsible to the rest of us to identify their sorties as just that—speculation. One may, according to his skill, find himself in the right a great many times, but for definitive knowledge of many hidden things, one simply must be shown what cannot otherwise be seen. And of course, while one always bases speculation on doctrine, it must never be done the other way around.

Karl Barth's observation on this subject (described well by Hans Frei in *Types of Christian Theology*, pp. 38–46) is that a great many theologians, liberal and conservative, go at their work by first engaging a general philosophical scheme, into which the language of revelation must be made to fit, and to which, therefore, revelation itself must ultimately be subject. But this, Barth insists, is putting the cart before the horse, since theology has been given the controlling paradigms of thought and language by revelation, and we are responsible before God to learn

what they mean and to bring what is apparently external and, at points, concep-
tually parallel to that revelation under the descriptive control of revelation itself. In
other words, when the philosophical science of being and theology as the discourse
of the Church consequent to revelation are brought together, one or the other
must control the field.

Barth insists that when theology is what it ought to be, it has the privilege
and responsibility to exercise this dominion. This means that while philosophy
can, at least in theory, be respected outside theology and used within it, it cannot
be allowed to dictate to it—not even at the fundamental level of imposing a rule
of noncontradiction—since philosophy does not know enough, nor does it have
the ability within itself, to make ultimate determinations about what is contradic-
tory and what is not. It can only guess. Barth makes it plain that philosophy,
driven by general doctrines of being and the logic that accompanies them, has
frequently attempted to impose its bad guesses on a theology built upon a revelation that calls it wrong.

A Family Discussion in the Occidental House

Let us return to St. Thomas here. I am still not approaching him as a critic, since
the answer I am looking for can only be given in light of a firm grasp of his thought
as a whole, which I do not have. Still, the question that must be posed to him and
to all other philosophers of being is whether God as Ineffable Being (even when
"being" is predicated analogically) is identical with the God of revelation, since
nothing in a mere philosophy or theology of being dictates the necessity past the
legitimate boundaries of what has been called natural revelation.

Discourse about God in terms of his being cannot be disallowed, since it is in
fact assumed by Scripture and the science of theology itself, as St. Thomas understood. But the science must accurately reflect *quasi per speculum* the reality about
which it speaks in order to be true. Philosophy, which at its base is discourse
about being in general, must be ancillary to theology when theology is the par-
ticularization of that discourse in terms of the self-revelation of God. Since (we
Christians believe) this revelation reveals a manifest community of likeness between God and man, one might therefore speak quite innocently of an analogy of
being, but this speech must ultimately be referred to and responsible to the
Christology in which it is concretized.

One may say, with St. Thomas, that being is predicated of God *per analogiam*, but in the mouth of a Christian this is usually less philosophy than apologetics: preaching doctrine to philosophy in terms that it can understand as a way of connecting its ideational forms with the symbolics of the apostolic faith. The formal test of St. Thomas's Christian philosophy, or of any other that claims to be such, is whether it (1) accurately reflects, in its own peculiar language, the faith revealed to the Church, and (2) acknowledges the final authority of revelation—describing as it does, reality, not simply theories about it—over general doctrines of being.

To the degree a philosophy and its doctrine of being accurately describe the truth of God in its own language, the theology of revelation recognizes it as symbolically true. If this were not so, *homoousias* could not be used in the Nicene Creed. This single-word explanation of Christ's relation to the Father is legitimized by revelation itself, since the reality it symbolizes is taught by revelation. To the degree philosophy or philosophical theology goes beyond revelation it is speculative—perhaps not wrong, but speculative, and should be treated as such. The recapitulation of the theology of revelation in philosophical (or other) terms is true only where the recapitulation is accurate, and always subject to revelation itself. And where philosophy and its attendant doctrines of being deny revelation—which has often been the case historically—theology, still the queen of the sciences, must correct it. Barth's many criticisms of school theology, Catholic and Protestant, probably center here. In light of the revelation given to the Church it is often wrong. Even when it is not demonstrably erroneous it tends toward speculation that it fails to identify as such, and so generates more confusion than light.

As a Protestant looking at Roman Catholicism, I believe that our most significant confessional differences occur not simply at places where we have different readings of the Tradition, but where the Catholic philosophical mind extends doctrine with logic while the Protestant holds back. For example, the Scriptures speak of a time of purification for believers: Purgatory as an extrapolation on this is eminently logical. But does revelation speak of purgatory, and are all Christians required to believe that it exists according to its Roman Catholic description? These questions would also apply where Marian doctrine or the matter of papal infallibility seem to go beyond Scripture. In each of these places a strong deductive logic appears to be at work, an "if this"—a beginning premise upon which Catholics and Protestants might agree—followed by a "then this" conclusion that

Protestants, and frequently the Orthodox also, question because it appears to go beyond what has been revealed to what we understand as the Church.

The Protestant protest on these matters cannot be final and dogmatic. We do not *know* whether the pope can speak infallibly, our Lady had no children of her body other than our Lord, or that we may ask for the intercession of departed saints. When reason and desire outstrip revelation, as we suspect they have done in these places, they need not be wrong (there are two nostrils—there might really be two lungs also!). But we hold judgment in abeyance, and so resile from Catholicism's *insistence* that its distinctive dogmas must be right, even when they are—as they always are—systematically grounded and supported by a driving logic. Conservative Protestants tend to have the same mindset as the Orthodox in such things and so have difficulty with what we think we see in Catholicism and know we see among religious progressivists. Something may be by all appearances *consistent* with apostolic teaching, but untrue. It is this, not necessarily an imperfect understanding of the character of Scripture, blindness to the authority of Tradition, or hostility toward our estranged Roman bishop, that keeps some of the most thoughtful Protestants protesting.

The *sola scriptura* of Protestantism, formally incorrect as it may be as a principle of authority, is best understood as a conservative response to what was perceived as theology's transgression of revelation within Roman Catholicism. Apropos St. Thomas's metaphysics, our observations of Catholicism incline us to approach cautiously, remembering what St. Paul said about philosophy, what Pascal said about the philosophers' god, and what Karl Barth said about the danger of a logicizing theology beginning in a general doctrine of being. Once again, this is not to say that such a theology is invariably wrong, but to note with appropriate emphasis its proclivity to wander from its allegiance to revelation back to its natal fields in which it again takes up an independent and only selectively Christian life of its own. It is these very fields in which we see so many Catholic theologians and philosophers, joining the liberal Protestants, at play since Vatican II. What has put them there seems less a Protestantizing aberration than a perennial aspect of the Catholic theological mind.

In the case of the ordination of women to the pastoral offices, upon which I began this train of thought, I spoke in my *Touchstone* article of a compelling scriptural logic upon which the institution could be based. It is essentially Marian— and *could* become Roman Catholic, if a theological idea, following popular sentiment, overcomes revelation—something we think we have seen happen in Catholicism before. If Mary, a woman, can be reckoned the minister of Christ par excellence, then counterarguments concerning iconic representation and divinely established male hierarchies can claim no inherent superiority over Marian arguments for priestesses. The decision as to whether to make women ministers of pulpit and altar could, with equal logic—logic with an apparent basis in scriptural revelation—go either way. There have been parallel cases, such as the question of whether Gentiles should be evangelized and admitted to the Church, and if so, on what terms.

What is needed in these cases is not a series of deductions based on general principles, even if the principles are drawn from Scripture (which indeed is what it seems we must sometimes settle for, but with which we should not be satisfied), but a word from God to settle the mind of the Church, a revelation to decide between contending arguments. In the case of Gentile accession, the required particulars were given to Peter at Joppa and to the apostles and elders at Jerusalem. With regard to the place of women in the Church, much has been given through Paul, and attempts to change the Church's understanding of what he meant or what it means for the rest of us, have shown themselves deeply suspect by being unable to alter traditional interpretations apart from bizarre exegesis or the practical denial of St. Paul's apostolicity.

A Matter of Submission

A distinctively revelational theology will always be, like the centurion of Luke 7, "a man under authority," defining its own science and its ancillary philosophies by what it perceives as revealed and refusing to grant canonical authority to speculation. Comprehensive thought systems, whether those of philosophy or philosophical theology, invariably have at their bases an idea, and by this we mean not merely a thought, but a thought pregnant with its logical consequences. (The Reformed philosopher Herman Dooyeweerd is particularly illuminating on how this happens.) Some of these ideas are better than others. The systematic fruit they bear when worked out will complement, recapitulate, and even explain something of what has been given in revelation. The closer the idea comes to what is Given, the more tempting it will be for the Christian thinker to adopt it as the key to knowledge—the more useful and dangerous it becomes.

The analogy of being is one of these. It can be used, on one hand, to explain to us the nature of the similarities and differences between us and our Creator, and can serve the Church as long as it is referred ultimately to, and controlled by, the doctrine of being implicit in orthodox Christology, described authoritatively in personalistic terms in Scripture and in apologetic terms in the Christological decrees of the ecumenical councils. It, however, like any philosophical ground-idea, is wild and unstable when not controlled by revelation. It can very soon seize the prerogatives of its divine mistress, leading us off into thinking that God and creation are related in ways they are not, allowing for the construction of systems of thought at variance with the revelation that mediates reality to us.

The point of revelation, which so frequently appears illogical or oppressive to those who stand outside it, is not to make the world narrow, but to show us the door to life by defining creation in terms of the Door itself, making all things lead us to God in Christ. Creatures who acknowledge themselves confined in both finitude and sin must think that the way into the life of God is something like a gate or a door, something relating to this confinement not in general but particular terms, terms that answer to the condition we are in both personally and as a race, with the power and authority to conform what *is* to itself. Christ is God occurring in the scandal of the particular, who could be prophesied confidently (since prophecy is revelation), but predicted only with the greatest caution and reserve. The story of the Magus at Bethlehem is that of the natural philosopher, the empirical scientist of being, of the abstract thinker concerned with truth, seeking the revelation before which he knows his science must bow, the uncanny place where general truth joyfully submits to the Particular from which it came.

Reprinted from Touchstone: A Journal of Ecumenical Orthodoxy, *Spring 1995, Volume 8, Number 2.*

DAVID MILLS

MEET THE LATCONS

The Trouble with Latitudinarian Conservatives

A s the Los Angeles Raiders' Napoleon McCallum planted his right leg to cut towards the line, a lineman drove down into his shin. His thigh snapped forward 90 degrees, tearing apart the tendons and vessels in his knee. He was carried to the bench, where he almost died, because bodies are made to bend, but only in certain places and only so far.

A body must bend, and bend a great deal, to move at all. An unbending body is a corpse, or about to become one. But a body that is bent too far breaks, especially when it is hit too hard, or hit in the wrong places. Even when it does not break, a body that is bent too far too often will be slower and clumsier than it should be, unable to dodge tackles or outrun pursuit, too crippled to attain the goal.

This is true also for religious bodies, and religious people. I am talking about those I call "Latitudinarian Conservatives." They are not skeptics or rationalists or unbelievers. They believe the Bible and want to be orthodox Christians. They will call themselves "biblical Christians" or even "traditionalists." They simply bend much farther than they ought, and not on any articulated principle, but in response to cultural changes and personal temptations.

"Latcon" parishes are often the largest and liveliest in their churches. They take more seriously than almost anyone biblical imperatives like evangelism and Bible study, and are often more convinced than "traditionalists" of God's presence and work today. They must be understood if the future of the church in America is to be understood, and to prevent their obvious sincerity and success from seducing traditional Christians desperate for an effective opposition to increasingly secular churches and society.

As far as I know, the distinctiveness of latitudinarian conservatism has not been recognized before. More traditional Christians dismiss them as liberals, and liberal Christians dismiss them as fundamentalists. Both are wrong, because latitudinarian conservatism is an unstable mixture of traditional Christianity and liberalism, and being unstable can very quickly become more fully one or the other.

A Latitudinarian Conservative is a Christian whose faith is for the most part traditional or conservative in form and content but held emotionally and instinctively. This faith is not exactly classical Christianity because it is undogmatic, both in being unsystematic and imprecise and in having no settled belief in the authority of inherited doctrine and practice. It is not simply liberalism because it includes belief in a definitive revelation and therefore asserts the truth of certain illiberal beliefs.

The Presence of Latcons

The largest group among the consciously biblical in the mainline churches, the Latcons produce many of the fruits of faith, and with a passion and commitment lacking in many more traditional Christians. They run soup kitchens and food banks and "ex-gay" ministries, pay for missionaries, homes for unwed mothers, and the like, go around the world to build schools or dig irrigation ditches, give up hours of their lives to tell others about the Lord. They convert people and change their lives.

And their numbers will grow, not only because the fruits of their faith are so evident, but because more and more people are searching for a supernatural religion conformable with middle-class society. This is the problem, and the reason they are worth examining. The Latcons succeed because they are orthodox and offer people a life-changing gospel, and also because they are inconsistently or rather selectively so, and offer that gospel with some of its costs removed.

Thus their theology is not completely or precisely orthodox, and to some extent their appeal depends upon their not pressing certain discomforting demands.

And even were I wrong about this, because they bend much farther than they ought, and not on any articulated principle, they will find it very difficult to hold to Christian orthodoxy in a rapidly secularizing culture, especially when certain orthodox teachings offend the self-interest of their members or the required doctrines of civil society.

Latcons can be found in every church, and I suspect become so for many different reasons. In the Episcopal Church, as far as I can tell, they are mainly cradle Episcopalians whose hearts but not minds have been strangely warmed by charismatic experiences, and converts from Rome and Evangelicalism running away from "dogmatism" or "rigidity" or a church that claims any right to tell them what to think and do. (Others, I suspect, simply found the comprehensive faith of traditional Christianity too difficult and decided to concede its most unfashionable demands.)

The charismatics did not stop after their conversions to relearn Christian doctrine but exchanged one sort of experiential theology for another. They think insisting on dogma is a retreat from renewed life in Christ or a sign of a merely intellectual religion. The converts often knew Christian doctrine but did not like particular doctrines or the idea of a settled and binding doctrine. They think insisting on dogma is a restraint on their freedom in Christ or a reactionary refusal to accept new truths and insights.

These are generalizations, but not unfair ones. I am writing of circles I know, and people I often admire. I often hear charismatics repeat some version of the popular and high-minded line, "doctrine divides, but experience unites," or declare of an open heretic that "he really loves the Lord," though that heretic does not believe the Lord to be God the Son. I once attended a parish composed mostly of converts and at coffee hour they would explain their conversions by saying, "The Episcopal Church doesn't tell you what to believe," or "The Episcopal Church lets you think for yourself," or "The Episcopal Church is so open," or tell stories of how closed and narrow, how simply unaffirming and life-denying, was their fundamentalist or Roman Catholic upbringing.

Of the two, the charismatics are the easier to reclaim for classical, dogmatic Christianity. They are moving toward something, and something good, and can sometimes be brought to see that traditional doctrine expresses and guards the good thing they have found. The converts are moving away from something itself good even if the version they knew was distorted and perverted, and can only with difficulty be made to turn around.

Latcons, Doctrine & Tradition

Latcons are not doctrinal liberals. They do hold most orthodox doctrines, but the problem is that they do not hold them doctrinally. What doctrines they hold are mostly instinctive or retained from their past, and thus tend to be lost if their lives or culture changes. They hold quite strongly to the "authority" of Scripture, but will not call it inerrant or infallible. They dislike exegetical sermons, particularly those on the theological subtleties of St. Paul or the doctrinal demands of all the New Testament writers, and prefer devotional sermons from the sunnier parts of the Gospels.

They rarely have any theological system, so that at one moment, they speak the language of therapy or community or inclusivity, and the next, the language of fundamentalism. Being instinctive and unsystematic, their doctrine tends at some times to turn into a form of moralism, at least about sexuality, or rather sexualities to which they are not themselves tempted, and at other times into a kind of therapeutic antinomianism in which an avuncular God helps people find happiness and contentment on their own terms.

A Latcon will bring out Romans 1 against homosexuals, but five seconds later speak glowingly of change and growth and renewal—and sometimes the guidance of the Holy Spirit—to justify multiple marriages. They will insist that homosexuals must be celibate, and that God will help them be so, but also that we must be "pastoral" and accommodate the needs of divorced heterosexual people. I have never yet succeeded in convincing one of them that he had contradicted himself, I think because he feels good about appealing to the Bible, and feels equally good about appealing to growth and pastoral compassion.

Though hostile to homosexuality, they support "women in ministry" (as they put it, revealingly), have only a loose marital discipline, and sometimes treat the Bible as a sort of divinely inspired self-help manual for those with low self-esteem or a low self-image or any of the self-regarding maladies of the bourgeoisie. They like to speak to people "where they are" without saying too loudly or insistently where God would like them to be.

They assert very strongly what they call "the core" or "the essentials" of the gospel, but act as if these can be separated from the other teachings of the New Testament. These essentials are mainly the biblical statements and ideas bearing most obviously upon salvation. By this I do not mean that they hold to the traditional Western belief in diversity in *adiaphora* or "things indifferent," of variety in the ways the New Testament revelation can be expressed.

What they mean is there are not only essential biblical teachings a Christian must hold, but also a number of teachings that some Christians believe biblical, and that in fact might very well be biblical, but may not be held, or may be set aside for the moment when the "essentials" are being challenged. The obvious example is women's ordination, which they will usually admit seems to be against the biblical revelation, but is, they say, a secondary issue compared to the more pressing issue of the divinity of Christ.

Thus, of dogma they have little, and of a submission to the mind of the Church they have almost none. The result is that the theology of the self-consciously "biblical" wing of the mainline churches is increasingly an acculturated, mobile conservatism, with no fixed principles or boundaries, and only the vaguest and most flexible respect for the Tradition of the Church, or even the confessions of their own churches. It is culturally selective in what it chooses to conserve and easily blown about by winds of doctrine, at least those that blow in the suburbs.

A comparison with the classically orthodox will show the effect of the Latcon's latitudinarianism upon his witness. Though he shares many commitments with the classically orthodox, the Latcon does not share their "dogmatism" or their submission to the mind of the Church, and finds reasons to accept what has usually been held intolerable, or at least to avoid taking a position.

The classically orthodox Christian accepts not only the orthodox doctrines but also the negations they require, and believes himself bound by the Great Tradition. The other, the Latcon, is happy to be orthodox as long as that will not earn him the label "fundamentalist." He respects the Tradition as a sort of wiser uncle, to be listened to, certainly, but being somewhat old-fashioned and set in his ways, not necessarily to be followed.

His approach to abortion shows how the Latcon defines being orthodox. He is happy to be "pro-life" as long as he does not have to be publicly anti-abortion. He will help women with difficult pregnancies, but will rarely say from the pulpit that aborting a child is a sin. Those who say so, no matter how gently, he will tend to call "strident" and be careful not to be seen in their company.

The question of women's ordination shows how Latcons treat the Tradition. It in particular is a problem for them. Not only does tradition insist on certain now unfashionable practices, but on some issues on which Latcons desire latitude, it is not as malleable as biblical texts taken by themselves. The Tradition says, "Scripture prohibits the ordination of women," but Scripture never says explicitly, "Women shall not be priests," and therefore can be manipulated into allowing the innovation.

The Latcon will say how important tradition is, but is never clear how authoritative or binding it is. He will declare our need for roots and the wisdom of the past, and the importance of history in forming our communal identity, but will not reject a position merely because it violates the consensus of Christians since the beginning. At this point, he will usually take his stand upon the Bible alone, with perhaps a nod to "our developing understanding" or its "new answers to new problems" or his experience of the innovation being proposed.

He is eager to support the "ministry of women," and will downgrade the Tradition by pointing to the effects of the clericalism and chauvinism of the past. He will often just say that he does not have a problem with it, and invoke the names of talented women priests he has known. He might grant that the weight of the New Testament seems to be against the innovation, but will treat the ambiguities in the New Testament as allowing it.

Postmodern Conservatives

Not surprisingly, a more sophisticated version of latitudinarian conservatism is to be found among academic Christians. These I call "Postmodern Conservatives." By this I mean people, generally academics and well-read clergy, who are for the most part traditionally orthodox in private belief but speak the relativist, postmodern language of the academy and try very hard to avoid being labeled "fundamentalist" or "traditionalist." As with the Latcons, belief in the headship of women and a laxity in marital discipline are their usual concessions to liberalism.

They often favor something called "dynamic orthodoxy," though without defining it. (The intended sneer at the traditionally orthodox is obvious.) They do not mean the truth lived out with power, nor a changing truth, nor changing expressions of truth, but something that is not traditional orthodoxy but is not liberalism either.

They tend to treat the Bible as a story, for example, and to talk much about "narrativity" and "canonical reading" and "the whole of the biblical witness." Against conservatives, they will denounce "proof-texting" and "literalism," and argue that some inherited beliefs—male headship—are actually culturally conditioned and do not express the Bible's real teaching. Against liberalism, they will stress the biblical narrative and the historic interpretation as establishing our identity as Christians, as being "our community's common memory."

In either case, what is avoided is the question of whether the Bible conveys binding propositional truth, and how that truth is to be known—whether, for example, the Great Tradition is to be trusted even when it contradicts contemporary convictions. A Postmodern Conservative will rarely, if ever, say, "St. Paul said" to settle a question.

Postmodern Conservatives tend to accept the protocol of academic discourse, in which one may not hold a question to be settled. They like to say that they "might be wrong" about moral teaching, without giving their grounds for assuming they might be wrong about that but not about the Resurrection, to which they hold firmly.

Some of this is obviously posturing, but it is worrisome posturing, because they concede the possibility of error on the point they are actually challenged by the culture and hold to the Tradition on a point the culture does not care about. In our culture, one may believe in the Resurrection because that is religion, and thus a private matter, but one is not supposed to hold that homosexuality is wicked, because that is morality, and thus a public matter, on which you must not "impose your personal beliefs."

The Effects & Our Rebellion

In either version, latitudinarian conservatism has four effects on those who choose it. First, it weakens their witness to the gospel, which converts and changes people because it comes as a word—a definitive, unbreakable, and eternal word—from the Lord. The effect of their doctrinal vagueness is to make the gospel a subject for negotiation, in effect to offer God fidelity to most of his demands in exchange for freedom from others.

Second, Latcons fail to speak the word their churches and our society need to hear. Perhaps it would be fairer to say they do not speak the exact word we need to hear, though one that is still offensive enough—heaven knows enough people reject even their gospel—to seem complete. It is good, but not enough, to tell men to be faithful to their wives; they must also be told to take authority. Many men today find chastity easier than headship, I think because chastity requires only control, but headship requires action and sacrifice. But if St. Paul is right, a man is not fully or truly a husband unless he is the head of his wife, as Christ is the head of the Church.

Latcons do much good, certainly. But I wonder how much of the good they do reflects not the power of the gospel to change lives, but the suburban habit of volunteering and the effects of natural kindness and friendship upon hurt and lost people. And I also wonder how much bad they do inadvertently, by allowing so much latitude: How many marriages would they save, for example, if they held to a stricter standard and expressed the principle of male headship in their worship?

Third, they cannot effectively resist the liberalization of their churches. This is especially true because most liberals—with the exception of such sixties tradition-alists as the bishop of Newark, who still use the "prophetic" rhetoric of the past—have now mastered the language of Evangelicalism, and speak easily of "mission" and "spirituality" and "evangelism." In battle, Latcons have no fixed home to de-fend, and in fact are sometimes not even sure there is an enemy to fight.

Because their faith is mainly instinctive and emotional, they are easily fooled by those whose instincts and emotions seem the same. Liberalism almost always makes a plausible case for laudable ends—equality or reconciliation or unity or mission. Its errors lie in the way it defines these words and in the way it defends them, which is to say in its doctrine. Thus Latcons, with their unsettled attitude to dogma and tradition, cannot easily see the errors, and therefore tend to accept the sentiment.

And fourth, the practice of latitudinarian conservatism easily leads to the prac-tice of unqualified latitudinarianism, when the culture changes or they are tempted personally. The Latcons have partly let go of a binding revelation and an authorita-tive interpretive tradition. In a rapidly secularizing culture, how long can they remain even Latitudinarian Conservatives without these? Without a fixed doc-trine, they can easily come to conserve the bad, even the wicked.

Some will recognize the inconsistency of their position and convert to a more thoroughly biblical view, but the rest, I think, may continue a long time in their latitudinarianism, because they can bend a very long way without realizing they are bending. They are able to accept almost any doctrinal innovation, and nearly any moral innovation, while continuing to talk about "a personal relationship with Jesus Christ." The problem, of course, is that they mean a relationship with

Jesus that does not require faithfulness to the words of those he authorized to speak for him, and that is not guarded by the consensus of the wise and godly people after them.

It seems wrong to argue against people whose lives and ministries have borne such fruit. Because of them, men are raising families and telling strangers about Jesus Christ and leading Bible studies—men who once sodomized other men several times a night or drank themselves into a rage and beat their wives or lived only to make money. You can't, it is said, with some biblical precedent, argue with success.

But of course you can, and often must. Strait is the gate, and few there be that find it. The details of the biblical revelation matter, all of them, and no latitude is given us to reject or ignore what God has revealed. We are asked to get right even the finest details, and believe and practice even the smallest doctrine. The doctrine has been well articulated, and there is no excuse for bending farther than we are allowed to bend.

We are also warned in Scripture that what we have gained—the personal and corporate successes, which are real and cannot be denied—we may yet throw away. The sodomite might return to his sodomy, the wife-beater go back to beating his wife, the robber baron once more plot to rob the poor. For the want of a nail, goes the nursery rhyme, a kingdom was lost. For the want of a doctrine a soul or a church may be lost.

As readers may already have realized, we are all, with the exception of the occasional saint, Latitudinarian Conservatives. The very doctrines we find most offensive, the doctrines on which we would like the most latitude, are often the truths against which we still rebel. Latitudinarian conservatism allows us to continue in rebellion while telling ourselves that we are good and faithful servants. It lets us bend our bodies into the shape necessary for hell while thinking that we are very good—very moral and very orthodox—people indeed.

Reprinted from Touchstone: A Journal of Ecumenical Orthodoxy, *Winter 1996, Volume 9, Number 1.*

DAVID MILLS

EVADING THE CREED

*The Various Attacks on the Faith
of the Church & Why They Fail*

NOT ONLY THE VARIOUS CLAIMS in the Christian Creed, but also
the authority of the Creed is under attack, and at high levels. The
direct assaults upon orthodox Christianity by would-be heresiarchs
receive all the attention, but a greater threat to the faith has gone more or less
unnoticed. This threat is the popular attempt to keep the Creed in a place of
authority while draining its meaning and drastically reducing its effect on the life
of the Church. It dissolves the hold of the Creed upon the minds and allegiance of
the faithful by reinterpreting its plain and obvious and hitherto accepted meaning
and by changing its place in the Church's life. It does not discard the Creed but
evades it.

I will take examples only from my own church, the Anglican Communion,
but the phenomenon is one with which any member of a major church, with the
temporary exception of Orthodoxy, will be familiar. By "Creed," I mean not only
the authoritative creeds established by church councils and the dependent doctrines that follow from the creeds and are usually included in the fundamentals or
essentials of the faith, but also the creedal or dogmatic mind that knows doctrinal
precision to be necessary to the faithful Christian life. In this sense, a fundamentalist who does not even know the Apostles' Creed may be a creedal Christian, and an

Anglican archbishop or a Roman cardinal deeply learned in the subtleties of theology may not be. By "the Creed" I mean the historic creeds themselves.

In the major churches of Western society, belief in the Creed is, speaking precisely, uncharacteristic. It does not characterize them, it is no longer a mark of their lives. This odd attitude to the Creed is not something found in the growing churches of Africa or in the churches that have heroically resisted Communist regimes. They understand that the power of the gospel to convert and sustain rests upon the truth of its doctrines. Christians faced with vigorous Islamic movements have complained that the writings of modernist Anglicans like the bishop of Durham are used by Muslim evangelists to devastating effect. They know what heresy does, and are not inclined to dilute the Creed of their salvation.

The Creed is evaded commonly or typically in four ways. The most popular and subtlest attempts to transcend the creeds, to go beyond and behind them to find their real meaning. The second puts the Church's institutional interests over the truths of the Creed, by treating the historic creeds as temporary expressions of the community's self-understanding. The third claims that we simply don't know enough to have an authoritative creed or, alternatively, that the truth is ever beyond our grasp. And the fourth claims that the Creed is all right as far as it goes, but that it needs enriching or expanding to satisfy new needs or conform with new insights.

These methods complement one another and are frequently combined, and anyone who holds one is likely to hold them all. Someone who believes that we do not know enough to have an authoritative creed (the third method) will almost certainly want to reinterpret the Creed as it stands (the first method), while adding new and more congenial teachings (the fourth method), and while retaining some sort of continuity with his tradition by stressing his primary commitment to his Church (the second method).

The "Real Meaning" of the Creed

Perhaps the best example of the first method of evasion in Anglicanism is the influential theology of the Reverend Dr. John Macquarrie, until recently the Lady Margaret Professor of Divinity at Oxford University. His *Principles of Christian Theology*, written in the 1960s when he was a Presbyterian disciple of Heidegger and slightly revised after he became an Anglican, is the standard theological text in many if not most Episcopal seminaries.

Of the creeds themselves, he seems to have a high opinion. Rejecting them "cannot take place in Christian theology," he writes at one point, and later that "they set forth the authentic faith." He uses them as an authority against any attempt to remove Jesus entirely from history. But though he asserts their authority, he refuses to grant such authority to their historic meaning. Though "the modern theologian cannot turn his back on creedal symbols that have become elements in the community's identity," he could not

> simply repeat these unaltered. This would be quite unintelligent deference to tradition. He is not to reject symbols that declare the Church's common mind, but he must . . . penetrate behind the possibly quaint and even alien language of the dogma to the existential issues that agitated the Church at the time of the dogma's formulation, and appropriate for our own time and in our own language the essential insight which the dogma sought to express. Every interpretation, in course of time, demands a new act of interpretation.

In other words, the words of the Creed have authority because they help define the community and declare its common mind. What those words meant when they were written, however, is only authoritative insofar as it expresses the doctrine's "essential insight" in "our own language"—as judged, presumedly, by a higher authority, whom Dr. Macquarrie does not specify. Here lies the problem.

Macquarrie's method of penetrating and appropriating is to explain what every doctrine really means by turning it into a metaphor for a statement of existentialist philosophy. We can, he tells us, no longer transpose "the history of Jesus into a mythological framework where he is seen as a supernatural pre-existent being who had come down from heaven." The Incarnation "is to be understood as the union of a being with Being in the fullest and most intimate way possible." In other words, the creedal declaration that God loved us so much that he took a human body and let himself die in agony means only that Jesus showed us how to be authentically human—"to be all that you can be," as the army has advertised its own form of salvation. The biblical story of the Incarnation is only a poetic way of putting it.

The present bishop of Durham, in his straightforward way, has put this more bluntly. "The older I get," he said in a videotape he produced for his diocese, ". . . I find I am not really interested much either way in the Virgin Birth—is it true, is it literal—but only what does it stand for." He added, perhaps in mitigation: "As I get older I seem to believe less and less, and yet to believe what I do believe more and more."

Another, less philosophically sophisticated version of going behind the Creed is the attempt to go beyond and behind it, not to its alleged meaning, but to Jesus himself. A recent article in *The Living Church* (a popular Episcopal weekly) said that "doctrines, by their very nature, set us apart. If we ever hope to unify Christ's church on earth, we must turn away from unifying doctrines, and turn toward the unifying love of Christ."

Community over the Creed

The second method of evading the Creed elevates the Church's existence and institutional processes over any creed it may have inherited. In 1976, the Church of England's doctrine commission could not reach sufficient agreement to make a common declaration (unlike the first Council of Nicaea, which had 33 times as many members). They decided to issue a collection of essays instead of a definitive statement. The collection's title, *Believing in the Church,* cleverly communicated the commission's emphasis on the institution; for some members, the Church was almost all they could be said to believe in. It was for many the only thing they were unwilling to bargain away.

In one essay, the then Lady Margaret Professor of Divinity at Cambridge, G. W. H. Lampe, declared that "unity in the future will be a unity in asking questions rather than agreeing to answers" (a claim criticized by Dr. Macquarrie, of all people). The chairman of the commission, the bishop of Winchester, John V. Taylor, added that "believing is mainly belonging." The archbishop of Canterbury, knowing the beginning of an unending controversy when he saw it, dissolved the commission.

The presiding bishop of the Episcopal Church (U.S.A.), in his opening sermon to the 1988 General Convention, announced that "the process of our decision making has taught us that we often arrive not at the ultimate solution but at a new understanding of being in community"—a statement at odds with other parts of the sermon in which he read the obstinately orthodox out of the church. Later in the sermon he added that the convention's task was not to "solve forever" the questions of women's ordination, sexual morality, and political involvement, but "to discern God's mission for the Church." One was left to believe that being in community and the church's mission had nothing to do with discerning truth—solving a question "forever," in his characteristically prejudicial way of putting it. The Holy Spirit is not leading us into all truth, as our Lord promised, but into a different form of fellowship.

Too Humble for a Creed

The third method of evading the Creed is quite attractive in its assumption of humility. It claims either that we do not know enough to have authoritative doctrines or that truth is something we may pursue but not grasp.

In some formulations, it seems—modernists are often startlingly vague—that the creeds are not authoritative because definitive truths are unattainable. The presiding bishop recently wrote to the clergy of the church of "the progressive revelation of God in human history." The "traditions and teaching of the Church," he wrote,

> have grown, must grow, and will continue to grow because times change. . . . The truth is that what The-Church-Has-Always-Taught is that God is changing us as individuals and as a community. This is the witness of the Bible and of our Church Fathers and Mothers.

(A cruder version, characteristic of the 1960s, was the claim that "you can't put God in a box," invariably thought a rebuttal to God's self-revelation. Today feminist liturgies are defended by the similar observation that "God is greater than our categories.") There are, in other words, no settled, authoritative doctrines. The Church has not taught truth but only the inevitability of change. The only eternal truth is that there are no eternal truths.

In other formulations, it seems that the creeds are not authoritative because we are being led into ever deeper truths that somehow so supersede those before them as to invalidate them. We are said to be on a journey or pilgrimage, though apparently without a compass or a map or even a known destination. The most radical implications of this idea were drawn, predictably enough, by the bishop of Newark, John Spong, in his recent declaration that doctrines were merely "images that bind and blind us all" and that one religion was as good as another. "The challenge before Christians today," he wrote, is to find new answers and more inclusive ways to respond to God's truth in our time. Faithfulness to Christ for me means saying no to the strictly defined alternatives of yesterday's religious enterprise, even while I seek to say yes to those truths into which I believe this century is calling Christians.

In a more restrained way, the managing editor of *The Episcopalian,* then the church's semi-official newspaper, wrote that he was "alternately frightened and bored" by a group who "held the same point of view on every question." (Revealingly unlike the psalmist who, one remembers, spoke of "how good and how pleasant it is for the brethren to dwell together in unity," but then the psalmist was not a relativist.) He preferred "to think of the Church as on a pilgrimage," as of necessity do most who are agnostic about the Creed, because it seems to free them from the need to be anywhere in particular.

In their 1987 *Pastoral Letter*—ghost-written, I am told, by the bishop of Newark—the Episcopal bishops announced that God

is fashioning a Church that is willing to lay aside all claims to the possession of infallible formulations of truth. God is instead fashioning a Church that will always be open to new insights, a Church that participates in the journey into God's purpose.

To the extent this phrase has any discernible meaning, it indicates that such doctrinal certainty as has usually been expected of Christians is in fact resistance to God's leading and therefore, though they do not say so, a sin.

Adding Truths

The fourth method of evading the Creed assumes that the Creed is too limited by its origins in a primitive, hierarchical, patriarchal culture and (in the case of the Nicene Creed) by its use of Greek philosophy to be accepted as it stands. The method therefore adds truths in response to new needs, insights, and discoveries. At best the Creed is thought to be inadequate to the needs of the day, written as it was so long ago, by men who knew rather less about some things than we do. At worst it is an instrument of oppression and exploitation, serving the interests and power of those who composed it and of their descendants.

In the Episcopal Church, such an evasion supports the "inclusive language" liturgies, which assert that the fatherhood of God is a partial and by itself a misleading understanding of God, and that feminine images must be introduced to give a better picture, though these images have no basis in the Creed.

The official explanation of the new liturgies suggested that

> to introduce the simile of God as mother . . . into our liturgical repertoire, not as substitute for Father, but as a means of reminding ourselves that the attributes of divine fatherhood which we invoke are unrelated to gender or sex, is one way to attempt to manifest a more complete image of God in the liturgy. . . . It does not destroy the metaphor of the God and Father of our Lord Jesus Christ, but it gives us a fuller and more comprehensive picture, one more intimate and personal than "Creator."

Masculine "images" of God, like Father and Son, it continues, "have been historically conditioned by the patriarchal nature, not only of Jewish but also of much of Christian society." And so the names used in the Creed must be joined by others more reflective of modern realities and modern needs.

The Appeal of Evasion

These are the characteristic methods by which Episcopalians try to dissolve the authority of the Creed while keeping it in a place of authority. In one, the "real meaning" behind the metaphor of our doctrines is sought. In another, the existence of the community is made more important than its inherited beliefs. In the third, the mystery of God is held to be too great to be put into words. In the last, new and deeper truths than the Creed contains are held to be necessary for modern belief.

It is a question why these methods are so attractive. The Creed declares, after all, that the Creator of the universe is not just "Deity" or "The Force" or "the ground of our being" but our Father. And further, that when we spat in his face, our Father loved us enough to send his Son to become a man just like us, and the Son willingly died for us to save us from the inevitable and deserved results of our own rebellion. And further (blessing piled on blessing), that the Son will someday come back to bring us to be with him forever, but while we are waiting, he has left us the Holy Spirit and the Church to sustain and comfort us.

I find it hard, as have most Christians throughout the ages, to understand why this vision does not satisfy, why it does not thrill and hearten, why it is not sung as the anthem of a conquering army. Next to the Creed, the evasions do not satisfy. I do not know why anyone would ever want to replace it with philosophical abstractions, or ignore it to stay close to those who reject it, or presume to revise it as if we knew better than God what we need.

For some, these methods allow them to give proper respect to the institution that employs them and to care for their people, while preaching and teaching what they think to be the truth. In a crasser form, such as that proposed for the reinterpretation of Scripture by the feminist theologian Elisabeth Schüssler Fiorenza, the Church is too useful for political and social change to be abandoned, and so some way is needed to adapt its foundational documents to that end.

Others believe that the "real" truths of Christianity must still be promoted by changing the meanings of now misleading formulations too deeply ingrained in the Church to reject. They do not believe that Jesus was the Son of God, but they still believe that he was a very good, perhaps even unique, example of what God wants every man to become. Yet others, more radical, agree that Christianity is unique, but only for those in a particular situation. For them, Christianity is the only way Westerners raised in the Church can apprehend universal truths. Thus, an explicit rejection of Christian institutions, though perhaps logically justified, would be spiritually suicidal.

Others have effectively lost their faith but not their attachment to the ethos of Christianity. For them, *something* in Christianity is true, or at least very helpful, which would be lost entirely by a direct denial. Evading the Creed provides a way to be in the Church but not of the Church.

Finally, these methods have a strong moral attraction. To look behind the creeds is to claim a depth of insight beyond one's literalistically minded fellows. To found the Church on the community rather than its doctrines is to claim a concern for peace and brotherhood beyond one's dogmatic fellows. To stop speechless before the mystery of God is to claim a humility beyond one's presumptuous fellows. To add new doctrines is to claim a sensitivity to history and present needs beyond one's reactionary fellows. We should not minimize the attraction of such easily acquired sanctity.

Though each attempt to maintain the authority of the creeds while rejecting their historic meaning fails logically rather badly (about which, more below), the methods can be applied successfully and with an orthodox intent. It is true that a change of vocabulary or emphasis or philosophy (the first method) can illuminate doctrines. It is true that belonging to a community (the second method) is in some ways prior to accepting its beliefs, and that controversies are resolved more successfully within the community than without. It is true that we see in a glass darkly (the third method) and that our limitations and sinfulness need to be remembered when we speak of things eternal. It is true that the Creed does not contain every truth necessary to the faithful Christian life (the fourth method). But in practice, the popular methods of evading the authority of the Creed push things too far. They apply these truths as governing principles—if not as final judgments upon the Creed—and not as limited insights which may aid our understanding.

Most importantly, their advocates lack that respect for the Tradition and for inherited wisdom required of Christians. They too quickly reject the possibility that, unlikely as it may seem to them, the original meanings of the Christian doctrines and Creed may be true and irreplaceable. They do not consider that something essential may be lost by reducing the authority of their rather straightforward and plain intent. As Chesterton said somewhere, a Catholic is someone who knows that something else is smarter than he is. Beyond the lack of a proper Christian humility toward the inherited wisdom, however, each alternative to creedal orthodoxy proves unsatisfactory on logical grounds.

The Failure of the Attack

The first evasion of creedal authority, the attempt to find its alleged meaning, fails in a number of ways. First, it leaves unanswered the crucial question of what gives authority to any particular proposal for its real meaning. The original meaning was at least defined by an authoritative church council and supported by a consensus of the faithful and intelligent since then. The proposed real meaning has only the authority of a clever theologian, or at most the general assent of a large number of educated Christians in one culture at one time. Macquarrie's vocabulary of "Being" is of limited popular appeal, as tested by the difficulty one would have in preaching from it.

A second problem is that a historical event proclaimed in the creeds does not "stand for" anything, as the bishop of Durham supposes. If it actually happened, it "stands for" itself, and any further meaning is dependent upon its reality. As a New Testament scholar, Bishop Donald Parsons, said to me: "The trouble with Bultmann is that he thought Jesus carried a message, when the New Testament tells us he *was* the message." The bishop of Durham presumably means by "What does it stand for?"—"What does it tell us about God?" But it only reliably tells us anything about God if it is true and "literal."

A third problem is most apparent in the less sophisticated version, which calls us to go behind the creeds to our Lord himself. One can't go to Jesus without having some substantive idea of who he is. "The unifying love of Christ" that the writer I quoted demands supposes a developed doctrine of Christ, which, to be effective, must be the unifying doctrine the author was trying to avoid. Once one has a doctrine of Christ, a host of other doctrines support and follow from the central doctrine, at which point controversy becomes inevitable.

Finally, it is questionable whether such reinterpretation is even needed. Very little of the Nicene Creed can plausibly be said to be in "alien language." Even a phrase such as "of one substance with the Father" is not all that difficult to explain. The heart of the Creed declares realities—some supernatural realities, certainly, but realities nevertheless—that are either true or false. They can be adequately understood by the least educated believer.

The "average man," who is, after all, the intended beneficiary of this reinterpretation, doesn't find the Virgin Birth incomprehensible even when he does not believe it. He knows that if God created the universe, he could cause a woman to become pregnant without a human father. Of the entire project of reinterpretation, one has to ask: Was it really necessary? Did it help anyone to believe? The evidence suggests that, in its radical form, as with Macquarrie and Bultmann, it did not. Quite to the contrary.

The response of the average man is to reject either the new interpretation or the Creed itself. To keep the Creed while draining it of meaning is the sort of compromise that would only appeal to people tied personally or financially to the historic institution while harboring grave doubts about its historic beliefs. If the Creed is only a collection of "symbols that have become elements in the community's identity," as Dr. Macquarrie believes, then the average man will ignore it. He won't believe more, he will believe less.

The second method of evading creedal authority, the attempt to elevate the community above its inherited beliefs, also fails. First, if a doctrine is true, it is true, whatever effect it has on the community, as a theological relativist like the bishop of Durham believes when he demands the immediate ordination of women, whatever the effect it will have on the community. "Believing is mainly belonging" is an utterly impractical doctrine. It does not work out that way. On the contrary, men are so created that they put truth before community.

Its advocates confuse community of faith with its institutional expression. The former depends for survival upon a general agreement in belief, the latter does not, or does so to a much smaller degree. The Church of England, and to a slightly lesser extent the Episcopal Church, is not a single institution but a collection of almost completely discrete communities, divided from one another by questions of belief and doctrine. It would be a mistake to base an approach to the Creed upon one of the world's more eccentric religious bodies.

In his convention sermon, the presiding bishop tried to avoid this problem by announcing that we have discovered "a new understanding of being in community." But an enduring, stable, healthy community not characterized by agreement in belief is a thing not elsewhere known to anthropologists and historians. A "community" without shared beliefs does not work, however, because it can't possibly decide what to do—and even if it did in some way work, it would not be a church. Perhaps sensing this problem, the presiding bishop announced that though we couldn't find reliable answers on fundamental questions, we nevertheless could discern God's will for us.

The third method, the declaration that we do not have or cannot grasp eternal truths, denies the experience of the truths of the Creed, attested by too many witnesses to be disbelieved so easily. It is a dogmatic atheism, whose advocates do not, as far as I have seen, make an adequate argument for it. If we cannot "put God in a box," God can certainly box himself—and, of course, it is a fundamental Christian claim that he has done so, in the Incarnate Body of his Son.

It also unfairly stresses one side of the tension in which men live. Christians since St. Paul have understood that God is greater than us yet has given us some necessary truths; we see in a glass darkly, but we still *see* in a glass darkly. Other than a dogmatic rejection of revelation and a dogmatic acceptance of historical relativism, there is no reason to believe that historic doctrines are only "images that bind and blind us all." We must choose between dogmas. And one can make a rather stronger argument, simply on the grounds of historical success, for the orthodox dogma.

The fourth method, that new truths must be added to the Creed, is no more successful than the others. Like the third method, it denies truths attested by far more reliable judges than the leadership of several rapidly shrinking mainline churches in the late twentieth century.

Like the first method, it lacks any authority for its additions and any real evidence that they are needed, beyond the cries of a small but effective political lobby, nor has it any evidence that it will heal wounded men and women as well as the Christianity of the Creed. As even some feminists have argued, replacing God the Father with an androgynous or feminine deity or with impersonal titles like "Creator" will not heal women hurt by men, but only leave them trapped in their pain. To be healed, they must be brought to the Father himself, to find what real men are supposed to be like.

The End of Evasion

This concludes a brief tour of the ways in which some modern Christians try to avoid the truth and authority of the Creed that billions of Christians before them have believed and for the truth of which countless martyrs have given their lives.

Whatever the apologetic intentions of their advocates and their temporary success in keeping some within the institutional church, these methods of evasion can work, or seem to work, only for a short time. When the Creed's meaning is drained and replaced with something more to contemporary tastes, it will inevitably disappear, even as a mere memorial of the community's history. The methods of evasion are thus only rest stations on the way to a fully acknowledged unbelief—and, therefore (for men cannot live without doctrines and dogmas), to the adoption of a more worldly and less demanding creed. If, as orthodox Christians believe, the Creed proclaims the truths of our salvation from sin and damnation, such evasions are profoundly inhuman and cruel.

Reprinted from Touchstone: A Journal of Ecumenical Orthodoxy, *Summer 1990, Volume 4, Number 1.*

PAUL V. MANKOWSKI

A FIG LEAF FOR
THE CREED

"Inclusive Language" Comes to Mass

CONSIDER, IF YOU WILL, the sad but instructive case of Brother Paulinus Riordan of the Society of Jesus. In the late forties and fifties, Br. Riordan worked in the library of the novitiate of one of the midwestern Jesuit provinces. He could often be seen of a morning, so I've been told, sitting at his desk with a pair of scissors, a pot of glue, several sheets of thick colored paper, and a magnifying glass. His goal—that is, the Final Cause of his efforts—was to help preserve the purity of Jesuit novices, an entirely honorable task. His means consisted of snipping tiny bikini bras and panties out of the paper and carefully pasting them in position over the photographs of tribal women that appeared in *National Geographic* magazine, so that no unwary reader be led astray into unchastity. For the fact of the matter is that, though his work was known and approved by his superiors, Br. Riordan was insane.

Let us turn then to a more contemporary setting: the National Conference of Catholic Bishops. In a memorandum distributed to bishops last summer by the chairman of the Bishops' Committee on Liturgy, the recipients were asked to consider and vote on nine alternative translations of a line in the Nicene Creed. The phrase deemed defective, *Et homo factus est,* is currently rendered "and [he] became man." The options listed were these:

1. and became truly human
2. and became a human
3. and became a human being
4. and became one in Being with us
5. and became of one Being with us
6. and took our human nature
7. and assumed our human nature
8. and assumed our humanity
9. and became one of us

What we have here, I shall argue, is the spectacle of roughly 300 grown men with scissors and paste, clumsily trying to install a kind of fig leaf over something they consider unseemly in the Nicene Creed: an occasion of sin—not impurity, in this instance, but injustice. What they believe they have found in the text, what they find an affront and a scandal, is of course "gender-exclusive" language. I intend to demonstrate that their scruples, though as well-intentioned as those of Br. Riordan, are no less beside the point.

The Fallacy of Inclusive Language

There is *no such thing as exclusive language.* It is undeniably true that one can use speech to urge the consideration that women should be excluded from this or that enterprise, just as one can use speech to demean tomatoes or to insinuate that baritones should have no active role in the social order. But the language in and through which these injustices are advanced can of itself be no more gender-exclusive than it can be tomatophobic or soprano-centric. The concept of inclusivity (as its partisans would have us understand it) is a phantasm, a category mistake, a chimera buzzing in a vacuum. Exclusion and inclusion have a political valence, but not a linguistic one, and the attempt to pretend otherwise is itself a politically motivated fraud.

If a set A is so treated that subset B is distinguished within it, the label or name given to A will have two meanings (or two uses): first, the general or universal meaning, and second, that of all non-B members of A. Linguists refer to the use of B as "marked" and that of A as "un-marked." For example, if next to the word *pig* we introduce the word *piglet, piglet* is marked (for size) and *pig* is the unmarked form. Because it is unmarked, *pig* has (along the axis) two meanings: pig *in se,* and adult pig. In the sentence "I have one pig and eight piglets" the word *pig* means the adult; in the sentence, "I bought three goats and six pigs" we cannot know how many adults and how many piglets made up the purchase. The second example is not an instance of exclusive language; no potential piglet is left out of the discourse; *pig* is simply unmarked for size.

Gender contrasts are treated linguistically the same way. When a form marked for gender is introduced, its correlative assumes two uses: the gender alternate to the marked form, and the usage non-specific as to gender (not the same as neuter). Thus we have *poetess,* which is marked for gender, next to *poet,* unmarked. It is important to stress that the marked/unmarked distinction is entirely independent of the sex or social status of the speaker and even of the surface grammar of the language. We find the feminine as the marked form in languages whose only adult speakers are women. The feminine appears as the marked form in Sumerian, the oldest of all written languages, which has no grammatical gender whatsoever; yet we have unmarked *dumu,* son or child, versus marked *dumu-munus,* daughter.

The point of all the foregoing pedantry is this: Regardless of the language, regardless of the speaker, regardless of the pertinent semantic axis, the marked/ unmarked contrast is ineradicable. To stigmatize one particular operation of this contrast as sexist is as pointless as damning the distinction between odd and even numbers as elitist.

The usage that the U.S. bishops apparently wish to stigmatize is the word *man* employed generically, on the grounds that the generic sense has been lost in contemporary English and hearers today do not feel that women have been included by the use of the term. But of course *man* is unmarked not only for gender but also for a theoretically infinite number of qualifications. Consider this sentence: "The men and officers of the second battalion will return to winter quarters on Monday." Here the word *man* is being used exclusively (i.e., non-generically), but it means, of course, not "non-females" but "non-officers." The word *man* is not only unmarked for gender but also unmarked for military rank. Accordingly, in different sentences it can serve the broader or the narrower function, usually without ambiguity. There are, of course, certain linguistic situations in which it may be difficult to tell which use is intended. For example, in a pub you overhear a stranger say, "Jack's a man in my regiment." Does he mean man/non-officer or generic man? A speaker of even modest skill can ordinarily indicate his meaning clearly.

Now suppose for a moment you're serving as a military chaplain somewhere and have just conducted a Mass in which you recited the Nicene Creed according to the conventional translation. How would you deal with a red-eyed infantry colonel who buttonholes you in the sacristy and complains in a trembling voice that he feels the words, "For us men and for our salvation he came down from heaven," exclude officers from the ambit of divine salvific activity? If you have bought into the standard inclusive-language mindset, you're in a tough bind, for according to the mindset, it is the listener's subjective impressions that take precedence over standard usage and over the intentions of the speaker. So if you refuse to change the creed to read, "for us men and officers he came down from heaven," you're at a complete loss to explain your previous concessions to feminist critics. And if you do make the requested change, you're incapable of refusing with rational consistency the next madman who feels himself excluded by your language.

I want to stress that the jaws of this logical vice are formed not by contemporary social realities but by the nature of language itself. Thus, for every exclusivist usage the Thought Police successfully manage to stigmatize, another seven will spontaneously appear in its stead. For example, the U.S. bishops issued a statement which read in part, "the Word of God proclaimed to all nations is by nature inclusive, that is, addressed to all peoples, men and women." Yet by their own reasoning, "men and women" won't quite do. For it could be seen to exclude children and hermaphrodites, who are of themselves entirely human, in need of redemption and addressees of the Word. Yet even the correction, "men, women, children and those of indeterminate gender" will still leave our colonel sniffling in the narthex, and babies-yet-to-be-born certainly belong to "all the nations," but fit into none of the listed categories. Notice: This proliferation is stark nonsense, but the only objection that can be tendered by the champions of inclusive language— viz., that the unmarked locution includes the various marked forms—is one that undercuts their own argument. Either way their project fails; the dilemma is fatal.

The claim is sometimes made that the imposition of inclusive language is justified by the fact that language changes over time; words change their meanings,

and the proposed diction is simply a tardy recognition of what has already occurred. Well, it is true that the semantic range of a given word is susceptible of
change, and it is true that words referring to males and females are as susceptible as
any other, and it is true that marked/unmarked contrasts are sometimes redistrib-
uted. Thus, there is no reason why the particular word *man* could not become a
form marked for gender in the future. Yet this only points up the futility of per-
forming the kind of invasive surgery on living language that is demanded by the
inclusivist project. (This demand is hard to understand on its own terms; why so
much effort to direct us where we can't help going? A surgeon might alter a child's
arm so that it attained its adult length, but we would hardly call the process growth.)
As new words and new applications continue to be dumped into the active lexicon
of a language, they will continue to bud and fructify according to laws of linguistic
nature, not according to the strictures of political sensibility. You can see this on
any playground; and even in places where political gender-awareness has reached
its highest pitch, even in the U.S. divinity schools, a dyed-in-the-wool feminist
will run into a room full of women, or women and men, and say, "D'you guys
want to order out for a pizza?" The unmarked form can no more be pruned from
language than can semantic change itself.

A Linguistic Taboo

At this point in my argument someone may object, "I'm not impressed with
linguistic reasoning on this matter. Whatever you say, I know I feel differently now
when I hear the word *man* used generically than I did 15 years ago, and I think most
people of similar background share the same feeling." Now this curious feeling that
surrounds certain words is indeed widely shared; but it does not reflect a change
in language strictly speaking. Rather it reflects the operation of a supra-linguistic
phenomenon called a taboo. For reasons of religion, superstition, etiquette, and of
course politics, certain locutions are stigmatized in certain societies as unpro-
nounceable or unacceptable. Sometimes they are banned entirely; sometimes they
are excluded from certain levels of discourse. The word *left* in many cultures,
various common words for bodily and sexual functions, words referring to hell and
damnation—all are examples of natural language utterances placed under taboo.
On the political level, one of the clearest examples has been given by the sociologist
Peter Berger, who said:

My mother was from Italy and my father was Austrian. As a child I spent a lot of time in Italy. This was in the 1930s, when Italy was of course under Mussolini. Sometime during that period, I forget which year it was, Mussolini made a speech in which he called for a reform of the Italian language. In modern Italian—as in most Western languages, with the interesting exception of English—there are two forms of address, depending on whether you are talking to an intimate or to a stranger. For example, *tu* and *usted* are used in Spanish. In modern Italian *tu* is the intimate form of address, *lei* is the formal address. *Lei* happens to be the third person [feminine singular]. I do not know the history of this, but it has been a pattern of modern Italian for, I would imagine, some two hundred years. No one paid any attention to this. Even as a child, I knew what one said in Italian. It meant nothing.

But Mussolini made a speech in which he said that the use of *lei* is a sign of effeminacy, a degenerate way of speaking Italian. Since the purpose of the Fascist Revolution was to restore Roman virility to the Italian people, the good Fascist did not say *lei*; the good Fascist said *voi*—from the Latin *vos*—which is the second person plural. From that point on, everyone who used *lei* or *voi* was conscious of being engaged in a political act.

Now, in terms of the empirical facts of the Italian language, what Mussolini said was nonsense. But the effect of that speech meant an awful lot, and it was intended to mean an awful lot. Because from that moment on, every time you said *lei* in Italy you were making an anti-Fascist gesture, consciously or unconsciously— and people made you conscious of it if you were unconscious. And every time you said *voi* you were making the linguistic equivalent of the Fascist salute.

The "funny feeling" which we associate with generic *man* and with other instances of inclusive language is the same twinge of uneasiness that second-person *lei* would have prompted in Fascist Italy. The feeling is not a natural response but a conditioned response to the stimulus. We feel it because we have been coached to feel it. We feel it because, like rats repeatedly given a jolt of electric current when they move in a particular way, we have become aware of potential unpleasantness accompanying certain behavior. That is how a taboo works. The Italian who used stigmatized *lei* risked Fascist anger; the English speaker who uses stigmatized *man* risks feminist wrath, but the phenomenon is identical. The converse is also applicable. As Berger says, the accommodationist Italian who said *voi* was giving the equivalent of a fascist salute. The accommodationist bishop in our time who uses inclusive language is making a little genuflection, a curtsy, in the direction of feminism.

Natural Linguistic Change

I have conceded the possibility that the usage of *man* could change in the future in the direction that inclusive language partisans claim that it already has. How would we know when this change has indeed occurred? Only when classes of speakers insulated from taboos or indifferent to them spontaneously employ the new usages, and when cognitive errors spontaneously begin to multiply when the older usage is maintained. For example, when unsupervised schoolchildren speaking on the playground talk about a horror movie in which a mass of protoplasm is metamorphosized into Tom Cruise and they say, "In the last scene, the Blob assumed our human nature and became of one Being with us," then we can be confident semantic change has taken place. Or when an intelligent little girl dives into a tank at Sea World and is killed, innocently believing that the posted warning "Man-Eating Shark!" did not apply to her because she was female, then we'd have a respectable linguistic case for changing our liturgical language on the grounds that the natural language substrate had shifted already. Such shifts are possible. They are not inevitable.

Perhaps the quandary in which the U.S. bishops find themselves over the translation of *homo factus est* is not so surprising after all. There is one and only one obvious and adequate translation of the phrase, and that has been excluded by taboo—at least, by those taboos the bishops have chosen to take seriously. It is to be expected that there should be nine unsatisfactory circumlocutions in uneasy contention for the job of *man*. This is our language's way of telling us that it is in the throes of a nervous breakdown. You can't forbid a language to act according to its nature and then demand that it behave normally. You can't avoid saying certain ordinary words any more than you can avoid stepping on cracks in the sidewalk and not expect the manifold enfeeblements of neurosis. If you come to believe those who tell you that your mother tongue is wicked, then you either have to find yourself a new tongue, or a new mother. Neither replacement does credit to the innovator; neither enterprise gives honor to the Church.

I confess it is somewhat embarrassing to have to argue for the naturalness of nature, just as it is embarrassing to make the case for the wholesome effects of not putting knitting needles in one's ears. But the fact is that we are being invited, indeed by our bishops, to sit at the table with Br. Riordan and his scissors and paste and—significantly!—his magnifying glass, to scrutinize with him the occasions of sin he has diligently identified for us, to acknowledge those lusts buried so deeply within us that we are unaware of their existence, and to paper over the obsceneness of places where we find no obscenity. Br. Riordan's partisans in the 1950s may have justified his zeal on the grounds that he was so much more pure than the rest of his brethren that he was proportionately more sensitive to the nuances of impurity. I doubt it. And I doubt very much that the champions of inclusive language exist on a higher plane of appreciation and respect for women than the rest of us. In fact, though my experience is obviously limited and I have no hard statistical data on the matter, my own observations suggest that extreme sensitivity to exclusivism occurs in men and women who are radically unbalanced in their ability to treat women as human beings—as opposed, say, to treating them as means to political ends. When I see self-proclaimed advocates of gender inclusivity deal with those women who vocally resist feminist-inspired changes to liturgical or other language, I do not find in their demeanor the patience, attentiveness, humor, respect, or even elementary human sympathy for the struggles of others that would count as evidence for this Higher Justice they claim to have found.

Surprised? Then try to look at it this way: Would you really want your child to have for a babysitter someone who couldn't make it through this month's *National Geographic* without whiting out the photos? Would you really want your sister to date someone who couldn't make it through the Sacramentary without whiting out the pronouns? Exactly.

In sum: Inclusive language is a fraud. It may be a pious fraud, although I am inclined to think otherwise. In neither case does it make our thought more precise; in neither case does God's love for us shine more clearly through Sacred Scripture and sacred worship. I applaud the dignity of womanhood as I applaud the virtue of chastity. Yet, as Cardinal Heenan remarked during the last Council, *"Timeo peritos et dona ferentes."* I fear the little men with magnifying glasses; I fear the hypersensitive reformer with scissors and paste; I fear the experts, even when they bear gifts.

Reprinted from Touchstone: A Journal of Ecumenical Orthodoxy, *Spring 1994, Volume 7, Number 2. This article was adapted from an early version that appeared in* Voices (February 1994), *a publication of Women for Faith and Family.*

JAMES R. EDWARDS

NEW QUEST, OLD ERRORS

*The Fallacies of the New Quest
for the Historical Jesus*

N o INSTITUTION felt the impact of the Enlightenment more than the Church and orthodox Christianity. The sources of the Church's life, particularly its Scripture and creeds, fell under the lens of secular scrutiny. The Bible was subjected to the same literary and historical theories used to judge other literature. Among the many forms this new criticism took, perhaps none was more celebrated than *The Quest for the Historical Jesus*, to quote the English title of Albert Schweitzer's monumental book (1906). His quest was to uncover the "real" Jesus, the exclusively human Jesus, beneath the layers of dogma and ritual that had accumulated over the centuries. Although Schweitzer's *Quest* came after more than a century of debate, it did not end debate. In mid-century a more modest quest resurfaced, and since the late 1980s dozens of books have appeared on Jesus, indicating that the New Quest is in full swing.

All three quests, to be sure, are controlled by the presuppositions and methods of naturalism. That is to say, only evidence "from below" is admissible, i.e., what can be known about Jesus from history, literary sources, anthropology, and reason. Evidence "from above"—for example, the faith claims of the Apostles' Creed— falls outside admissible evidence, unless such evidence can be verified apart from the authority of Church, creed, and confession.

But in other respects today's New Quest parts company from Schweitzer's eloquently chronicled quest. The original quest, a nineteenth-century European

208

(largely German) endeavor, was the product of liberal Protestantism, whereas today's late twentieth-century New Quest is dominated by North Americans and includes not only Protestants and Catholics, but also Jews, New Agers, and people of no religious commitment, including Marxists and atheists. But perhaps most importantly, the first quest was sparked by the scientific method whose hallmark was rationalism, whereas the New Quest is the child of the social sciences and particularly the ideologies of liberation and cross-cultural anthropology.

The Jesus Seminar

The most publicized forum of the New Quest is "The Jesus Seminar," a highly publicized scholarly think tank of some 50 scholars that has met twice yearly since 1985 to vote on the historical accuracy of the sayings attributed to Jesus in the Gospels. The chief result of the seminar is a new translation of the Gospels, *The Five Gospels: The Search for the Authentic Words of Jesus*.[1] The fifth Gospel in the title is the Gospel of Thomas, which was discovered in 1945. The Gospel of Thomas generally is considered by New Testament scholars to be a tendentious product of a Gnostic Christian community in existence circa A.D. 100. But it is regarded by the Jesus Seminar as a more important source for the sayings of Jesus than any of the four canonical Gospels. The "Scholars Version," as the seminar refers to its translation, shuns pious and puritanical phraseology that, in its opinion, characterizes existing Bible translations, in favor of "the common street language of the original." The results vary from occasional fresh and insightful renderings to clearly affected and even sophomoric ones.

Seminar members cast ballots on each saying attributed to Jesus in the Gospels (including Thomas). A red ballot indicates that a given statement (or something like it) was spoken by Jesus; a pink ballot, that a statement resembles something Jesus might have said; a gray ballot, that, although the ideas may be close to those of Jesus, the statement did not originate with him; and a black ballot indicates a definite negative, that the statement derived from later tradition.

What is the final result of the seminar's deliberations? Eighty-two percent of the words attributed to Jesus were not spoken by him. Only one statement in the Gospel of Mark (which generally is regarded by New Testament scholars as the earliest and most reliable Gospel) is judged by the literati of the seminar to have come from Jesus ("Give to Caesar what is Caesar's, and to God what is God's," Mark 12:17). As for the Gospel of John, "the Fellows of the Seminar were unable to find a single saying they could with certainty trace back to the historical Jesus" (*The Five Gospels*, p. 10).

The conclusions of the Jesus Seminar have been publicized widely—by the seminar itself—as having achieved a final breakthrough in the Jesus quest. It seems that the Church, particularly Evangelical Christianity, has been living in a fog of deception and ignorance that has now been dispelled by the intrepid endeavors of the Jesus Seminar.

The impression of a new breakthrough, however, is itself a deception. In reality, the seminar plies the same trade and reaches similar conclusions to those that have been reached in liberal theology for decades. The introduction to the Scholars Version, a 35-page primer in higher criticism, parrots the standard theories and methods of the New Testament guild, including the two-source and four-source hypotheses of the Synoptic Gospels, the Q-hypothesis, and the standard criteria for determining the veracity of a given statement. Among the latter are the principle of *uniqueness* (a statement with no parallel in Judaism or Hellenism cannot have derived from the latter and may go back to Jesus); the principle of *difficulty* ("hard" sayings have greater claim to authenticity since they would less likely have been fabricated by the Church); and the principle of *multiple attestation* (the more often a saying is attested to in different sources, the greater its likelihood of authenticity).

Old Bias, New Saviors

The hype about the Jesus Seminar misses the real story. What is new is not methods and results, but a bent *against* the Church and orthodox faith. Not unlike the infamous Re-Imagining Conference of 1993 at which radical feminist theology was used to mock Christian dogma, the Jesus Seminar is not engaging in objective investigation but plying a theological bias that surfaces in undisguised iconoclasm towards Church, faith, and creed.

The Church is stereotyped as a medieval instrument of inquisition and censorship. In contrast, the Scholars Version is "free of ecclesiastical and religious control" and "not bound by the dictates of church councils" (p. xviii). Like Galileo, Thomas Jefferson, and David Friedrich Strauss, to whom *The Five Gospels* is dedicated, the seminar pretentiously hails itself as a liberator "from windowless studies and the beginning of a new venture for gospel scholarship" (p. 1).

Seminar members regard themselves as a Promethean breed: "The Christ of creed and dogma . . . can no longer command the assent of those who have seen

the heavens through Galileo's telescope." The "old deities and demons," they maintain, have been swept from the skies. "The refuge offered by the cloistered precincts of faith gradually became a battered and beleaguered position," before which
"biblical scholars rose to the challenge and launched the tumultuous search for the
Jesus behind the Christian facade of the Christ" (p. 2). Affecting high destiny, the
Jesus Seminar endeavors "to break the church's stranglehold over learning" and to
free Jesus from the "tyranny," "oppression," and "blindness" of his ecclesiastical
Babylonian captivity. The Apostles' Creed, asserts the Scholars Version, "smothers
the historical Jesus" (p. 7), overlaying and overwhelming him with the heavenly
figure of later Christian conviction (p. 24). Purged of the barnacles of ritual, creed,
and dogma, Jesus has been sanitized and de-Christianized for the academy and for
public consumption. Obedient to its heroic and historic destiny, the seminar has
dispelled the age of darkness by the light of reason: The wine of myth has become
the water of reality.

The idea that Jesus and the Gospels need to be "rescued" from the Church is,
of course, profoundly incongruous, for the Gospels are the product of the Church.
The New Testament, and the Bible as a whole, is uniquely the Church's book, not
the academy's. From its inception the story of Jesus was transmitted verbally and
scripturally by Christian faith communities who regarded themselves not as fabri-
cators or deceivers but as custodians of God's redemptive work in the world.
Throughout its history the Church has defended its story against detractors—
against Celsus in the second century and now the Jesus Seminar in the twentieth.
The scholarly triumphalism of the Jesus Seminar is thus rather melodramatic, and
has been rightly criticized as such.

The state of current Gospel research is in reality far different from the liberation from oppression and conspiracy theories presented in the Scholars Version
and propagated by media appearances of Seminar members. The situation continues to be—as it has been for many decades—a debate between a more naturalistic
liberal persuasion that minimizes or eliminates the supernatural in the life and
work of Jesus, and a more conservative and Evangelical persuasion that admits of
the possibility of Jesus being God's eternal Son in human form, and which finds
substantial evidence to that effect in the various strata of the Gospels.

The most misleading (and unscholarly) aspect of the Jesus Seminar is its black-
out of any position but its own (the seminar is a club of handpicked "members
only"), leaving the impression that conservative scholarship has nothing to say to
its speculations. For more than a century a pantheon of scholars, including Schlatter,

Lightfoot, Westcott, Manson, Cranfield, Bruce, Martin, Barrett, Cullmann, Schweizer, Stuhlmacher, Hengel, Metzger, Brown, Wright, and many more, have both studied and answered the methods and conclusions of liberalism. Their work may have been sidestepped by the Jesus Seminar, but it has not been refuted.

The Alternative Jesus

Who, then, is the Jesus of the New Quest? Two members of the Jesus Seminar, Marcus Borg and John Dominic Crossan, have written three books each on Jesus in the past decade. Their anthropological approach and the resultant picture of Jesus as a Jewish teacher of alternative wisdom is characteristic of the New Quest. The New Quest is concerned with the role of social forces in history. The main order of business is an examination of the social world of Jesus, about which more is known today than ever before.

The first axiom of the New Quest is that Jesus' society, and Jesus himself, was thoroughly Jewish. That may seem a commonplace, but given the history of anti-Judaism in Christianity, and the tendency to "Aryanize" Jesus by separating him from his Jewishness, it is an important acknowledgment.

Like all of Jewish society, maintains the New Quest, Jesus grew up in a patriarchal culture, which, in addition, was woven on the warp and woof of distinctions between clean and unclean, pure and impure. In contrast to Jerusalem Judaism, the Judaism of Nazareth and Capernaum where Jesus lived was peasant and rural, which colored his experience with a second contrast between ruling urban elites in Jerusalem and landed laborers in Galilee. In the minds of Borg, Crossan, and others, this social world produced an alternative social vision in Jesus, accompanied by a social passion for an egalitarian society, that broke down social barriers between fathers and families, men and women, learned and illiterate, observant and lax Jews, pious and profane, and even Jew and Gentile.

The role Jesus adopted to promote his vision, according to the New Quest, was that of itinerant teacher. Less Torah-bound than the average rabbi, Jesus appears in the New Quest as a teacher of alternative and subversive wisdom. The earliest and truest form of the gospel, in this view, was the wisdom teaching of Jesus, which is better preserved in "Q" (a hypothetical source of Jesus' sayings preserved in Matthew and Luke) and in the Gospel of Thomas than in the canonical Gospels with their later accretions of miracles, atonement, and resurrection.

New Questers hold that the original message of Jesus was incorporated into a later faith agenda of the early Church that, for better or worse, distorted the historical Jesus. In *Meeting Jesus Again for the First Time: The Historical Jesus and the Heart of Contemporary Faith*,[2] Borg calls these faith agenda "macro-stories." The task before the critical scholar is to liberate Jesus from such stereotypes. The method of preference of the New Quest for recovering the "real" Jesus beneath the Christ idealized by the faith and piety is a typology of religious leaders in general, especially that of the shaman or holy man.

The bottom line of the New Quest is that Jesus was a peasant Jew who, like Buddha or one of the Cynic philosophers, espoused a subversive view of traditional wisdom, and who both preached and practiced radical egalitarianism. He also gathered a group of followers and formed them into a movement (which was free from messianic or eschatological expectations). This Jesus had no messianic or divine self-concept, although most of the New Questers grant that he performed at least some healings by inducing trance-like states or by the powers inherent in him as "a spirit-person."

On this last point, an important distinction must be drawn between curing a "disease" (a biological malady) and an "illness" (a psycho-social experience). The "healings" of Jesus in the New Quest turn out to be more subjective than objective, i.e., they were changes in the psychological state of the patient rather than in the physical condition (unless the illness was psychosomatic and curable by suggestion). In *Jesus: A Revolutionary Biography*,[3] Crossan cites the healing of the leper in Mark 1:40–45 as an example. Jesus "did not and could not cure that disease or any other," states Crossan, but he was able to remove the shame of leprosy and its social ostracism. "Miracles," in other words, "are not changes in the physical world so much as changes in the social world" (p. 82).

The New Quest's profile admittedly omits a large—and for the Evangelical Christian, essential—body of the New Testament testimony to Jesus. In addition to eliminating miracles in the normal sense of the word (physical changes in nature), Crossan denies that Jesus called twelve apostles (too large a group to travel in rural Galilee), and denies that there was a Triumphal Entry into Jerusalem (a later scribal addition) or Temple cleansing (a later story symbolizing the destruction of Jerusalem) or Last Supper (since it is not in "Q" or Thomas). Jesus was indeed crucified as a suspected political subversive, but his death has no atoning significance and there was no Resurrection (Crossan attributes the resurrection

accounts to free associations by the early Church on the scapegoat theme in
Leviticus 16). Finally, insists Crossan, Jesus' body was eaten by dogs(!)—a
conclusion for which there is not a hair of evidence in the New Testament or
ancient Christian literature. Dogmatism and lack of historical evidence coexist in
trouble-free juxtaposition in the minds of Crossan and other New Questers.

But how can scholars assert things that are not in the Gospels, and deny things
that are? One answer is found in the premise that historical claims are valid only
where corroborated by external sources. Crossan, for example, says that unless a
biblical claim is paralleled in Josephus, early Christian literature (especially the
Gospel of Thomas), or cross-cultural anthropology it cannot be accepted. Crossan's
Jesus, not surprisingly, is a carbon copy of Josephus's description of Jesus in
Antiquities of the Jews (18.3.3)—a charismatic wiseman and wonder-worker
condemned by the Romans. It is important to understand the rules of play here—
that the criteria of truth claims exist only *outside* the body of evidence being investigated. That is indeed a dubious test of historicity—rather like writing the history
of a small town by excluding what the local newspaper says in favor of what might
occasionally appear in the *New York Times*.

More importantly, this rarefied or even contrary Jesus is achieved by subordi-
nating the Gospel accounts to a cross-cultural ideology. For instance, Crossan asserts
that "Jesus was illiterate"—a statement that flatly contradicts the New Testament.
Luke 2:46–47 and 4:16f, for example, claim that Jesus could and did read. Here is
the trail that leads to this incredulous conclusion: Crossan begins with the statement
in Mark 6:3 that Jesus was a *tekton* (usually rendered "carpenter"). Next, he quotes
a social historian (Ramsay MacMullan) who asserts that *tekton* is not, in fact, the
name of a trade, but a description of a social class of peasant expendables, like the
shudra caste in India. Third, Crossan asserts that 95 to 97 percent of Jews in first-
century Palestine were illiterate. Finally, Jesus' low social status placed him irrevo-
cably in this class of illiterates. Crossan concludes that the stories that Jesus was
literate "must be seen clearly for what they are: Lukan propaganda rephrasing Jesus'
oral challenge and charisma in terms of scribal literacy and exegesis" (pp. 24–26).

There is, of course, a headwall of contrary evidence to every point. To begin
with, all Greek lexicons render *tekton* "carpenter." Moreover, manual labor was *not*
a derogatory distinction in Jewish Palestine; the Mishnah, in fact, places the teaching of a manual trade on a par with the teaching of Torah. As for a 95 percent
illiteracy rate among Jews, that is simply inconceivable among a people whose

fathers were commanded to teach their sons Torah and who produced the large body of literature that distinguishes early Judaism. Never mind, finally, that a 95 percent illiteracy rate would obviate any reason to make Jesus literate. (Disciples of Siberian shamans do not portray their masters as graduates of the Sorbonne.)

Crossan is not unaware that his speculations are as fragile as hoarfrost. Indeed, he often follows his points by saying, "I realize how tentative all this is. . . ." Despite such caveats, however, he doggedly sides with his social theories. And where social theories, rather than primary historical evidence, determine truth, "history" becomes a very malleable matter.

False Assumptions, Right Pictures

The increase of knowledge about social conditions in first-century Palestine is clearly a valid and fruitful path of investigation into the life of Jesus. But to assume that a social context—even a correctly perceived one—captures the meaning of a person in it is rather like supposing that a resumé divulges the essence of an applicant. The chief problem with lives of Jesus exclusively "from below" is one of inadequacy. C. S. Lewis observed that "a naturalist Christianity leaves out all that is specifically Christian," and this is a telling critique of the New Quest. Each of the elements in its profile of Jesus—peasant Jew, movement founder, overcomer of social barriers, healer, ecstatic, and sage—is arguably a fair description of some aspect of Jesus. What is false is the attempt to package the list as the sum and extent of the historical Jesus.

There is an absolutism in the New Quest, as in all approaches that deny in advance the possibility that Jesus was God incarnate, against the fuller testimony of the New Testament to Jesus. The social world of Jesus, important as it was for certain necessary raw data, cannot account for who he was. That Jesus was a peasant or teacher or movement founder or even a Jew is, in the final analysis, secondary to the core claims of the New Testament that he was the unique incarnation of God, by whose death salvation is freely offered to the world. Every page of the New Testament clamors for this deeper, essential understanding. Every reconstruction of Jesus that denies this results in a paltry shadow. The question the New Testament puts inescapably to readers is not "What do you make of my social context?" but "Who do you say that I am?" (Mark 8:29).

Finally, a purely social reconstruction of Jesus cannot account for the effect that Jesus has had on history. To assume that the earnest though bewildered Jesus of the New Quest could have affected the course of human history as Jesus Christ really has is rather like stumbling upon a crater and supposing it the result of a cherry bomb.

All the various quests have critically erred in making what might be called the "assumption of discontinuity"—that the Jesus presented in the Gospels is essentially the fiction of the early Church and hence discontinuous with the historical Jesus.

Modern scholarship has rightly shown that the Gospels are not strict biographies but presentations of Jesus told from the standpoint of faith and for the purpose of furthering faith. Jesus, in other words, can be known only through the testimony of his followers. But it cannot be assumed from this—as liberal scholarship often has—that that testimony results in a distortion of the historical Jesus. Indeed, given the respect with which Jesus' words and deeds were held (e.g., 1 Cor. 7:6,12,25), it is more reasonable to think of the early Church as custodian rather than corrupter of the tradition.

The critical study of Jesus now has the momentum of more than two centuries behind it. In the history of the debate, four essential positions have emerged. In order to illustrate them, imagine four pictures on a wall. The first picture is a sharp black-and-white photograph of Jesus, the second a portrait of Jesus painted by an accomplished artist, the third an abstract painting with no discernible sense to it, and the fourth a mirror. The first represents the literalist who believes the Gospels deliver an exact, photographic likeness of Jesus. The second represents a moderate critical scholarship that affirms that although the Gospel portraits emphasize various facets of Jesus they stand in trustworthy continuity with the Jesus of history. The abstract art in the third frame represents radical critical scholarship that affirms that the historical Jesus actually existed, but it is disagreed on what, if anything, can be known about him. The mirror in the fourth frame represents a subjectivist approach that regards the study of Jesus as essentially autobiographic. That is, all statements about Jesus are in reality statements about ourselves that are projected onto Jesus.

The Jesus Seminar (and other studies mentioned) belong to one of the last two frames. Either their critical theories permit only the barest evidence and result in very selective outlines of Jesus, or they altogether fail to find a historical figure and compensate by projecting a Jesus of their own values and ideologies.

The photographic likeness is not an appropriate analogy, either. There are four Gospels—not one—each of which presents a unique profile of Jesus, depending on the special purposes for which it was written. Particulars in one Gospel are not always reconcilable with other Gospels. It is obvious to any sensible person that the same Jesus is the subject of all four Gospels, but the uniqueness of each of the four portraits makes it very difficult to produce from them a single harmonized life of Jesus. The photographic likeness is not dismissed out of irreverence or devaluation of the Gospel record, but simply because it is inappropriate to what God has given us in the Gospels. The Gospels are thus not distortions of the historical Jesus, but faithful depictions of him.

The modern critical distinction between the Jesus of history and the Jesus of faith is an essentially artificial and untenable distinction. In its endeavor to discern the historical Jesus, critical scholarship has exaggerated to an unwarranted degree the differences between the Jesus of history and the Jesus who is presented in the Gospels. Among the various arguments that can be made for the historical reliability of the Gospels, the following four are particularly important.

Christological Titles & Creativity

Some of the titles of Jesus found in the Gospels, such as Son of Man, Son of God, Lord, Messiah (or Christ), Prophet, etc., were used by Jesus of himself, whereas others were used only later of Jesus by the Church. The primary question, however, is whether any of these titles, especially the ones likening Jesus to God, can be said to represent Jesus' self-understanding.

It has become an axiom of New Testament scholarship to regard as secondary statements in the Gospels that attribute messianic or divine status to Jesus. The Christology of the Gospels, especially its titular Christology, is generally considered either to have arisen as a result of the early Church's encounter with the categories of Greek thought (e.g., "divine man," "son of God," etc.) in the Gentile mission, or to have been projected back onto the Gospel accounts by the early Church as a result of its desire to attribute to the historical Jesus an honor commensurate to the church's post-Resurrection experience of his Lordship.

This hypothesis has been around a long time, and its longevity has given it an appearance of credibility that is unwarranted. The idea that messianic titles and the divine status of Jesus first arose in the Gentile mission is neither a provable nor especially convincing premise. The first evangelists to the Gentiles were, after all,

Jewish Christians, and the elevation of Jesus to divine status, and the projection onto him of sayings and titles commensurate with that status, constituted no minor compromise to the monotheism that such Jewish evangelists held. The ace in the hand of every Jew in the face of Gentile polytheism and idolatry was the *Shema*, "Hear, O Israel: The Lord our God is one Lord" (Deut. 6:4). The hypothesis that Jewish Christians would be willing to surrender their trump card of monotheism in exchange for acceptance of the gospel by "Gentile sinners" (Gal. 2:15) and "idolaters" (Rom. 1:23), as Paul called them, is a very questionable hypothesis.

The hypothesis can, in fact, be tested to some degree in the New Testament itself. In its search for categories by which to describe Jesus, the early Church came perilously close at various points to calling Jesus God (John 20:28; Rom. 9:5; Titus 2:13), and it ascribed titles of ontological status to him, such as Lord and Son of God. Nevertheless, the New Testament is extremely reluctant to call Jesus God, which, given its monotheistic environment, is exactly what we would expect.

Think of the question this way: Is the deity ascribed to Jesus in the New Testament more likely to be the result of the early Church's desire to court the Hellenistic world (which it largely disdained), or to honor its experience of Jesus—despite the problems that it caused for its monotheism? By far the most satisfying answer to this question is the latter. The dominant gene of Jesus' self-consciousness was transmitted by Jesus to his followers. It was not a product of the early Church projected back onto the Gospel accounts of Jesus. It is, in other words, easier to start with the messianic self-consciousness of Jesus and explain the Gospel accounts than it is to start with the assumption that Jesus was simply a Jewish teacher or charismatic healer, for example, and imagine how his followers came to regard him as God—and fabricated the Gospel accounts accordingly.

This leads to a second axiom of liberal New Testament scholarship, that the early Church wildly invented sayings and stories of Jesus that reflected *its* needs and experiences rather than truths about Jesus himself. This supposed inventiveness of the early Church results in a puzzle that has never been adequately resolved: namely, how a simple first-century Jew, about whom little is known and who was uncertain (if not confused) about his identity, could have been recast as the unique revealer of God (Matt. 11:25–30) whose death was the once-for-all remedy for sin (Rom. 3:21–26).

There are, in fact, a number of "quality control" factors that argue strongly against the supposed fanciful and ultimately misleading inventiveness of the early

Church. It is possible to say with confidence that the Gospel writers did not wildly invent material about Jesus, but were quite careful with the entire Jesus tradition. Among those factors are the following:

A. Eyewitnesses of the events described in the Gospels were still alive at the time of the writing of the Gospels. Such eyewitnesses functioned as gatekeepers and custodians "of the faith that was once for all entrusted to the saints" (Jude 3). The wild inventiveness often attributed to the Gospel writers is, in fact, first evident in certain second-century documents (e.g., the Infancy Narratives of Jesus, the Protoevangelium of James) that were produced where Jesus traditions circulated in communities separated from the apostolic Church.

B. The rabbinic method of teaching by rote favored accurate and careful transmission of Jesus traditions as opposed to novel interpretation.

C. The presence of embarrassing and even problematic material in the Gospels (e.g., Mark 9:1; 14:71) speaks against the inventiveness of the early Church, even when the Church might have profited by it.

D. The absence of parables outside the Synoptic Gospels is the strongest possible argument for the authenticity of the parables deriving from Jesus.

E. A comparison of the Epistles with the Gospels reveals that neither Paul's words nor those of other New Testament writers have been projected back into the mouth of Jesus in the Gospels. This is a strong argument against the radical form critics, for example, who assert that the Gospels tell not the story of Jesus but the story of the early Church projected onto Jesus.

F. Paul is careful to differentiate between instructions from the Lord and his own opinions (e.g., 1 Cor. 7:10,12,25). Was Paul an exception in this matter, or typical of the Church as a whole? Surely the latter. It is highly doubtful whether Paul could have won acceptance from the Twelve and the Jerusalem leaders had he been known to play loose with the Jesus tradition.

G. It can be shown within the New Testament itself that *written* sources are handled with integrity (e.g., the generally faithful handling of Markan material by both Matthew and Luke). Is it not reasonable to assume the same care in the transmitting of oral tradition? One characteristic of children, primitive peoples, and religious groups is that they do not like to see their traditions changed. What evidence do we have to suggest that the early Church was an exception to this rule?

H. Finally, the supposed inventiveness of the early Church meets its strongest opposition in the Gentile question. According to Acts and the Epistles, the preaching of the gospel to Gentiles and their admission into the Church was *the* burning question of the early Church. This issue, however, is virtually absent from the Gospels. Had the Church actively engaged in framing "Jesus material" according to its needs and interests, surely it would have developed sayings on the Gentile question. The fact that such material is absent in the Gospels argues in favor of the historical reliability of the material that is there.

Jesus' Self-Consciousness

An earlier generation of liberal scholars was persuaded that Jesus' elevated self-concept, as shown by his presuming to forgive sins, cleanse the temple, and his authority to speak and act on behalf of God, would have been unthinkable within first-century Jewish monotheism. It was concluded that anything indicating divine awareness could not have come from Jesus himself but only from subsequent tradition ascribed to him by Hellenistic Christianity. Comparative studies within Judaism, made possible in part by the discovery of the Dead Sea Scrolls, have now sharply reduced the credibility of this view. The Teacher of Righteousness at Qumran, for instance, distinguished himself from the community to which he brought deliverance in these words:

> Through me hast Thou illumined
> the faces of full many,
> and countless be the times
> Thou hast shown Thy power through me.
> For Thou hast made known unto me
> Thy deep, mysterious things. (1QH 7)

Even more pronounced was Rabbi Hillel's self-understanding. "If I am here, everything is here; if I am not here, what is here?" (*b. Sukk.* 53a) declared the sage who died less than a decade before Jesus was crucified. Hillel was known to apply to himself biblical quotations that referred to God. "Hillel's self-understanding," says the well-known Jewish New Testament scholar David Flusser, "was so extraordinarily high that later rabbinic tradition often could not admit that Hillel had made such elevated claims for himself; it was asserted, rather, that Hillel was actually speaking of God."[4]

Such examples warn us against categorically discounting sayings of preeminence attributed to Jesus in the Gospels. Nevertheless, the self-consciousness of Jesus and his understanding of his place in God's economy are without parallel in ancient Judaism or Hellenism. To quote again from David Flusser:

> There is a great difference between Hillel and Jesus. Hillel's self-understanding was not limited to his own person, but was an archetype for each individual person. Jesus' understanding of his surpassing status . . . was linked to the knowledge that his person was not interchangeable with anyone else. He understood himself to be "the Son," and as such to have a central status and commission in the economy of God.[5]

This is a remarkable testimony coming from a Jewish scholar.

Jesus' consciousness of standing in a unique and sovereign relationship with God is the key that makes the Gospel accounts intelligible, without which the Gospels are reduced to a conundrum. We may briefly consider three apertures into Jesus' consciousness of Divine Sonship and messianic authority that are preserved in the Gospels: his calling of the disciples, and his use of *amen* and *abba*.

Unlike the rabbis, Jesus assumes a commanding role in calling his disciples (Mark 1:16–20; 2:13–17; 3:13–19). No Jewish rabbi called disciples. Rather, Jewish rabbis were chosen by their disciples, much like students today choose universities. Jesus, however, called his disciples, and not to Torah (as did the rabbis), but to himself. Moreover, rabbis assumed that gifted disciples might equal or surpass their understanding of Torah, eventually succeeding them. Jesus' disciples, however, can never equal him, much less succeed him. Finally, the fact that Jesus calls *twelve* disciples signals that he presumes to reconstitute Israel. The prominence of Jesus in the call of the disciples indicates that their response to Jesus determines their response to the kingdom of God itself.

A second insight into Jesus' divine self-consciousness emerges in his use of *amen*. The Old Testament prophet prefaced his pronouncements with "Thus says the Lord" as a guarantee of Yahweh's authority. Jesus, however, assumes that authority himself, solemnly pronouncing, "Truly I say to you" (*amen lego hymin*). Jesus' use of *amen* as an introductory formula, thereby attributing to his words divine authority, rather than as a concluding prayer response as was customary in Judaism, is, in the words of New Testament scholar Joachim Jeremias, "without any parallel in the whole of Jewish literature and the rest of the New Testament."[6]

A third insight into Jesus' Divine Sonship comes from his addressing God as *abba*, Father. Evidence in Jewish Palestine is extremely rare, if not entirely lacking, of "my Father" being used as an individual address to God. Jesus, however, addresses God intimately and personally as *abba* (e.g., Mark 14:36). T. W. Manson rightly recognizes that "The experience of God as Father dominates the whole ministry of Jesus from the Baptism to the Crucifixion."[7] Jesus' confidence in his unique placement and empowerment by God is the source of his filial consciousness and authority to speak and act on behalf of God.

Equally without precedent, yet present in all layers of the traditions, is Jesus' instruction to his disciples to address God as *abba*.[8] Nowhere is the unshared sonship of Jesus more evident than in the 51 occurrences (excluding parallels) of *Father* in the Synoptics, in which Jesus either speaks of God as "my Father" (29 times), or teaches his disciples about God as "your Father" (22 times), without, however, including himself with the disciples in addressing God as "our Father." The presence of *abba* in the Gospel traditions preserves a seminal memory of Jesus' filial consciousness not only in relationship to the Father, but also in contrast to the derivative sonship of his disciples.

The Historical Jesus of the Creeds

The most uncontested fact of Jesus' life is that he was crucified. The impression left by the Gospels is that the Jerusalem religious leaders instigated a procedure against Jesus that was finally executed by the Roman authorities. It is worth considering, however, exactly why Jesus was crucified. Jews, after all, did not randomly kill people, even over theological disagreements. The Mishnah, an 800-page Jewish sequel to the Torah that spans the time from roughly the birth of Jesus until A.D. 200, preserves thousands of differences of opinions among rabbis without one of them leading to a plot of death and execution. The fate of Jesus, in other words, was categorically different from that of other Jewish rabbis. Not the least formidable obstacle to the quest for a non-messianic Jesus who champions our causes and espouses our ideologies, to paraphrase a modern critic, is that such a Jesus would have scarcely gotten himself crucified.

There was, however, one ground for which Jews did impose the death sentence, and that would account for Jesus' execution: the charge of blasphemy. The earliest Gospel, in fact, preserves this charge in Mark 14:61–64. All the Gospel accounts agree that the point at which Jesus most threatened the Jerusalem authorities was his attack on the temple (e.g., Mark 11:27–33). What might have caused Jesus to presume to challenge the most sacred site of Judaism? Mark clearly indicates that Jesus understood his person to supersede the temple itself, and that makes sense only if Jesus understood himself to be divinely appointed and empowered. The Jerusalem authorities, of course, took both the deed and the word justifying it as a blasphemous presumption on Jesus' part, justly punishable by death. The charge of blasphemy testifies unmistakably—even if from his opponents—to Jesus' true mission and purpose.

Our examination of four aspects of the Gospel tradition allows us to affirm with confidence that the Gospels preserve a diverse and significant body of evidence of the *verus sensus Jesu*. Nowhere is the continuity between the memory of the early Church and the self-understanding of Jesus more discernible than in the many witnesses to Jesus' bearing, his consciousness of standing in an absolutely unique relationship to God as his Father, and his authority to speak and act on behalf of God in the world of humanity and nature.

There is a host of scholars who understand that the Gospels point to the Apostles' Creed, not away from it as the Jesus Seminar insists. The eminent Christian historian of Tübingen, Martin Hengel, lays an ax at the root of the modern presumption to find an adequate Jesus by the methods of modern historiography and sociology:

> Jesus' claim to authority goes far beyond anything that can be adduced as prophetic prototypes or parallels from the field of the Old Testament and from the New Testament period. . . . [Jesus] remains in the last resort incommensurable, and so basically confounds every attempt to fit him into the categories suggested by the phenomenology or sociology of religion.[9]

"Did Jesus know that he had an identity which his followers later came to understand in terms of his being God?" asks Raymond Brown, a Roman Catholic who stands at the apex of American New Testament scholars.

> If he was God (and most Christians do agree on that), did he know who he was? I think the simplest answer to that is yes. Obviously there is no way of proving an

affirmative answer because we do not have material describing all his life. Yet in the Gospel material given to us Jesus is always shown as being aware of a particular relationship with God that enables him to speak with awesome authority. There is never a scene in the Gospel portrait where he discovers something about himself that he did not know before. I realize that what I am saying runs against some popular views that would have Jesus discovering his identity at the baptism or some other time; but there is no evidence for such views. The baptismal scene is designed to tell the readers who Jesus is, not to tell him who he is.[10]

Statistics, it is often said, can prove anything. Likewise, critical theories about the Bible can produce various results, depending on the disposition of scholars. We have seen that some of the very theories and methods employed by the Jesus Seminar to discredit the New Testament portrait of Jesus when handled carefully and reasonably actually *underscore* the veracity of the account. The most reasonable answer to the question of why the Gospels present Jesus the way they do is that is essentially the way he was. The Gospels faithfully preserve the memory that Jesus left on his followers, that he was divinely legitimated and empowered to be God's Son and Servant.

Reprinted from Touchstone: A Journal of Ecumenical Orthodoxy, *Winter 1996, Volume 9, Number 1.*

ENDNOTES

1. *The Five Gospels: The Search for the Authentic Words of Jesus* (New York: Macmillan, 1993).
2. *Meeting Jesus Again for the First Time: The Historical Jesus and the Heart of Contemporary Faith* (San Francisco: Harper San Francisco, 1994).
3. *Jesus: A Revolutionary Biography* (San Francisco: Harper San Francisco, 1994).
4. *Entdeckungen im Neuen Testament. Band I: Jesusworte und Ihre Überlieferung* (Neukirchen-Vluyn: Neukirchener Verlag, 1987), p. 210 (my translation).
5. Ibid., p. 215 (my translation).
6. *New Testament Theology*, trans. J. Bowden (New York: Scribner's, 1971), pp. 35–36; also H. W. Kuhn, *"amen,"* EDNT 1.69–70.
7. *The Teaching of Jesus: Studies in its Form and Content* (Cambridge: Cambridge University Press, 1963), p. 102.
8. See J. Jeremias, *The Prayers of Jesus,* trans. J. Bowden (Philadelphia: Fortress, 1978), pp. 11–65.
9. *The Charismatic Leader and His Followers*, trans. J. Greig (New York: Crossroad, 1981), pp. 68–69.
10. *Responses to 101 Questions on the Bible* (New York: Paulist Press, 1990), p. 99.

CONTRIBUTORS

Philip G. Davis ("The Swiss Maharishi") is Professor and Chair of Religious Studies at the University of Prince Edward Island. He is the author of *Goddess Unmasked: The Rise of Neopagan Feminist Spirituality* (Spence Publishing, 1999). He and his wife have four children and are members of the Cathedral Church of St. Peter (Anglican) in Charlottetown, Prince Edward Island, Canada.

James R. Edwards ("New Quest, Old Errors") is Professor of Religion at Whitworth College, Spokane, Washington. An ordained Presbyterian minister, he holds a doctorate from Fuller Theological Seminary. The author of numerous articles, he is also a contributing editor for *Christianity Today*. He is the author of *The Divine Intruder: When God Breaks into Your Life* (NavPress, 2000) and several New Testament commentaries, including *The Gospel of Mark* for the *Pillar New Testament Commentary* (Eerdmans, 2002).

Steven Faulkner ("Century of Cyclops," "Workshop of Worship") received his doctorate in Creative Writing from the University of Kansas, Lawrence, where he teaches English. He lives in Topeka, Kansas, with his wife, Joy, and two of their seven children. He has completed a book about a two-month, thousand-mile canoe trip that he took with his son Justin from St. Ignace, Michigan, to St. Louis, Missouri.

Vigen Guroian ("Family & Christian Virtue") is Professor of Theology and Ethics at Loyola College in Baltimore, Maryland. Among the books he has written are *Incarnate Love: Essays in Orthodox Ethics,* 2nd edition (Notre Dame, 2002),

Inheriting Paradise: Meditations on Gardening (Eerdmans, 1999), *Tending the Heart of Virtue: How Classic Stories Awaken a Child's Moral Imagination* (Oxford University Press, 1998), and *Life's Living Toward Dying* (Eerdmans, 1996).

James Hitchcock ("Christ & Culture") is a senior editor of *Touchstone* and Professor of History at St. Louis University in St. Louis, Missouri. He has written numerous articles and books, including *Recovery of the Sacred* (Seabury, 1974; Ignatius Press, 1995), *Catholicism & Modernity: Confrontation or Capitulation?* (Seabury, 1979), and *What Is Secular Humanism?* (Servant, 1982). He and his wife Helen have four daughters. He is past president of the Fellowship of Catholic Scholars.

Thomas Howard (*"Brideshead Revisited* Revisited," "Recognizing the Church") taught for many years at an Evangelical college until he became a Roman Catholic in 1985. From then until his recent retirement, he taught English at St. John's Seminary College, the seminary of the archdiocese of Boston. He is the author of many books, including *Christ the Tiger* (2nd ed. Ignatius, 1990), *Evangelical Is Not Enough* (2nd ed. Ignatius, 1988), and *The Liturgy Explained* (Morehouse, 1981).

S. M. Hutchens ("The Professor & the Unicorn") is a senior editor of *Touchstone* and a librarian in Kenosha, Wisconsin. He holds a Ph.D. in Theology from the Lutheran School of Theology at Chicago. He and his wife live in Racine, Wisconsin, and have two daughters. His articles and reviews for *Touchstone* include a ten-part series on the Ten Commandments.

Russell Kirk (1918–1994) ("T. S. Eliot & Literary Morals") was the author of thirty books, including *The Conservative Mind: From Burke to Eliot* (7th ed., Regnery, 2001), *Eliot & His Age* (Random House, 1972), *Redeeming the Time* (Intercollegiate Studies Institute, 1996), and *The Politics of Prudence* (Intercollegiate Studies Institute, 1993). He also founded two journals, *The University Bookman* and *Modern Age*. His autobiographical *The Sword of Imagination: Memoirs of a Half-Century of Literary Conflict,* was published in 1995 by Eerdmans.

James M. Kushiner (Editor, Introduction) is the executive editor of *Touchstone: A Journal of Mere Christianity* and executive director of the Fellowship of St. James. He and his wife Patricia live in Chicago and have six children and six grandchildren. He is working on a book inspired by his pilgrimage to Iona, Scotland, during the terrorist attacks of September 11, 2001.

Paul Mankowski, S.J. ("A Fig Leaf for the Creed") is a lector in Biblical Hebrew at the Pontifical Biblical Institute in Rome. His essays have appeared frequently in *First Things* and elsewhere, and he is a contributor to *The Politics of Prayer: Feminist Language and the Worship of God,* ed. Helen Hitchcock (Ignatius Press, 1992). His scholarly work includes *Akkadian Loanwords in Biblical Hebrew (Harvard Semitic Studies #47),* (Eisenbrauns, 2000).

David Mills ("The Bible Tells Me So," "Meet the Latcons," "Evading the Creed") is a senior editor of *Touchstone* and director of publishing at Trinity Episcopal School for Ministry, where he edits the magazine *Mission & Ministry.* He is the editor of *The Pilgrim's Guide: C. S. Lewis and the Art of Witness* (Eerdmans, 1998) and the author of *Knowing the Real Jesus* (Charis Books/Servant Publications, 2001).

Leon J. Podles ("All That Separates Must Converge," "No Place Like Home") is a senior editor of *Touchstone* and has worked as a teacher and a federal investigator. He holds a Ph.D. in English from the University of Virginia and is the author of *The Church Impotent: The Feminization of Christianity* (Spence, 1999). He is working on a book on the recent scandals in the Catholic Church. He and his wife have six children and live in Naples, Florida.

Patrick Henry Reardon ("Classroom Chaos," "Christology & the Psalter") is a senior editor of *Touchstone* and pastor of All Saints Antiochian Orthodox Church in Chicago, Illinois. He is the author of *Christ in the Psalms* (Conciliar Press, 2000) and editor of the *St. James Daily Devotional Guide* (www.touchstonemag.com).

James L. Sauer ("Lessons from the Nursery," "An Everlasting Life") is Director of Library at Eastern University in St. Davids, Pennsylvania, and an elder in the Presbyterian Church in America. He has published over 200 essays, reviews, short stories, and poems. He and his wife Paula have seven children.

Huston Smith ("Scientism: The World's Littlest Religion") is the author of *The Religions of Man* (retitled *The World's Religions* [HarperSanFrancisco, 1992]), which has been a standard college textbook on the subject for several decades. An occasional visiting professor at the University of California, Berkeley, his most recent book is *Why Religion Matters: The Fate of the Human Spirit in an Age of Disbelief* (HarperSanFrancisco, 2000).

INDEX

A

Abolition of Man, The (Lewis), 164
abortion, 10–11, 150, 183
Abraham, household of, 97–99
Abraham, William, 19
ACLU. *See* American Civil Liberties Union
Adam, 148
Adams, Richard, 76
"Address on Vainglory and the Right Way
   for Parents to Bring Up Their
   Children" (Chrysostom), 97, 104
Aesop, 76
Africa, 189
After Strange Gods (Eliot), 58–62
Against the Opponents of the Monastic Life
   (Chrysostom), 99–101
Alabama, 28
Ambrose, Saint, 123, 154
American Civil Liberties Union (ACLU),
   23, 27
American Federation of Teachers, 23
American Humanist Association, 61
Amish, 10, 12
anaphora, 126–27
Anglicanism, 7
Antichrist, 169–70

Anti-Defamation League, 61
Antiquities of the Jews (Josephus), 214
Apostles' Creed, 108–14, 211
Appleyard, Brian, 14–15, 16
Aristotle, 26, 54, 166, 168, 169
Arius, 120
Arminius, 121
Ascension, 149
Assumption, 132
Athanasius, Saint, 157
atheism, public school education and,
   23–31
Augustine, Saint, 123, 136, 154, 157
Austen, Jane, 64, 65
Australia, 30

B

Baal, 15
Babbitt, Irving, 30, 59
Bachofen, Johann Jakob, 88, 89
   Bambi (Salten), 75–80
   Eros in, 76–77
   freedom in, 78
   as novel, 75–76
   treachery in, 78–79
Barry, Marion, 28

Barth, Karl, 165, 166, 169, 173, 174, 176

Basil, Saint, 93, 123

Beatitudes, 103–4

beauty, 44–45

Believing in the Church, 191

Bellah, Robert, 17–18

Benedict, 123

Berger, Peter, 5, 204–5

Bergson, Henri, 47–48

Bernard, 154

Bernays, Minna, 82

Beza, 168

Bible

    Christ and, 149–52

    Church and, 147–49

    fundamentalists and, 115–16

    God and, 144

    homosexuality and, 140–42

    liberalism and, 149–50

    morality and, 139–52

    public school education and, 26–28

    reading and studying, 142–49

    sexual morality and, 139–42

    as story, 184–85

Blessed Virgin Mary, 143

Bollingen Foundation, 82

Bookman, 76

Book of Acts, 97, 126

Book of Common Prayer, 117, 154, 158

Book of the Dun Cow (Wangerin), 76

Borg, Marcus, 18, 212, 213

Bouyer, Louis, 131

Boy Scouts, 4

Brideshead Revisited (Waugh)

    characters of, 68–70

    conversion in, 73–74

    moral imagination and, 63–65

    religion and, 65–73

    strategy in, 65–66

Brief History of Time, A (Hawking), 16

Brown, Raymond, 223–24

Buber, Martin, 170

Bultmann, Rudolph, 18, 19, 197

Bunyan, John, 49

C

California, 32, 84

Calvert School, 38

Calvin, John, 9, 121

Cambridge University, 38

Campbell, Joseph, 82

Canada, 30

Carter, Stephen, 15

Catechism of the Catholic Church, 132

Catholicism. *See* Roman Catholic Church

Catholic World, 76

Celsus, 211

Chambers, Whittaker, 76

Channing, William Ellery, 68

Chariots of the Gods (Daniken), 89

charismatics, 181

Chesterton, G. K., 24, 65, 143, 151, 196

children, poetry and, 51–57

Christ

    alternative, 212–15

    Bible and, 149–52

    of creeds, 222–24

    culture and, 1–13

    family and, 94

    invention of stories about, 218–20

    mysteries of, 156–57

    Psalms and, 153–59

    quest for historical, 208–24

    self-consciousness of, 220–22

    social reconstruction of, 215–16

    titles of, 217–18

Christ and Culture (Niebuhr), 6

Christian Coalition, 9, 10

Christian family. *See* family

Christianity

    Eastern vs. Western, 129–38

    media and, 11

    mere, xii

    persecution of, 2

Christianity Today, 121

Christian Left

    Christian Right vs., 8–9

    culture and, 7

Christian prayer. *See* prayer

Christian Right
 Christian Left vs., 8–9
 culture and, 6, 7, 9
 family and, 11
 importance of, 5–6
 media and, 5–6
 politics and, 12
 technology and, 7–8
 theocracy and, 9
Christians
 democratic participation by, 10–12
 divisions between, xi–xii, 8
Christo, Gus, 99
The Chronicles of Narnia (Lewis), 37
Chrysostom, Saint John, 136, 154
 ecclesial vision of, 93–106
 family and, 93–96, 99–101
 household and, 96–99
 marriage and, 101–3
Church
 antiquity of, 122–23
 authority of, 123-24, 165
 Bible and, 147–49
 creed and, 121–22
 culture and, 96
 division of, 129–30
 Eastern vs. Western, 129–38
 family and, 93, 96
 feminism and, 137
 five marks of, 122-128
 homosexuality and, 136
 liturgy of, 126–27
 meaning of, 119–22
 sacraments of, 127–28
 tradition of, 147, 156
 unity of, 124–26
 women in, 162–63, 173, 177, 182–84
Church Dogmatics (Barth), 169
Church of England, 67, 191, 198
Civilization of the Goddess, The
 (Gimbutas), 89
Clement, Saint, 122, 123
Clinton, Bill, 29
Cobb, John, 19

collective unconscious, archetypes of,
 86–90
Communist dictatorships, 2
community, creed and, 191–92, 194,
 197–98
"Comparison Between a King and a
 Monk, A" (Chrysostom), 97
Comus, 59
Constantine, 4, 96
Continual Feast, A (Vitz), 42
conversion, 73–74
Council of Nicaea, 191
Crammer, Archbishop, 154
Creation Science, 25–26
creed
 adding truths to, 193–94, 199
 Church and, 121–22
 community and, 191–92, 194, 197–98
 evading, 188–99
 historical Jesus of, 222–24
 humility and, 192–93, 198
 inclusive language and, 194, 200–207
 meaning of, 188–91
 Scripture and, 120
Creuzer, Friedrich, 88
Crick, Francis, 49
Criterion, 59
Crossan, John Dominic, 212, 213–15
Crossing the Threshold of Hope (John Paul
 II), 129
Cruise, Tom, 206
culture
 autonomy of, 12
 Christ and, 1–13
 Christian Right and, 6, 7, 9
 Church and, 96
 definition of, 1
 elitism and, 3–5
 religion and, 1–2, 6
 state and, 1–4, 11
 technology and, 8
Curran, Charles, 134
Cyprian, Saint, 123
Cyril, Saint, 123, 154

D

Dallas Seminary, 125
Daniken, Erik von, 89
Darby, J. N., 121
Dark Ages, 10, 21
Darwin, Charles, 18, 49
Darwin's Dangerous Idea (Dennett), 16
Darwinism, 16
David, King, 54, 155
Dawson, Christopher, 1, 2, 4, 59
Dead Sea Scrolls, 220
Decalogue, 26–27
Declaration of Independence, 28
Defense of Poetry (Sidney), 45
Degenerate Moderns (Jones), 82
de la Mare, Walter, 53
democracy, 3, 7
Democritus, 25
Denmark, 30
Dennett, Daniel, 16
De Quincey, Thomas, 46
Descartes, Rene, 47, 53–54
Deschooling Society (Illich), 35
Dickens, Charles, 48
Dirt, Greed, and Sex, 141
Dooyeweerd, Herman, 177
Dostoevsky, Fyodor, 142
Drew University, 19

E

education
    Evangelical Protestantism and, 30, 32
    history of, 34–35
    home-based, 30, 32, 37–39
    Plato and, 51–52
    private, 32–34
    school learning and, 35–37
    socialization and, 33, 39
    Supreme Court and, 23–24, 25
    See also public school education
Eliade, Mircea, 88
Elijah, 15
Eliot, George, 60
Eliot, T. S., 63

After Strange Gods of, 58–62
    liberalism and, 58
elitism
    culture and, 3–5
    private education and, 33–34
Enarrationes (Augustine), 157
England. *See* Great Britain
Enlightenment, 3–4, 208
Enquiries into Religion and Culture
    (Dawson), 1
Ephesians, 93, 104
    ecclesial marriage and, 101–3
Episcopalian, The, 193
Europe, totalitarianism in, 2
Eusebius, 97
Eustathius, 154
Eutychius, 119
Evangelical Protestantism
    culture and, 6
    education and, 30, 32
    Roman Catholic Church and, 116–17
    sexual morality and, 42
Evdokimov, Paul, 137
Eve, 143, 148
Evil Spirit, 59–61
evolution, public school education and,
    24–26

F

Faerie Queene, The (Spencer), 64
Faith and Life series (Ignatius Press), 42
family
    Christ and, 94
    Christian Right and, 11
    Church and, 93, 96
    ecclesial vision of, 93–96
    as mission of Kingdom of God, 99–101
    modernism and, 11–12
    society and, 94
    Supreme Court and, 12
    virtues of, 103–5
*Family Matters: Why Homeschooling Makes
    Sense* (Gutterson), 42
Fascism, 2, 205

Faust (Goethe), 83
feminism
   Christian, 168
   Church and, 137
   gender-inclusiveness and, 158
   inclusive language and, 206
   religious, 167
   fiction, moral imagination in, 63–65
Fielding, Henry, 64
Fiorenza, Elisabeth Schüssler, 101, 195
Five Gospels, The (Jesus Seminar), 209, 211
Flusser, David, 220–21
Forgotten Truth (Smith), 21
Forster, E. M., 68
Fox, Matthew, 134
France, 30
Frei, Hans, 173
Freud, Sigmund, 21, 81–82
Frost, Robert, 53
Fuller Seminary, 125
fundamentalists, politics and, 9, 11

G

Galileo, 210, 211
Gardner, James, 86–87
Geneva, 9
Germany, 30, 84
Gerohus, 154
Gibson, Mel, 36
Gimbutas, Marija, 89
Gingrich, Newt, 28
God
   Bible and, 144
   doctrine of being and, 170–71
   existence of, 15–16, 26, 28
   poetic knowledge and, 46–47
   understandings of, 165–71, 175–76
   worship of, 1
Goethe, Johann Wolfgang von, 83
Gorgias, 25
Grail Psalter, 159
Great Books program, 39
Great Britain, 30, 67
Great Chain of Being (Lovejoy), 79

Green, Arthur, 18
Greer, Mary K., 86
Gross, Otto, 89
Gutterson, David, 42–43

H

Haeckel, Ernst, 83
Hamlet, 36
Hannah, 99–101
Hard Times (Dickens), 48
Hardy, Thomas, 60
Harnack, Adolf von, 165
Harvard University, 38
Hauerwas, Stanley, 95
Hawking, Stephen, 16
Heenan, Cardinal, 207
Hegel, Georg, 168, 172
Heidegger, Martin, 18, 19, 189
Hengel, Martin, 223
Hermetic Order of the Golden Dawn, 86
hierarchy, 19
Hilary, Saint, 123
Hillel, Rabbi, 220
Historic Reality of Christian Culture, The
   (Dawson), 1
   history, religion and, 1
History of Christian Spirituality (Bouyer
   and Leclerq), 131
Holland, 30
Holy Spirit, 123, 150, 182
home-schooling
   advantages of, 37–41
   obstacles to, 39–41
   religion and, 41–43
homosexuality
   Bible and, 140–42, 145–46
   Church and, 136
   latitudinarian conservatism and, 182
Honegger, J. J., 88
Horton Hatches the Egg (Seuss), 75
Horton Hears a Who (Seuss), 75
household, "ecclesial," 96–99
Hughes, Langston, 52
humanitarianism, 59

humility, creed and, 192–93, 198
Huyuk, Caral, 89

I

iconoclasm, 5, 135, 210
Ignatius, Saint, 122, 123
Ignatius Press, 42
Illich, Ivan, 35, 42–43
Immaculate Conception, 132
imperialism, scientism and, 15–16
impiety, Psalms and, 158–59
Incarnation, 157–58, 190
inclusive language
    creed and, 194, 200–207
    fallacy of, 201–4
    feminism and, 206
India, 5
Irenaeus, Saint, 123
Irons, Jeremy, 65
Italy, 205

J

James, Henry, 64, 68
Jefferson, Thomas, 211
Jeremias, Joachim, 221–22
Jesus (Crossan), 213
Jesus Christ. *See* Christ
Jesus Seminar, 209–12
John, Saint, 209
John Paul II, 129, 137–38, 166
Johns Hopkins University, 17
Johnson, Samuel, 59
Jones, E. Michael, 82
Journal of Biblical Literature, 18
Journal of the American Academy of Religion, 18
Joyce, James, 60
Jung, Carl, 137
    collective unconscious and, 86–90
    Freud and, 81–82
    modernism and, 90–91
    New Age and, 86
    occultism and, 82–84, 85–86
    rebirth and, 84–85

religious legacy of, 81–91
Jung Cult, The (Noll), 82–83, 86
Justin, Saint, 123
Justinian, Emperor 96

K

Kant, Immanuel, 45
Kennedy, John F., 8
Kentucky, 26–27
Kierkegaard, Soren, 171, 172
Kirk, Russell, 27
    moral imagination and, 63
    Touchstone and, xi–xii
knowledge, poetic, 44–50, 56
Kropp, Arthur, 29

L

Ladner, Gerhardt B., 96
Lampe, G. W. H., 191
Language of the Goddess (Gimbutas), 89
Lasch, Christopher, 53
latitudinarian conservatism
    distinctiveness of, 180
    doctrine and, 182–84
    effects of, 185–87
    homosexuality and, 182
    postmodern conservatives and, 184–85
    theology of, 180–81
    Tradition and, 183–84
Lawrence, D. H., 59, 68, 60–61
Laws, The (Plato), 52
learning, school, 35–37
Leclerq, Jean, 131
Leisure, the Basis of Culture (Pieper), 45
Levi, Eliphas, 86
Lewis, C. S., 164
    Christianity and, xii, 215
    image of Christ and, 150–51
    poetry and, 48–49, 54
liberalism
    Bible and, 149–50
    Protestantism and, 117–18
    sexual morality and, 118, 139–40
    worship and, 117–19

Liebenfels, Jorg Lanz von, 84
Light Princess, The (MacDonald), 75
Lippmann, Alter, 20
List, Guido von, 84
liturgy, 126–27
Living Church, The, 191
Living in Sin? (Spong), 140
Louisiana, 25
Lovejoy, Arthur, 79
Luke, Saint, 143
Luther, Martin, 121, 125, 154

M

MacDonald, George, 75
MacMullan, Ramsay, 214
Macquarrie, John, 189–90, 191, 197
Manson, T. W., 222
Maritain, Jacques, 45, 50, 54
Mark, Saint, 209
marriage
   Christian, 94
   ecclesial, 101–3
   sanctity of, 64
   sex outside, 140, 145–47
Marsden, George, 18
Marx, Karl, 10, 18, 21, 177
Matthew, Saint, 212
Maximilian Kolbe, Saint, 134
Mead, G. R. S., 88
Measure for Measure, 64
media
   Christianity and, 11
   Christian Right and, 5–6
Meeting Jesus Again for the First Time
   (Borg), 213
Melchizedek, 155
Mere Christianity (Lewis), 150
meritocracy, 3–4
Middle Ages, 34, 46
Midgley, Mary, 57
Milton, John, 53
Mishnah, 222
Mithraism, 88
modernism

essence of, 4–5
family and, 11–12
Jung and, 90–91
modernity vs., 4
modernity
   as exhausted, 13
   modernism vs., 4
   technology and, 8
Mollenkott, Virginia, 125
monasticism, 10
monogamy, 140
moral imagination, 63–65
morality
   Bible and, 139–52
   public school education and, 26–28
   sexual, 118, 139–42
Moral Majority, 9, 11
Mother-Right (Bachofen), 88, 89
Muggeridge, Malcolm, 67
Muller, Steven, 17
Mussolini, Benito, 205

N

National Association of Evangelicals, 125
National Conference of Catholic Bishops,
   200
National Council of Churches, 61
National Education Association, 23
National Endowment for the Arts, 2
National Geographic, 37, 200, 207
National Public Radio, 44
National Review, 86
New Age, 82, 86
New Class, 4, 6
New England, 9
New Jerusalem Bible, 159
Newman, John Henry, 48, 56, 57
New Quest, 212–13
Newton, John, 118
New York, 58, 59
New York Times, 59, 86, 214
Nicene Creed, 119, 164, 175, 193, 197,
   200–201
Nicholas, Saint, 42

Niebuhr, H. Richard, 6–7, 9
Nietzsche, Friedrich, 21, 83–84
Noll, Richard, 82–86, 88, 89

O

occultism, Jung and, 82–84, 85–86
Oden, Thomas, 19
Order of the Solar Temple, 86
Ordo Templi Orientis, 86
Oxford Movement, 149

P

Packer, J. I., 121
papacy, role of, 133–34
Parsons, Donald, 197
Pascal, Blaise, 164, 171
Pastoral Letters, 193
patriarchy, 19–20
Paul, Saint, 143
    Epistles of, 126
    family and, 101–2
    sexual morality and, 145–46
    women in Church and, 163
pederasty, 5
Peninsula Bible Church, 125
People for the American Way, 29
Percy, Walker, 64–65
Peter, Saint, 116
Pieper, Josef, 45–46, 57
Pilgrim's Progress, 75
Pittsburgh Post-Gazette, 28
Plato
    education and, 51–52
    poetry and, 53
Pledge of Allegiance, 28
poetic knowledge
    need for, 44–50
    worship and, 56–57
poetry, children and, 51–57
Poetry of Pope, The (De Quincey), 46
"The Poison of Subjectivism" (Lewis), 54
politics
    Christian participation in, 10–12
    Christian Right and, 12

fundamentalists and, 9, 11
salvation and, 12–13
withdrawal from, 9–10
Polycarp, Saint, 122, 123
Popper, Karl, 20
postmodern conservatives, 184–85
Pound, Ezra, 59
prayer
    prohibition of, 24, 28–30
    Psalms and, 153–59
    public school education and, 24, 28–30
    Supreme Court and, 28
Preiswerk, Helene, 84
Princeton University Press, 86
Principles of Christian Theology
    (Macquarrie), 189
private education, 32–34
    elitism and, 33–34
Progress and Religion (Dawson), 1
Protestantism
    Catholicism and, 175–76
    liberalism and, 117–18
Psalms, 118
    impiety and, 158–59
    prayer and, 153–59
    sacraments and, 156
Psalms Anew, 159
Psalter for the Christian People, 153, 158, 159
public school education
    alternatives to, 23
    atheism and, 23–31
    Bible and, 26–28
    complacency about, 32
    evolution and, 24–26
    homogeneity in, 5
    morality and, 26–28
    prayer and, 24, 28–30
    reform in, 30–31
    social engineering and, 11
Puritanism, 7, 9

Q

Q-hypothesis, 210, 212
Quest for the Historical Jesus, The

(Schweitzer), 208
Quay, Rev. Paul, S.J., xv

R

Reardon, Patrick Henry, 162
Re-Imagining Conference, 210
religion
  autonomy of, 12
  Brideshead Revisited and, 65–73
  conversion and, 73–74
  culture and, 1–2, 6
  emotion and, 6
  history and, 1
  home-based education and, 41–43
  human discoveries and, 6
  United States and, 15
Religion and the Modern State (Dawson), 1
Religion and the Rise of Western Culture
  (Dawson), 1
revelation
  logic of ideas and, 171–74
  speculation and, 162
  submission and, 177–78
Rieff, Philip, 5
Roman Catholic Church
  Evangelical Protestantism and, 116–17
  Protestantism and, 175–76
  sexual morality and, 42
  See also Church
Roman Empire, 2, 10
Rosicrucianism, 86
Rule of St. Benedict, 153

S

Sabellius, 120
sacraments, 127–28, 156
Sagan, Carl, 16
Salten, Felix, *Bambi* of, 75–80
salvation, 12–13
Salzmann, Siegmund. *See* Salten, Felix
Samuel, 99–100
Sauer, Mary Denise, remembering, 108–14
scholasticism, 164
school learning, dynamics of, 35–37

Schweitzer, Albert, 208
science. *See* scientism
Science of Logic (Hegel), 172
scientism
  imperialism and, 15–16
  science vs., 15
  Scriptures and, 18
  theology and, 14–21
  universities and, 17–21
Scripture
  abortion and, 150
  authority of, 140–42, 182
  creed and, 120
  liberalism and, 118
  science and, 14
  scientism and, 18
Seuss, Doctor, 75
sexual morality
  Bible and, 139–42
  liberalism and, 118, 139–40
Shakespeare, William, 45, 52, 53, 109
Shoemaker, Sam, 125
Sidney, Sir Philip, 45, 48, 52
Sir Gawain and the Green Knight,
  63–64
Skinner, B. F., 82
social engineering, 2–3, 6, 11
socialization, education and, 33, 39
society
  definition of, 1
  family and, 94
  theology and, 16
Socrates, 25, 30
"Solar Phallus Man," 87–88
Sola Scriptura, 119, 176
Soul of the American University, The
  (Marsden), 18
Southern Methodist University, 19
Soviet Union, 2
speculation, revelation and, 162
Spinoza, Baruch, 15
Spong, John, 140–41, 192
St. John's College, 39
Stalin, Joseph, 143

state
    culture and, 1–2, 2–3, 4, 11
    definition of, 1
Stern, Karl, 47–48
Stevenson, Robert Louis, 53, 55–56
Stott, John, 125
Strauss, David Friedrich, 211
Supreme Court
    education and, 23–24, 25
    family and, 12
    public prayer and, 24
    religion and, 6
Surgeon General, 23
Sweden, 5
Switzerland, 84
Sword of Honor trilogy (Waugh), 65
Synoptic Gospels, 210

T

Taylor, Hudson, 125
Taylor, John V., 191
technology, 7–8
Teilhard, Pierre, 18, 19
Ten Commandments, 27
Tennyson, Alfred Lord, 53
Teresa, Mother, 140, 143
theocracy, Christian Right and, 9
Theodore of Mopsuestia, 157
Theodoret of Cyrus, 157
theology
    Creation Science and, 25–26
    scientism and, 14–21
    society and, 16
Thomas, Gospel of, 209, 212
Thomas Aquinas, Saint, 25, 47, 131, 164
    understanding of God of, 168–70,
        175–76
Tillich, Paul, 168
Tolkien, J. R. R., 65
Tolstoy, Leo, 65
Torah, 18, 222
totalitarianism, 2, 4
Touchstone, xi–xii
tradition

    of Church, 147, 156
    endurance of, 58–59
    latitudinarian conservatism and, 183–84
Trollope, Anthony, 64
Twain, Mark, 49
Types of Christian Theology (Frei), 173

U

Understanding the Present: Science and the
    Soul of Modern Man (Appleyard), 14
United States
    culture of disbelief in, 15
    public school education in, 5
    religion and, 15
universities, scientism and, 17–21
University of Kansas, 53
University of Virginia, 58

V

Vitz, Evelyn, 42
von Balthasar, Hans Urs, 136

W

Wagner, Richard, 84
Walton, E. H., 76
Wangerin, Walter, Jr., 76
Warren, Robert Penn, 53
Washington, D. C., 33
Watership Down (Adams), 76
Watts, Isaac, 117
Waugh, Evelyn
    bravado and, 66
    Brideshead Revisited of, 63–74
    strategy of, 65–66
Weekly World News, 38
Wellesley College, 41
Wesley, Charles, 117, 118
Wesley, John, 121
Whitefield, George, 121
Whitehead, Alfred North, 18, 19, 168
Whitman, Walt, 54
Wilder, Laura Ingalls, 34
Will, George, 21
Willimon, William H., 95–96

Wimber, John, 125
Wittgenstein, Ludwig, 21
women, Church and, 162–63, 173, 177, 182–84
Women of the Golden Dawn (Greer), 86
Woolf, Virginia, 64
World Evangelical Fellowship, 125
worship
    liberalism and, 117–19
    poetic knowledge and, 56–57

Wright, Charles, 44
Wycliffe, John, 166

Y

Yeats, William Butler, 59, 60
Yoder, John Howard, 101

Z

Zimmer, Heinrich, 88
Zwingli, Ulrich, 121, 125, 135